Modern Critical Views

Modern Critical Views

Modern Critical Views

OCTAVIO PAZ

Edited and with an introduction by
Harold Bloom
Sterling Professor of the Humanities
Yale University

CHELSEA HOUSE PUBLISHERS
Philadelphia

Printed and bound in the United States of America

10 9 8 7 6 5 4 3 2 1

Library of Congress Cataloging-in-Publication Data

Octavio Paz / edited and with an introduction by Harold Bloom.
        p. cm. – (Modern critical views)
   Includes bibliographical references and index.
    Contents: The poetry and thought of Octavio Paz / Kosrof Chantikian -- The surrealist
mode / Rachel Phillips -- Mentalist poetics, the quest, "fiesta" and other motifs / Jason
Wilson -- Flowing rivers and contiguous shores : the poetics of Paz / Julia A. Kushigian
-- Arborescent Paz, interlineal poetry / Djelal Kadir -- The poetic revelation / Frances
Chiles -- Octavio Paz : poetry as coded silence / Jaime Alzraki – Irony and sympathy in
Blanco and Ladera este / Manuel Duran – Reerberation of the stone / Ricardo Gullon -
Towards the other shore : the latest stage in the poetry of Octavio Paz / Manuel Duran –
Octavio Paz : critic of modern poetry / Allen W. Phillips.
      ISBN 0-7910-6334-8 (alk. paper)
      1. Paz, Octavio, 1914---Criticism and interpretation. I. Bloom, Harold. II. Series.

PQ7297 .P285 Z873 2001
861'.62--dc21   2001047212

Chelsea House Publishers
1974 Sproul Road, Suite 400
Broomall, PA 19008-0914

http://www.chelseahouse.com

Contributing Editor: Aaron Tillman

Contents

Editor's Note

My introduction centers upon the two major prose works by Octavio Paz, *The Labyrinth of Solitude* and *Sor Juana, Or, The Traps of Faith*, in order to supplement the critical essays reprinted here, which concern themselves primarily with Paz's poetry.

Kosrof Chantikian, introducing Paz's poetry, explores the high idealism of his enterprise, while Rachel Phillips analyzes the influence of Surrealism upon Paz throughout the 1950s.

For Jason Wilson, Paz is a poet of visionary quest in the tradition of William Blake as well as the Surrealists, seeking to restore an Adamic Golden Age. Julia A. Kushigian examines the profound influence of Asian thought upon Paz, who for six years was the Mexican ambassador to India, and she provides us with an exegesis of his vital poem, "Blanco."

A Tree Within, a crucial volume of Paz's later poetry, is studied by Djelal Kadir, with particular emphasis upon its elegiac celebration of the Cuban poet José Lezama Lima. Frances Chiles, considering Paz's treatment of poetic inspiration, shows how authentic, difficult, and rare his moments of revelation tend to be.

The metaphor of silence in Paz's poetry is investigated by Jaime Alazraki, who follows his poet's idealism in believing that this figurative silence is the authentic voice of poetry. Manuel Duran, in the first of his two essays reprinted here, was more pragmatic in his view of "Blanco," finding in it the meeting of Mexico and India.

Ricardo Gullón deals with the extraordinary *Sunstone*, finding in the poem Paz's personal revelation, after which Manuel Duran returns, to discover in Paz's later poetry a dialectical resolution of contraries. In this volume's final essay, Allen W. Phillips makes a high estimate of Paz's value to younger Mexican poets as a critic of their work.

Introduction

Paz received the Nobel prize for literature in 1990, one of the sounder choices. He possessed, and retains, an unique eminence in Mexican literature up to this time. Primarily a poet-critic, nevertheless his most influential books are likely to be *The Labyrinth of Solitude* (1950), which is a quest for the Mexican identity, and *Sor Juana, Or, The Traps of Faith* (1988), a critical biography of the poet Juana Raміréz, who became *Sor Juana Inés De La Cruz* (1651?-1695), the major literary figure of the City of Mexico in seventeenth-century New Spain.

An eclectic and idiosyncratic international poet-critic, and certainly one of the principal Spanish-language poets of the twentieth-century, Paz paradoxically is most original in his exploration of the very vexed question of Mexican national identity. Doubtless there are and will be rival attempts to define what might be called the genius of Mexico, and some Mexican feminists already denounce *The Labyrinth of Solitude* for implicitly taking the side of what it exposes and criticizes, the Mexican male myth that their women first betrayed them to, and with, the invading Spaniards. And yet I cannot see how Paz could have been clearer:

> In contrast to Guadalupe, who is the Virgin Mother, the *Chingada* is the violated Mother. Neither in her nor in the Virgin do we find traces of the darker attributes of the great goddesses: the lasciviousness of Amaterasu and Aphrodite, the cruelty of Artemis and Astarte, the sinister magic of Circe or the bloodlust of Kali. Both of them are passive figures. Guadalupe is pure receptivity, and the benefits she bestows are of the same order: she consoles, quiets, dries tears, calms passions. The *Chingada* is even more passive. Her passivity is abject: she does not resist violence, but is an inert heap of bones, blood and dust. Her taint is constitutional and resides, as we said earlier, in her sex. This

1

passivity, open to the outside world, causes her to lose her identity: she is the *Chingada*. She loses her name; she is no one; she disappears into nothingness; she is Nothingness. And yet she is the cruel incarnation of the feminine condition.

If the *Chingada* is a representation of the violated Mother, it is appropriate to associate her with the Conquest, which was also a violation, not only in the historical sense but also in the very flesh of Indian women. The symbol of this violation is Doña Malinche, the mistress of Cortés. It is true that she gave herself voluntarily to the conquistador, but he forgot her as soon as her usefulness was over. Doña Marina [The name given to La Malinche by the Spaniards.] becomes a figure representing the Indian women who were fascinated, violated or seduced by the Spaniards. And as a small boy will not forgive his mother if she abandons him to search for his father, the Mexican people have not forgiven La Malinche for her betrayal. She embodies the open, the *chingado*, to our closed, stoic, impassive Indians. Cuauhtémoc and Doña Marina are thus two antagonistic and complementary figures. There is nothing surprising about our cult of the young emperor—"the only hero at the summit of art," an image of the sacrificed son—and there is also nothing surprising about the curse that weighs against La Malinche. This explains the success of the contemptuous adjective *malinchista* recently put into circulation by the newspapers to denounce all those who have been corrupted by foreign influences. The *malinchistas* are those who want Mexico to open itself to the outside world: the true sons of La Malinche, who is the *Chingada* in person. Once again we see the opposition of the close and the open.

The Mexicans thus see themselves as the sons of La Malinche, and regard her as the *Chingada* personified. Since Paz was writing as a poet, he received all the misunderstandings that he risked: "an elegant insult against Mexican mothers." More accurately, as Paz remarked, *"The Labyrinth of Solitude* was an attempt to describe and understand certain myths; at the same time, insofar as it is a literary work, it has in turn become another myth." Involved here is a disagreement on Paz's part with Claude Lévi-Strauss, set forth in a wise little book (1967):

... Lévi-Strauss affirms that there is a real kinship between myth and music and not between myth and poetry. Myth as distinguished from poetry can be translated without any appreciable loss in the translation...

Paz adds that translation, for a poem, "implies transmutation or resurrection." A poem by Paz, translated into English by Elizabeth Bishop or Mark Strand is another poem and yet the same poem. This is a version of the Mexicans respecting their President, while behind the respect is the traditional image of the Father. Yet Paz ends his *Labyrinth* on an ominous note:

Every moribund or sterile society attempts to save itself by creating a redemption myth which is also a fertility myth, a creation myth... The sterility of the bourgeois world will end in suicide or a new form of creative participation.

Paz has been dead for more than two years, and his Mexico currently is becoming both more bourgeois and more Catholic. A superb Surrealist poet, whether in verse or prose, Paz founders in prophecy, as everyone has done in opposing the endlessly driven onward march of bourgeois societies. But that does not lessen the insight nor the visionary power of *The Labyrinth of Solitude*. Himself of mixed Spanish and Indian ancestry, Paz explains Mexican "solitude" by the original trauma of the Spanish Conquest, though as a diplomat and world-traveler he came to know that there are different modes of "solitude" in every national culture.

The starting-point for Paz in defining the difference between the United States and Mexico is that the Native Americans were essentially nomads, while the native Mexicans were settled peoples, farmers rather than hunters. To this was added the differences between Protestant England and the Spain of the Counter-Reformation. So far, that seems obvious enough; Paz manifests his particular genius for locating differences by passing beyond historical origins to spiritual insight:

The Mexicans' vision of death, which is also the hope of resurrection is as profoundly steeped in Catholic eschatology as in Indian naturalism. The Mexican death is of the body, exactly the opposite of the American death, which is abstract and disembodied. For Mexicans, death sees and touches itself; it is the body emptied of the soul, the pile of bones that somehow, as

in the Aztec poem, must bloom again. For Americans, death is
what is not seen: absence, the disappearance of the person. In the
Puritan consciousness, death was always present, but as a moral
entity, an idea. Later on, scientism pushed death out of the
American consciousness. Death melted away and became
unmentionable. Finally, in vast segments of the American
population of today, progressive rationalism and idealism have
been replaced by neo-hedonism. But the cult of the body and of
pleasure implies the recognition and acceptance of death. The
body is mortal, and the kingdom of pleasure is that of the
moment, as Epicurus saw better than anyone else. American
hedonism closes its eyes to death and has been incapable of
exorcising the destructive power of the moment with a wisdom
like that of the Epicureans of antiquity. Present-day hedonism is
the last recourse of the anguished and the desperate, and
expression of the nihilism that is eroding the West.

Capitalism exalts the activities and behavior patterns
traditionally called virile: aggressiveness, the spirit of
competition and emulation, combativeness. American society
made these values its own. This perhaps explains why nothing
like the Mexicans' devotion to the Virgin of Guadalupe appears
in the different versions of Christianity professed by Americans,
including the Catholic minority. The Virgin unites the religious
sensibilities of the Mediterranean and Mesoamerica, both of
them regions that fostered ancient cults of feminine divinities,
Guadalupe-Tonantzin is the mother of all Mexicans—Indians,
mestizos, whites—but she is also a warrior virgin whose image
has often appeared on the banners of peasant uprising. In the
Virgin of Guadalupe we encounter a very ancient vision of
femininity which, as was true of the pagan goddesses, is not
without a heroic tint.

There is much here to acknowledge, and much to argue. Paz had a
limited understanding of the American Religion, which he identified with
Puritan New England. But the United States, since about 1800, has not been
Protestant in the European way, and instead has developed a complex
configuration of new faiths that are more than sects: Southern Baptists,
Adventists, Mormons, Pentecostalists, and others. Our hedonists are not that
different from those of other nations, and our denial of death has something
to do with the astonishing national belief (eighty-nine percent, according to
Gallup) that God loves each of us on a personal and individual basis. Sane

Mexicans do not walk and talk with Jesus; an astonishing number of ordinary citizens of the United States do.

And yet Paz troubles me when he opposes Mexico's vision of femininity to that of the United States, though in this area someone regularly condemned as a "patriarchal critic" had better exercise wariness. The myth of La Malinche or the *Chingada*, unforgettably expounded by Paz, is alien to the United States, yet it is the center of *The Labyrinth of Solitude*, which on rereading flowers into a two-hundred-page prose-poem, rather than what Paz himself describes as "a book of social, political and psychological criticism."

Halfway through his *Labyrinth*, Paz gives us a remarkable excursus upon Sor Juana, which decades later exfoliated into his superb biography of the first major Hispanic poet in the New World:

> Despite the brilliance of her career, the pathos of her death, and the admirable geometry that shapes her best poetic creations, there is something unrealized and fragmentary in the life and work of Sor Juana. We can sense the melancholy of a spirit who never succeeded in forgiving herself for her boldness and her condition as a woman. Her epoch did not provide her with the intellectual nourishment her appetite required, and she herself could not—and who can?—create a world of ideas in which to live alone. An awareness of her singularity was always very alive in her:
>
> "What can women know except the philosophy of the kitchen?" she asked with a smile. But the wound hurt her: "Who would not believe, hearing such general applause, that I have voyaged full-sail on the handclaps of popular acclamation?" Sor Juana was a solitary figure. Indecisive and smiling, she lived an ambiguous life; she was conscious of the duality of her condition and the impossibility of her task. We often hear reproaches against men who have not fulfilled their destinies. Should we not grieve, however, for the ill fortune of a woman who was superior both to her society and her culture?

Eloquently plangent, this still would not have prepared me for Paz's Sor Juana, which is a baroque masterwork, and though a critical biography in form, fulfills the project of The Labyrinth of Solitude, and perfects Paz's lifelong meditation upon Mexican identity. What emerges most vividly from Sor Juana, aside from its depiction of the culture of later seventeenth-century Mexico, is the poetic splendor and final personal tragedy of Sor Juana, destroyed by "the traps of faith," the spiritual tyranny of a Church resisting

all enlightenment, and obliterating a woman poet of genius for the sole sake
of eliminating an anomaly, an autonomous creative spirit:

> It is scarcely necessary to point out the similarities between
> Sor Juana's personal situation and the obstacles we Mexicans
> have experienced during the process of modernization. There
> was an insoluble contradiction between Sor Juana and her world.
> This contradiction was not merely intellectual; it was
> fundamental, and can be located in three main areas. The first
> was the opposition between her literary vocation and the fact that
> she was a nun. At other moments, although not in New Spain,
> the Church had been tolerant and had harbored writers and
> poets who, often in blatant disregard of their religious
> responsibilities, had devoted themselves exclusively to letters.
> Their cases, however—the most notable being those of
> Góngora, Lope de Vega, Tirso de Molina, and Mira de
> Amescua—differ from that of Sor Juana in an essential point:
> they were poets and dramatists but not intellectuals. Both
> vocations, poet and intellectual, converged in Sor Juana. In late
> seventeenth-century Spain and its domains, a priest or nun with
> an intellectual vocation was restricted to theology and sacred
> studies. This incompatibility was aggravated y the fact that Sor
> Juana's extraordinary intellectual restlessness and her
> encyclopedic curiosity—Sigüenza's also—coincided with a
> moment of paralysis in the Church and exhaustion in Hispanic
> culture.
>
> The second area of discord was Sor Juana's gender. The fact
> that a woman—what is more, a nun—should devote herself so
> single-mindedly to letters must have both astounded and
> scandalized her contemporaries. She was called the "Tenth
> Muse" and the "Phoenix of America": sincere expressions of
> admiration that must have set her head spinning at times. She
> tells us in the *Response* that no lack of criticism and censure
> accompanied this praise. The censure came from influential
> prelates and was founded on a point of doctrine. It was not by
> chance that in his appeal to Sor Juana asking her to forsake
> secular letters the Bishop of Puebla quoted St. Paul. It was one
> thing to be tolerant with Lope de Vega and Góngora, both bad
> priests, and another to be lenient with Sor Juana Inés de la Cruz.
> Although her conduct was beyond reproach, her attitudes were

not. She was guilty of the sin of pride, a sin to which the vain feminine sex is particularly susceptible. Pride was the ruin of Lucifer, because hubris leads to rebelliousness. Sor Juana's critics saw a causal relationship between letters, which lead a woman from her natural state of obedience, and rebelliousness. Sor Juana had disproved the inferiority of women in intellectual and literary matters and made her attainments a source of admiration and public applause; to the prelates this was sin, and her obstinacy was rebellion. That is why they demanded a total abdication.

As Paz shows, Sor Juana's great, Hermetic poem, *First Dream*, differs profoundly from the visions of St. John of the Cross and of St. Teresa. John of the Cross quested to get to a point where there was no knowing, and St. Teresa wished to be possessed by God's light. Both were impatient with reason, but Sor Juana, sublimely reasonable, desired to illuminate all things, in a quest both more Neoplatonic and more encyclopedic than it was specifically Christian. She was the last great poet of Spain's Baroque Age, and that the Church violated her creative integrity was its own sin against the spirit.

Paz, an eclectic religionist, more Hindu and Buddhist than Christian, had an instinctive empathy for Sor Juana's doomed Hermeticism. She stands in his work as the other personification of the scapegoated *Chingada*, at the other end of the historical and spiritual world from the reviled La Malinche. It fascinates me that Octavio Paz, a great erotic poet and universal critic of poetry, composes his two major prose achievements upon two victims of what has to be called the vision of Mexican masculinity, the nature of which remains so resistant to change.

KOSROF CHANTIKIAN

The Poetry and Thought of Octavio Paz:
An Introduction

I The Poet

In his foreword to the first edition of *El arco y la lira (The Bow and the Lyre)*, Octavio Paz puts a question to us and to himself: "From the time when I began to write poems, I wondered whether it was worth while to do so: would it not be better to transform life into poetry than to make poetry from life?" Like all authentic questions, this is really an invitation for us to enter into a living dialogue with the Poet. And like all true questions, the shadow of an answer is already implicit within it. Let us ask then what Paz's question means for us.

In an essay delivered in 1942, "Poesía de soledad y poesía de comunión" ("Poetry of Solitude and Poetry of Communion"), Paz declared that "poetry is neither moral nor immoral, just nor unjust, false nor true, beautiful nor ugly. It is, simply, poetry of solitude or of communion." This is an astonishing statement for Paz to have made before an audience gathered in Mexico City to celebrate the fourth centenary of the birth of San Juan de la Cruz. And perhaps Paz felt a little strange saying this because several pages on in the essay, he plainly contradicts himself: Poetry, he says, is nevertheless a great force which reveals to us our hidden longings and dreams and allows us to actualize them. The Poet, by teaching us what our dreams are (and in fact demonstrating that *we have dreams*), shows us at the same time that we

From *Octavio Paz: Homage to the Poet*, edited by Kosrof Chantikian, © 1980 by Kosrof Chantikian and KOSMOS.

are not simply machines created for the purpose of following commands or spilling blood "to enrich the powerful or to maintain injustice in power" and that we are more than mere statistics or pieces of goods that can be inventoried. And poetry in directly manifesting these dreams "invites us to rebellion, to live our dreams awake: to be no longer the dreamers, but the dream itself."

Can such a *force*, an invention of the soul of such magnitude that it teaches us to invent ourselves and even if necessary to rebel, can such a poetry be called "neither moral nor immoral, just nor unjust, false nor true, beautiful nor ugly"? Can a poetry which declares *dream what you might be*, can such a poetry be not committed to a higher vision of our potential? And can a poetry which reveals to us our hidden depths, which teaches us about ourselves, and which therefore embraces and advances a consciousness of superior authenticity, can such a poetry be other than moral and just? Can we not therefore legitimately call such a poetry true and beautiful? Paz himself acknowledges that *El arco y la lira* is the maturing and correction of his "distant" essay, but we are warned that his question ("Would it not be better to transform life into poetry that to make poetry from life?") is not to be taken as a proposal to make life more beautiful. Guillermo Sucre, for example, paraphrasing Paz, declares "Life is neither beautiful nor ugly, noble nor ignoble." Sucre adds that Paz is proposing instead to have everyone base their lives on the principle of poetry—where contraries are fused into a unity, where contradictions become resolved, where fragmentation is healed and where dichotomy is finally negated.

Let us note first here that "life" is what we invent for ourselves out of ourselves. This inventing of life is an act, it has the force of intentionality, a consciousness behind it. It is therefore a *value*: One chooses to live in *this way* rather than in another way, to be this type of person rather than that type. This entails a commitment whose freedom is the foundation of the act. To make the claim as Sucre does, that life is neither beautiful nor ugly is already to have committed himself to a particular value. A pretending not to take a stand, not to make a decision, is already to have acted. Neutrality, like the denial of freedom, is an illusion, a self-deception, a lie. It is therefore clear that we have a right to judge whether certain acts undertaken in our inventing ourselves and one another may be called "good" or "bad," "reasonable" or "fanatical", "beautiful" or "ugly."

To say that life is neither this nor that is a verbal confusion. "Life" refers to human beings who create, invent, discover themselves in this world, who act and interact, who speak and are spoken to, who listen and are listened to, who touch and are touched, who commune and participate with others, who are transfigured by the world and who in turn transfigure it.

"Life" is time in the historical continuum out of which all of us arise; the sum total of our acts from our birth, our first movements as conscious beings, to our last, to our death. Thus the structure of action which posits itself through an intentionality, a freedom, a consciousness, can never possess a neutrality. Furthermore, what could it possibly mean to say that Poetry (whose fundamental foundations are the Imagination, Possibility, Eroticism and Love) governs our experience except that utopia has been found? Being a construction of the Imagination and Will, the act of founding this utopia *is a value*. What shall we name this value? Beautiful! Sucre is thus mistaken when he claims that Paz's question has nothing to do with "life": with its beauty or ugliness, its sublimity or wretchedness.

Paz himself understands this very well when he points out that all great poets at one time or another have believed in a revolutionary, libertarian society which would at last resolve the contradictory tensions between the simultaneous affirmation and negation of history perpetually residing in the center of the Poem's Being. In this revolutionary society poetry would finally become, as Lautréamont predicted in his *Poésies*, practical and for *everyone*! Since the reformation and critique of language must be the basis of the reconstruction of philosophy and thought, the very *least* that would occur in such a community is the creation of a pure Language! Would such a new Language, the speaking of it purely, transform our lives, make it that is, "more beautiful"? Of course it would! Thinking's foundation *is* Language. A pure Language would be unrestrained, liberating, free of bureaucratic jargon, and unmanipulative as Orwell prophesied. In such a sustaining environment thinking and intuition would more closely approach their potentiality to re-create ourselves through a genuine self-consciousness, a consciousness, that is, no longer chained, muzzled and entombed. This gain in a pure Language (or at least the *movement toward it*) then would obviously be the beginnings of the creation of utopia.

In such a society consciousness would undergo a metamorphosis, a transfiguration: the transcending of linear time and the overthrow of a history of mutilation into a new time, a *present*, where love is neither a solitary instance nor an accident nor a stroke of luck, but an awaking to the Poetic Instant, the present, here, today. This present, as Paz says, is what poets and artists continually seek even though they are not always aware of it. And how will we know this present, this new time? "Perhaps," Paz says, "the alliance of poetry and rebellion will give us a vision of it." This merging of poetry and rebellion must be possible only because there exists an affinity between the two. What is this affinity, this analogy, between poetry and rebellion? First, authentic poetry (as all true art) reveals to us the *hidden*: poetry places our consciousness above the usual noise of chatter, it reveals, the other to us; in so doing, poetry rips off the mask that hides the world by re-creation of the world as a *presence*. Rebellion also reveals the world to us because its function is to demystify society. Both poetry and rebellion destroy deception; both are subversive to the established norms; both transform the given reality; both are a criticism of society: of its myth of progress, of linear time, of language.

Against Sartre who claims that literature is an illusion, that we never live as well as we might dream or write about living, Paz observes we have no choice: we are human because of language: "Living implies speaking and without speech humankind cannot have a full life. Poetry, which is the perfection of speech—language speaking to itself—is an invitation to enjoy the whole of life." What then is the basis of this invitation from poetry? From where does it arise? Let me repeat: to enjoy the fullness of life must mean to live in such a way that not only am I happy—but you, the *other*, the shadow of myself, are also happy. A world without poetry is logically possible, but morally, aesthetically, a contradiction. Who would want to live in that hell? Isn't this proof that poetry is an essential ingredient of our soul? Moreover, doesn't the very concept of "living a full life," a life based on authenticity, entail "truth" and "beauty"? Poetry sustains and nourishes the Imagination; it raises consciousness, as Rimbaud would have said, to a higher power; and because of its living energy and erotic tension, poetry reminds us of *life*, of a superior way to be, of the power of love, of who we are and who we may become.

C. M. Bowra has pointed out in his preface to Paz's *Anthology of Mexican Poetry* that a nation's character may be deduced from its poetry, what it has sought to preserve as a true reflection of its spirit. Thus, poetry, or rather the poem which is a work, contains within itself a universe of experience: of a "poplar of water" or of gas ovens, of a remainder that love will never die or of torture. "To love is to struggle," says the Poet, "and if two people kiss / the world is transformed." Poetry and the experience found in the poem, a *work*, is always more than the artist intended: the poem, any work of art, is a living being, always independent of its creator. We can see this in any of Paz's great works, in *Piedra de sol*, for example:

> amar es combatir, si dos se besan
> el mundo cambia . . .
> . . .
> amar es combatir, es abrir puertas,
> dejar de ser fantasma con un número
> a perpetua cadena condenado
> por un amo sin rostro;

el mundo cambia
si dosse miran y se reconocen,
amar es desnudarse de los nombres
. . .

. . . mejor ser lapidado
en las plazas que dar vuelta a la noria
que exprime la sustancia de la vida,
cambia la eternidad en horas huecas,
los minutos en cárceles, el tiempo
en monedas de cobre y mierda abstracta

(to love is to struggle, and if two people kiss
the world is transformed . . .
. . .
to love is to struggle, to open the doors
to stop being a ghost to a number
condemned to life imprisonment
by a faceless master:
                                   the world is transformed
if two people look at and recognize each other,
to love is to rid ourselves of names
. . .
better to be stoned to death
in the town square than tread the mill
that squeezes life's substance dry,
turns eternity into empty hours,
minutes into prisons, and time
into copper pennies and abstract shit).

The meaning of this fragment from *Piedra de sol* (as in any work of art) is the image and only the image. And though it is futile to try to "explain" a poem, it is also true that the poet and artist believe their "images tell us something about the world and about ourselves and that this something . . . really reveals to us who we are." This is precisely the aesthetic power of a great art and within it lies a *force* capable of disclosing to us the lost secret of a time in which humankind had not yet served itself from being at one with the universe: *wisdom*. The poem is thus a negation, a criticism, of the world's reification and an attempt to represent the actual goal of rebellion (and revolution): liberation and happiness of the individual. The subversive nature of the poem is not based merely on the knowledge of things, of the world, which it puts before us in its re-creation of reality, though that is certainly true; it is rather, something much more. The poem is subversive because its foundation, mediated by experience, is a "higher knowing": *wisdom*. This wisdom from which the true poem is born is the reason it is able, through the image, to tell us about the world and reveal to us ourselves: the elemental power of the poem, in this sense, is of the same undiminished magnitude as Socrates' moral dictum: *Know Thyself.*

Our question which all artists conscious of their work and of the historical continuum in which we all live, create and transform the world (and are in turn transformed by) must eventually face, is answered as soon as it is posed. We'll see that rather than being antagonistic and irreconcilable, the two elements of our question (transforming life into poetry—making poetry from life), because of their dialectical nature, are inseparably intertwined and converge upon one another relentlessly, having the same tendencies, characteristics and functions: to change, transmute, reshape, metamorphosize and revolutionize the given.

Though it is true to say that we choose ourselves, we decide who we are and who we will become, it is equally true that this freedom-of-Being has a certain intrinsic, inescapable relation with necessity, with the world: the unavoidability of a Poet being a Poet. One chooses to be a Poet, it is true; but the Poet who chooses must choose. How could it be otherwise? This contradiction worries philosophers and they sometimes have nightmares over it. For it is they who have chosen to regard analytical reason rather than the Imagination as the sole unifying principle of the world. They forget, these professors, that after class they will return to their homes, converse with a friend, exchange thoughts, intuit feelings, make love, touch the night, dream. These events and their participation in them: are they capable of being reduced to a deductive logic, a mathematical identity, an *a priori* truth?

The contradiction of choosing to be and simultaneously having to be a Poet can be put in a more general way: Finding ourselves surrounded *by* and *as history* and therefore being formed by it, how much is it possible to poetically create ourselves and thus to invent History? Dreams of transforming life into poetry vs. making poetry out of life: are not these ultimately the same processes? Is not the first dream simply the other side of the second?

What is it to say we will transform life into poetry but another way of speaking of change, metamorphosis, transmutation and revolution? And the Poem: what is its function except to return us to the origin of time (our childhood), the beginning of beginnings (our birth), the starting point of our Being (consciousness of our authentic experience), all of which take place at once, now, here, this instant?

Poetry does this by negation, alchemy, magic, desire, eroticism, by daring language to sing, and by singing—existing. In other words, by destroying history in order to find, that is, to compose, to invent History. Unlike the existing situation today where history (worship of a technology and "progress" that sputters forth its specter of ideological tentacles and bureaucratic control) daily conditions a petrified consciousness into its grave, this new History will be one born, nourished, comprehended and so actually invented and shaped by a Consciousness immediately and spontaneously aware of its intentionality.

This Consciousness is another way of speaking of the new Person who will be born in History; who will appear by a negation and destruction of the presently dominant form of (a masochistic-sadistic) consciousness. Consciousness will now create History instead of history overpowering, enslaving, terrorizing consciousness. But this is precisely the goal of revolutionary Marxism: to dismantle the existing superstructure of society, to destroy a "false consciousness" and to transform history into History, into universal socialism; to make, in other words, the new Person.

The revolutionary Being of Poetry is its ability through its own directive to authentically ground our Being-in-the-world, to throw ourselves out-of-our-selves so we may be able to fundamentally comprehend our existence, so that we may essentially and supremely recognize ourselves as beings whose deepest recesses and foundation is Love. The task of humanity is to restore to itself, to recapture, above all to remember its original Being— now lost, buried, forgotten in its frenzied "pursuit of happiness," in its insatiable hunger for more technology, for "progress," in its lust to conquer nature. Until that time when our original Being (which is the Being-of-Love) is restored to us, it is only Poetry which will allow us to comprehend in a truly fundamental way the Being toward which we must become.

Paz's thoughts parallel Heidegger's, whose own dialogues with Hölderlin and Rilke emphasize that the being of existence *is* the being of song. In his third *Sonnets to Orpheus*, Rilke says: *Gesang ist Dasein*—Song is Existence. Rilke's Imagination which has equated authentic song with authentic existence undermines the established norms of society. "Song is Existence" is a revolutionary declaration. It renounces technology which cannot commune either with nature or ourselves; it laughs at the religion of ideology (politics); it is the disinfectant for the abscess of bureaucracy. Thus Poetry which is grounded and arises from Language-Thought-History, from the Imagination, is revolutionary.

Poets and other artists who understand this revolutionary, trans-muting, erotic, subversive (and necessary) element of art cannot disown their work without destroying themselves. And it is Paz himself who reminds us that the Poet and the Poem are one: how could Baudelaire be Baudelaire apart from his poems? Poets who abandon Poetry abandon themselves. Poets who write "verse" for the state will end up themselves as enforcers of ossified codes, as mere functionaries of a bureaucratic, frozen ideology, as bullies. Memory will not allow us to forget the murders, suicides, tortures and silencing of Poets. Whoever condemns Poetry condemns in the same breath the sky and the air; whoever condemns Poetry also condemns at the same time the possibility of a general revolt against pertification of the human spirit. Poetry and revolt must come to meet, to share one another's presence. Let there be no doubt however, that it is the Poet who prophesies this communion.

Paz's question with which we began: "Would it not be better to transform life into poetry than to make poetry from life?" has haunted him since he began to write. The implication is not solely an aesthetic judgment, but is also a moral one: that it would be "better" to give up creating poems and instead change life, the world, into poetry. But how can we transform the world into poetry? How is it possible to create a universal Poetic Consciousness? The very being of society is anti-poetic. Poetry has no exchange value in society. It is looked upon as impractical, useless. How then shall we negate existing society and reshape it into a Creative Community of Beings, each of whom is *antonomous*, each of whom is both *law-maker* and *law-obeyer* in this new society? The underlying catalyst can only be either a persistent application of pressure for gradual reform (including rebellion) or a more sudden, catastrophic, upheaval—revolution, since the being-of-society is deeply antagonistic to the Being-of-Poetry. (Paz chooses rebellion over the violent excesses evoked by modern revolutions.)

Furthermore, a Poetic Community which implies an Autonomous Community is irreconcilable with existing history. An Autonomous Poetic Community is the destruction of this history into a History. Implicit in Paz's question is thus a value judgment: transformation of society into a Poetic Community is more important than a mere creation of poetry from a world which at the present moment is, among other things, filled with brutality, murder, hunger, poverty, disease and ignorance.

Paz's question is a dialectic: each element of which attempts to break away, to flee, to suck-up the other, but cannot because each is contained in the other: first, the beginning of the transformation of life into poetry is the invention of a Poetic Consciousness, a return to original time before fragmentation severed the unity of the world's Being, before a dichotomy arose between Freedom and Existence, Reason and Imagination, Love and Eroticism, Culture and Society, Art and Work, Work and Pleasure. . . . And second, the creation of poetry from life is the opening up of Possibility, unleashing the full revolutionary and erotic potential of the Imagination into a metamorphosis: of the given into a Creative Community, of history into a History and of consciousness into a Consciousness which at last directs and is the foundation of History.

We have said that the Poet cannot abandon Poetry without being destroyed. Let us for the sake of argument assume this is now possible. Poets will renounce the inventing of poems and instead, transfer all their energies toward the reconstruction of life into poetry. I ask: with Poetry abandoned how will we *know* Poetry? How will we recognize it? Since life is to be transformed into Poetry, it is obvious we need to remember what Poetry was, how it existed, in order to *know how to make life into it!* How will life know it has become poetic with Poetry under embargo? From the past? But what is the point of returning to the past if we abandon Poetry in *our own time*?

This situation collapses upon itself: in order to create (life as) Poetry, we abandon (the making of) Poetry; in order to make life poetic (which is really to say: in order to make life more *human*—since the history of the world is the history of Language, and so thinking), we turn away from song, from dance, away from existence! How then will poetic life dwell if the Imagination is forsaken?

To pose our question, I said earlier, is already to have answered it because a questioning, a looking, a touching, a writing (of a poem, a book) can never be an empty or neutral event. To pose a question is to hope, to desire contact, to commune with another human being, to commit ourselves to a value, *to act*. Paz returns to his (and our) question near the end of *El arco y la lira*. His answer is quite a natural outcome of the dialectical being of the question: it is *impossible to choose between* Society and Poetry, between Life and Language, between Existence and Song. Each is the umbilical cord and source of the other. Society without Language would be like a body without a heart, a being in search of a brain. Such a society not only would hardly be worth preserving, it could not exist. No one would speak. And Language without society—how is this even conceivable? Language is what makes society possible. It is, according to Heidegger, the dwelling place of Being, that which gathers everything into itself and then returns every being to its own self.

To transform life, existence, society, from its common, stupid, painful being, into the Creative Being of a Poem; or to create Poetry from the presence from which it must be born: the choice is neither one nor the other. It would not be a choice! As soon as one attempted to isolate, to separate, to mutilate, to take one from the other, both would simultaneously vanish (like a collision between a particle and its anti-particle). Poetry is Language, purely, originally. A society that abolished Poetry would be committing in the same act suicide. To condemn Poetry is to condemn Language and as a consequence, thinking!

Between Doing and Being; between Knowing and Being; between the Evening and Morning Star; between the Imagination and the Body—how do we "choose"?

II The Poetry

Eruption, woman, nakedness, embrace, blood, dust and ashes, death, abandons, world, leaves, pomegranate trees, noon, sun and moon, water, air, fire, earth, stars, flying, bodies, you, we, language, words, dreams, time, history, autumn, night, breast, existence, eyes, silence, solitude, the empty space of writing.

To discover the inventions and language of Paz is to experience a primordial beginning of ourself, a return to the origin of the world, a relearning of our forgotten erotic dances, of the Imagination venturing to the abyss in order to arrive at an open space where it will touch Song and Existence, where Body becomes Imagination.

In *Libertad bajo palabra*, a collection of five volumes of Paz's poetry, we find an inexhaustible energy moving simultaneously through dimensions of thinking and feeling with a magnitude of the spectrum of autumn colors. One of these poems "Hacia el poema" ("Toward the Poem") is from the volume *¿Águila o sol? (Eagle or Sun?)*:

I

Damos vueltas y vueltas en el vientre animal, en el vientre mineral, en el vientre temporal. Encontrar la salida: el poema.

. . .

Arrancar Ias máscaras de la fantasía, clavar una pica en el centro sensible: provocar la erupción.
Cortar el cordón umbilicla, matar bien a la Madre: crimen que el poeta moderno cometió por todos, en nombre de todos. Toca al nuevo poeta descubrir a la Mujer.

. . .

II

Palabras, frases, sílabas, astros que giran alrededor de un
centro fijo. Dos cuerpos, muchos seres que se encuentran
en una palabra. El papel se cubre de letras indelebles,
que nadic dijo, que nadic dictó, que han caído allí y
arden y queman y se apagan. Así pues, existe la poesía,
el amor existe. Y si yo no existo, existes tú.
. . .

El poema prepara un orden amoroso. Preveo un hombresol
y una mujer-luna, el uno libre de su poder, la otra
libre de su esclavitud, y amores implacables rayando el
espacio negro. Todo ha de ceder a esas águilas
incandescentes.
. . .

Todo poema se cumple a expensas del poeta.
. . .

Cuando la Historia duerme, habla en sueños: en la frente
del pueblo dormido el poema es una constelación de
sangre. Cuando la Historia despierta, la imagen se hace
acto, acontece el poema: la poesía entra en acción.

Merece lo que sueñas.

I

We turn and turn in the animal belly, in the mineral
belly, in the belly of time. To find the way out: the
poem.
. . .
To tear away the masks of fantasy, to drive a lance into
the nerve center: to incite the eruption.

To cut the umbilical cord, to kill the Mother: crime the
modern poet has committed for all, in the name of all:
It is up to the new poet to discover Woman.
. . .

II

Words, phrases, syllables, stars which turn about a fixed point. Two bodies, many beings that find each other in a word. The paper is covered by indelible letters, that no one said, no one pronounced, that have fallen there and blaze and burn up and die out. In this way, poetry exists, love exists. And if I do not exist, you do.
. . .

The poem prepares a loving order. I foresee a man-sun and a woman-moon, he free of his power, she free of her slavery, and implacable love streaking through black space. Everything must give way before these incandescent eagles.
. . .
Every poem is realized at the poet's expense.
. . .
When History sleeps, it speaks in dreams: on the brow of a sleeping people the poem is a constellation of blood. When History wakes, the image becomes act, the poem happens: poetry moves into action.

Deserve what you dream.

This is a poem not so much of exploration, every good poem is certainly that and incalculably more. It is the being-of-exploration: between the Poet and Time, Time and History, History and Language, Language and the Poet. As always the beginning is the belly, the womb, the starting place, the point of departure. And it is by and through the elemental unit of the phrase this poem will begin, be upheld and continue. Only Language which begins our journey can take us to the opening, the threshold, the world, into existence. But if it is necessary to cut the umbilical cord which has given us life and the strength to begin our journey of becoming, why must the modern Poet commit murder in the process? How is this crime committed in the name of us all? And who or what is the Mother being killed?

The answer is tradition, history, ideology, Christianity. A severing of eternal time, of paradise, of tradition, is accomplished, a necessary act, so that History may become the beginning of the future—which is now, this moment, the Present. The new Poet is the first who will rediscover Woman. It is Woman who has been buried 5,000 years by a patriarchal consciousness.

In discovering Woman, the Prophetic Poet discovers the other side of our world, that lost part of ourselves, that part killed, made silent, ridiculed, neglected; that element of the world, yin, without which its contrary and complement, yang, cannot exist: History, Wisdom.

This is the Poet's relation, obsession and yearning for original time, the beginning before the world was tempted by a lust to seize control of Nature, before fear and hatred had become an excuse to acquire power over another; a time before the discovery of inauthenticity, stupidity and inequality. This original time will be once again, now: original time-future time and future time-original time:

> The poem prepares a loving order. I foresee a man-sun and a woman-moon, he free of his power, she free of her slavery, and implacable love streaking through black space. Everything must give way before these incandescent eagles.

It would be a mistake here to think that man is only sun (reason-thinking) and woman only moon (intuition-emotion). Thinking-emotion (reason-intuition) are another of a pair of contraries which cannot exist separately. The unifying tension and force which require Thinking and Emotion, Intuition and Reason, Sun and Moon, Man and Woman, Desire and Knowledge, Freedom and Necessity, Energy and Delight to indissolubly embrace is the same as that which for us invents the universe: the Poetic Possibility of the Human Imagination.

The sublime strength, high tension and erotic quality in the language of this great Poet has still not found its potential audience in the North. Of his poetry, only *Early Poems, Configurations, Eagle or Sun?, Renga: A Chain of Poems*, (a colaboration with Jacques Roubaud, Eduardo Sanguineti and Charles Tomlinson), and *A Draft of Shadows* have been translated and published in book form here. In fact, more of Paz's critical writings abound in English than his poetry.

Paz's insatiable mind which extends to philosophy, anthropology, linguistics and literary and art criticism tends to overshadow his poetry. But it is for his poetry that he first attracted attention and it is his poetry which of all his writings is most unique. It is above all, his poetry which for us matters most:

> Allá, donde terminan las fronteras, los caminos se borran.
> Donde empieza el silencio. Avanzo lentamente y pueblo
> la noche de estrellas, de palabras, de la respiración de un
> agua remota que me espera donde comienza el alba.

Invento la víspera, la noche . . .
. . .
Allá, donde los caminos se borran, donde acaba el silencio,
invento la desesperación, la mente que me concibe,
la mano que me dibuja, el ojo que me descubre. Invento
al amigo que me inventa, mi semejante: y a la mujer, mi
contrario . . .

Contra el silencio y el bullicio invento la Palabra, libertad
que se inventa y me inventa cada día.

Over there, where frontiers end, the roads are erased.
Where silence begins. I advance slowly and I people the
night with stars, with words, with the breathing of a remote
water that waits for me where the dawn begins.

I invent the evening, the night . . .
. . .
Over there, where roads are erased, where silence ends,
I invent passion, the mind which conceives me, the hand
which designs me, the eye which discovers me. I invent
the friend who invents me, my counterpart; and woman,
my contrary . . .

Against the silence and noise I invent the Word, freedom
which invents itself and invents me every day.

In Octavio Paz we have found what has been forgotten in our day:
the Poem and the Poet are the same. If we are told it is the Poet who sits
down at a desk to create, to fashion phrases into the living being of a Poem,
I will add that it is the Poem which causes the Poet to invent those phrases
which the Poem will become. The freedom of the Poet—the Poet's
Imagination—creates, shapes, invents, transforms, metamorphosizes the
Poet in this very act. To our list of contraries which require themselves to
exist only when their complementary elements have a like presence in the
world, we must add Poet-Poem.

Against silence and noise (each a movement and negation into the
other) Paz invents the Poem, aware that it is always the Freedom of the
Poem which invents himself and us everyday. Language: words, phrases,
poems, become the being of thought, passion, song; and in turn, invent
Language which discovers itself, and allows us to discover ourselves.

Language—Thought—Freedom—Song—Existence—Language. Each is for the other, each discovers and invents the other.

Paz's origin and thus source of strength is Mexico: place of Toltec Pyramids, Aztec gods, land of Spanish subjugation, U.S. domination; a nation looking for its past with its arms flung open to "progress." If it is this Mexico which has partly invented him, as all of us are invented in one way or another by a collective history a unique time and place, it is also his prophetic vision, his dialectical language, his contradictory tensions and his lyrical eroticism all interwoven at once, here, now into a *Presence*, into a whole tapestry of Being which has made him a universally great Poet—one who easily transcends the stupid boundaries and arbitrary divisions of land masses still archaically called "nations."

III The Poet—The Poetry

It is the Poet who in a time of destitution, a time that is, when the world is so destitute it has little awareness even of its destitution, journeys to the abyss, experiences it, comprehends it and returns with a vision, a warning: either the world must fundamentally turn away from this abyss or annihilate itself. It is the Poet's task to venture to the abyss because only the Poet is venturesome and daring enough to do so. Dante descends into hell while still a mortal in order to comprehend how and where he went astray from the true path, to recapture his original being and to recount his experiences to us so we may know of the dangers of living inauthentically, of fragmenting ourselves from the world.

Society must learn to listen to the prophetic voice of its Poets. Hölderlin, who first poses this question in his poem "Brod und Wein" ("Bread and Wine"): ". . . und wozu Dichter in dürftiger Zeit?" (". . . and what are Poets for in a destitute time?") brings us full circle back again to our question: "Would it not be better to transform life into poetry than to make poetry from life?"

In Nature, in the world's original time, there was no contradiction between Love and Eroticism, Reason and Intuition, Being and Authenticity, Desire and Knowledge, Action and Thought, Community and Creativity. But today the world is split up. Original time has been lost, forgotten, mutilated. Nature has been conquered by tools. Adolescents carry calculators to school but have no knowledge, no comprehension of the foundations of mathematics. Imagination is an orphan, unwanted, called impractical, and treated as a vestigial oddity having no utility. And thought vitiated gives birth to that twin mutation, technology and "progress," a hydra difficult to extirpate. Is it therefore utopian to conceive that society can be transformed into an integrated Poetic Being and that Love will undergo a genuine metamorphosis—rediscovering its authentic Being, its eroticism?

Paz is echoing the revolutionary prophecy of Lautréamont when he said that *poetry should be made a "practical truth" for everyone*, and Rimbaud, when he declared that *Love needed to be reinvented*! Will everyone create poetry? Can Love undergo a fundamental transformation? Each question (and therefore the answer given it) is contained in the other.

Poetry is a revolutionary vocation because its deepest foundation is Love: and Love in its original state is equivalent to the Erotic in our authentic Being in Nature (original time). Thus Love and Eroticism, which are inseparable from each other and commune by virtue of the Imagination are the original subversive elements in the world. Until a time comes (and it will) when society is metamorphosized into one where history's negation has become a *History* being invented and directed by Consciousness, Poetry will remain practically the only avenue open for the world to comprehend itself. I have said and let me repeat—that it is for this reason, if no other, that true Poets can never abandon Poetry without eventually destroying themselves. (The case of Rimbaud, one of our greatest Poets, is no exception. After abandoning poetry at nineteen his life ever after was, as his letters show us, one of constant worry, self-doubt and pity, drifting from one place to the next until his death at thirty-seven.)

Poetry is the Imagination and the Body together, Desire and Knowledge, Pleasure and Work, Love and Eroticism, Intuition and Reason, Sun and Moon, Knowing and Being, Existence and Song, Venture and Daring, Action and Thought, Energy and Delight, Life and Language, Freedom and Necessity.

Our goal is and will always be both Society and Song; and because Song is, as Rilke has said, the same as Being, it is the Poet who teaches us who we are, who we may become, from where we have traveled and even, through the magic and power of prophecy, that Poetry and History will someday embrace. Husserl once remarked that philosophers were the civil servants of Humanity. I will add: Poets are its Soul!

RACHEL PHILLIPS

The Surrealist Mode

There is a definite period in Octavio Paz's career when his poetry may be considered as set in a surrealist mode. Chronological precision is impossible when dealing with the intangibilities of a creative psyche, and traces of a predisposition to a surrealist outlook appear early. Yet the three collections in which this mode is most apparent are those which contain Paz's writing of the 50s: *¿Aguila o sol?*, the prose poems of 1949–50 *La estación violenta*, which appeared in 1957 and contains major works from 1948–57, and *Salamandra*, whose poems are from 1958 to 1961 and which appeared in 1969 in its second edition. Paz was closely associated with the surrealist group in Paris when André Breton returned there after the Second World War, and there is obviously a correspondence between his own years in Paris and his change in literary style. Yet Paz never gave up his poetic independence to become a committed member of this group, and so did not assume the title of surrealist proper. It is more accurate to say that he found in the ideas and practices of the Surrealists' affinities with his spiritual state and his linguistic theories at that time. The Surrealists' exploration of the whole self by taking into account the individual's dream and fantasy worlds as well as his conscious level of existence tends towards a unitive view of the psyche which echoes in all Paz's writings in one form or another. Again, the deliberate dislocation of the image in order to shock the recipient into a new vision is particularly apt

From *The Poetic Modes of Octavio Paz* by Rachel Phillips, © 1972 by Oxford University Press.

for the expression of a state of mind which is 'out of joint' with itself and its universe. This is, in fact, the prevailing mood of *Salamandra*, and is implicit in the linguistic and imagistic struggles of *¿Aguila o sol?* In terms of the mythic cycle which I see as the structure basic to Paz's work, the anguished rites of initiation preceding spiritual rebirth gain in poignancy when set in a mode which explores the underside of the mind as an indispensable complement to the conscious.

Paz's prose writings make constant reference to the Surrealists, Breton and Peret, for instance, as well as to writers considered precursors of the movement, Lautréamont and Apollinaire. Apollinaire was the first to coin the term 'surréalisme', when in 1917 in a programme note to the Satie–Massine–Picasso ballet *Parade*, produced by Diaghilev, he called this unique collaboration a kind of 'surréalisme'. André Breton seized upon the new term as applicable to his own vision of art a few years later, though he hesitated between this and Gérard de Nerval's 'supernaturalisme', feeling that: 'Il semble, en effect, que Nerval posséda á merveille *l'esprit* dont nous nous réclamons, Apollinaire n'ayant possédé par contre, que *la lettre*, encore imparfaite, du surréalisme et s'étant montré impuissant à en donner un apercu théorique quinous retienne.'

Breton himself is quite explicit in his description of this new spirit which was to combine the world of reality with the dream world 'en une sorte de réalité absolue, de *surréalité*, si l' on peut ainsi dire'. Breton's knowledge of Freudian theories and his application of these in his work in neuro-psychiatric centres during the First World War are apparent in his formal definition of the term in the 1924 *Manifeste*:

> SURREALISME, n. m. Automatisme psychique pour par lequel on se propose d'exprimer, soit verbalement, soit par écrit, soit de toute autre manière, le fonctionnement réel de la pensée. Dictée, en la pensée, en l'absence de tout contrôle exercé par la raison, en dehors de toute pré-occupation esthétique ou morale.
>
> ENCYCL. *Philos.* Le surréalisme repose sur la croyance á la réalité supérieure de certaines formes d'associations négligées jusqu'à lui, à la toutepuissance du rêve, au jeu désintéressé de la pensée. Il tend à ruiner définitivement tous les autres mécanismes psychiques et à se substituer à eux dans la résolution des principaux problèmes de la vie. . . .

Breton then points out how many writers have in fact been unwitting surrealists in certain aspects of their writings, a statement which supports exactly the present view of surrealism in Paz's work: 'Swift est surréaliste dans la méchanceté. Sade est surréaliste dans le sadisme. . .'.

Because surrealism became for its true adherents so much a way of life and an all-pervading outlook, it is most easily discussed in purely literary terms if broken down into some of the elements most crucial to it. Paz's work can then be examined in more concentrated focus. Thus three categories seem most important as common denominators in surrealism proper and in Paz's poetry: emphasis on the word, the treatment of the image, and the figure of the double, crucial to exploration of the psyche. Naturally surrealism did not depend exclusively upon these three basic approaches; categories galore can be isolated within the movement, from metaphysical systems to creeds of social action. It is merely to avoid dissipation that these three have been chosen as links between Paz in his surrealist mode and the hard-core movement which guided him. Paz was surrealist in technique as and when it suited him, using depersonalization of emotion and dislocation of image to heighten the anguish which he was communicating through the poem. It could even be said of Paz, as Paul Ilie has said of Cernuda, that he is 'a surrealist only to the extent that his compositional needs are being satisfied. . . . Indeed we may almost speak of an aesthetic accidentalism, an expedient borrowing of techniques from the French school simply because they are the most appropriate means available for the immediate context. Given the affinity which Paz feels for Cernuda's poetry, this remark seems particularly applicable to his also.

The Word

The Surrealists tried to restore to the word its original purity, a preoccupation in which Mallarmé had preceded them when he claimed that one must 'donner un sens plus pur aux mots de la tribu', though his active verb 'donner' does not apply to the Surrealists. They saw the process more as a removal of a falsifying exterior, and the word as source of the energy which alone could do justice to the surrealist vision. It was this energy which all their techniques strove to release. This awareness of language as such has entered the bloodstream of contemporary poetry, as testified by Sartre among many others: 'L'homme qui parle est au delà des mots, près de l'object; le poète est en deçà. Pour le premier, ils sont domestiques; pour le second, ils restent à l'état sauvage.' The liberty which the Surrealists demand for the imagination must be realized through the power of the word.

There is an obvious desire in surrealism to step beyond the bounds of the human condition. In this respect there exists a continuity between the Surrealists and the 'Orphic' poets, Nerval, Hugo, Baudelaire, and Rimbaud, with their efforts to cut through the limitations of the conscious mind.

Surrealists were drawn by a desire for transcendence in that their subjectivity and introspection led them through realms of the unconscious from which emergence was the prize of anguish. Yet the 'surreal' is not the 'super-natural', and many Surrealists denied the idea of God while feeling drawn to some awareness of the Infinite. The resolution of resultant tensions between the conscious and the unconscious and between the imagination and the reason occurred for the artist in the possibility of creation. Where the expression of inner visions was possible the psychic balance was restored. Where the conflict became too great between the creative impulse and the imperfection of the medium, alienation took place, silence in the case of Rimbaud, madness in that of Antonin Artaud. The word, then, is not only the means by which the poet descends into the unconscious depths of his mind, formulating for himself and for others the obscure impulses found there, but also the vital medium of adjustment by which man retains contact with both the inner and the outer worlds. Hence the obvious connections between surrealism and psycho-analysis, with similar emphasis on dreams and on the verbal expression of these dreams as well. In both cases the word is clearly the means of survival.

Paz's poetry from first to last shows his obsession with his medium. His early collection, *A la orilla del mundo* (1942), opens with the poem 'Palabra', which elevates language to the mystical heights of the sacramental:

> Palabra, una palabra,
> la última y primera,
> la que callamos siempre,
> la que siempre decimos,
> sacramento y ceniza.

His poetry from here on abounds in similar expressions of frustration at the sheer impossibility of there ever existing a sufficiently viable bridge between the experience and the expression of it. Yet talking about the frustration is also conquering it, and the very form given to the despair is the vehicle of salvation. Thus the bridge which sanity demands between the ineffable and the attempt to express it is created even by cries of despair at the impossibility of the task. In the state of mind which accompanies Paz's surrealist works this is the cry most often heard, and it becomes more poignant through the abandonment of logical discourse which surrealism prescribed.

The whole first section of *¿Aguila o sol?* in fact deals with the nature of the poet's task. 'Trabajos del poeta' is the longest single confrontation of the poet and the word in a struggle which Paz sums up in the small preface which precedes it: '*Ayer, investido de plenos poderes, escribla con fluidez sobre cualquier hoja disponible. . . Hoy lucho a solas con una palabra. La que me pertenece, ala que pertenezco: ¿cara o cruz, águila o sol?.*' The two most impressive facts about this struggle are the personification of the words as assailants (and consequent depersonalization of the poet) and the extraordinary verbal agility in which it is described. Words are in fact the challengers on two levels: the imaginary, which lines them up in fantastic battle array, and the technical, in which the poet literally twists, distorts, and remakes all the components of language to suit his ends. All sixteen sections involve a narrator who gives a first-person account of his trials and torments and whose presence provides the unity of the work. Thematically the work can be discussed in three divisions, though the transitions are so smooth that no distinct breaks occur. But for convenience Sections I to VII may be dealt with as a first theme, divided from their development by the insomnia of Section VIII. The last five sections, XII to XVI, link the inner sufferings of the narrator to the wider arena of suffering around him.

The frustrations of the narrator in the first unit are twofold. First he is prey to attack by myriads of unwanted elements of language which catch him unawares and force themselves and the nightmare they conceptualize into his consciousness. They present themselves 'desgreñados al alba y pálidos a medianoche . . . dientes feroces, voces roncas, todos ojos de bocaza.' They must be fought off, or else they will take control and the consequences will be disastrous. Sections I and II thus show the conscious mind receptive to the impulses of the subconscious and aware of the horrors and the treasures of that realm: 'También debo decir que ciertos días arden, brillan, ondulan, se despliegan o repliegan. . . .' The narrator faces the teleological issue raised by this contamination of the conscious by the unconscious mind: is it providential design or mere fortuitousness which governs this invasion of the psyche? Secondly, there is the urgent need for the right word which will be the poet's bridge back into the mysteries of the imagination and out into the world of human contact. This Word, which Paz capitalizes to add an element of sublimity, comes in moments of silence or inattentiveness, and must be seized if this is possible. Often, as in Section III, the narrator misses his chance: 'Lo inesperado del encuentro me paralizó por un segundo, que fue suficiente para darle tiempo de volver a la noche.'

Section IV explores silence, a silence pulsing with the rhythm which links all layers of creation, from the heart of man to the waves of the sea. Section V breaks the cosmic mood in a brilliant tussle between narrator and language: 'Te desfondo a fondo, te desfundo de tu fundamento. Traquetea tráquea aquea. El carrascaloso se rasca la costra de caspa. Doña campamocha se atasca, tarasca.' Words are coined, rhymed, used alliteratively, played with, and mangled as the narrator bests his adversary. The result is whirlwind chaos ending in breathless mastery: 'Jadeo, penduleo desguanguilado, jadeo.'

The first unit ends with two moments of introspection. In Section VI the narrator considers the disillusionment and the grief of the purification which those who serve poetry must go through. No other process will create the empty expectancy where the Word may some day be heard. The sacrifice of identity must be made, for rewards which are doubtful: 'A veces, una tarde cualquiera, un día sin nombre, cae una Palabra, que se posa levemente sobre esa tierra sin pasado. El páajaro es feroz y acaso te sacará los ojos. Acaso, más tarde, vendrán otros.' Section VII is concerned with words which by their numbers exclude the one magic syllable. The narrator is writing on and on until he realizes that 'un simple monosílab bastaría para hacer saltar al mundo.' Yet he has cluttered himself with the inessential so that there is no longer room for what would take him to the heart of things.

After the anguish of insomniac introversion in Section VIII, the three sections of the second unit develop in different ways the power of man over language. Section IX picks up the earlier personification of words as inhabitants of some monstrous other-region who can be manhandled and debased at will once they have been cowed into submission: 'A la palabra odio la alimento con basuras durante años, hasta que estalla en una hermosa explosíon purulenta, que infecta por un siglo el lenguaje'. Next the narrator repudiates traditional beliefs along with traditional language, while dreaming up a new fabrication of words which will wipe out the old and clear the ground for a new order: 'Hoy sueño un lenguaje de cuchillos y picos, de ácidos y llams. Un lenguaje de látigos. Para execrar, exasperar, excomulgar, expulsar. . . .' And finally the fantasy of the word 'Cri' which becomes an elusive will-o'-the-wisp, drawing the hunter-fisherman after it, but never caught, again symbolic of the tantalizing promise of that one word which, if found, will provide a key to all secrets.

The third unit widens the horizons by moving both deeper into the narrator's psyche and further out into the surrounding world. Sections XII and XIV are moments of intense introspection in which preoccupation with language is replaced by deeper feelings of spiritual anguish. The alternating sections move outwards to the sufferings of the narrator's unnamed country, first with the touching parable of Tilantlán, and secondly in a lament for a people whom even hope has passed by: 'Todas las palabras han muerto de sed. Nadie podrá alimentarse con estos restos pulidos . . . Esperanza, águila famélica, déjame sobre esta roca parecida al silencio.' The last section transcends the struggle with language itself to arrive at the implications of speech, and the responsibilities of the artist: '. . . tú, mi Grito, surtidor de plumas de fuego, herida resonante y vasta como el desprendimiento de un planeta del cuerpo de una estrella . . . .' The final justification of the 'trabajos del poeta' is here not only an artistic but a humanitarian one. The inner world of the imagination has been explored and allowed to enrich the workings of the conscious mind. Then the resources of both have been allowed to combine in a universal plea which takes the poet back out from surreality into the world of concrete reality around him. The result has not been an escape, but an enrichment of commitment.

Many poems in *Salamandra* deal in a purely literary or meta-physical framework with the poet's struggle to govern his idiom. Paz's exploration of his Mexican roots does not end after 'Piedra de sol', but recedes into wider concerns. Certainly preoccupations with the creative function of the poet grow more obvious. In 'Disparo' the struggle with language is couched in a series of images which treat the word as an entity with its own energy and animation. It leaps ahead of thought and sound, like a horse ahead of the wind, 'Como un novillo de azufre'. It leaps through the night to lose itself in the sleeping poet's brain. Now the metaphors grow wilder and human anatomy mingles with its surroundings, while sensations of sight and touch are called into play:

> En la cara del árbol el tatuaje escarlata. . .
> En la espalda del muro el tatuaje de hielo
> En el sexo de la iglesia el tatuaje eléctrico. . .

The image of the wild beast returns but gives way to that of the sunflower turning towards whiteness, 'Hasta el grito hasta el basta'. Sound and sight fuse in contorted images—'la firma del sin nombre', 'el grito que ciega', 'la imagen que ríe', and the word which 'revienta las palabras'. And the poem ends with seven vertiginous lines of imagery in which one female figure follows another—'la desaparecida en mitad del abrazo . . . ,' 'la mendiga profética'—until the final release:

> la muchacha que en mitad de la vida
> me despierta y me dice *acuérdate*

It is as always for this poet: the poetic faculty itself provides the moment of awakening from the nightmare. There is the pain of initiation, in this case of struggle with incoherence or with the inexpressible, and there is the eventual crystallization of the poem itself which, along with passion and the plenitude of Nature, shows man's transcendence of the limitations of solitude, alienation, and silence.

There are two pairs of poems in *Salamandra* which emerge in very different ways from Paz's need to examine the links between himself, his experiences, and his language. The first pair, 'La palabra escrita' and 'La palabra dicha', experiment with the naming process itself, a self-conscious manipulation of the machinery of language. 'Aspiración' and 'Espiración' use language experimentation as an end in itself, ignoring the means. But both pairs depend upon the ability of the artist to exploit his medium, just as the process was described in 'Trabajos del poeta'. Behind all four poems—and these are chosen merely as examples of a continuing process—lies the conviction cherished by the Surrealists that language could be a tool used to reach and express the subconscious side of the mind. Words, if allowed to emerge from free association of sounds and fantasies, provide one of the most important keys to that integration of the real and the 'surreal' at which surrealism aimed.

Such premises do not make for easily explicated poems. Both pairs depend on antithetical concepts and are related formally, but at this point comparisons cease to be valid. 'La palabra escrita' is a poem so cryptic in form that it opens itself to many depths of interpretation. There is a creative inspiration, be it on the aesthetic level of the poet or the mystical plane of God, or a combination of both, which provides a leitmotiv recurring six times throughout this comparatively short (thirty-one lines) poem. This phrase, 'Ya escrita la primera / Palabra', is the only one not parenthesized, and it is never made into a complete sentence. Instead it is complemented by what might be called the self-evident reality as opposed to the ontological: parenthetical portions of a scene which involves the sun and a face both reflected in a well. Into this well a stone, objective correlative of the word, is dropped, with the consequent breaking up of the reflected images. When the ripples cease the images return, and the stone/word lies forgotten at the bottom. The poem ends with the antithesis between the absolute first Word and the finite reality which our language can grasp:

> Ya escrita la primera
> Palabra (sigue,
> No hay más palabras que las de la cuenta)

'La palabra dicha' cuts through the polemics of the linguists, following the word from the page into the intricacies of the ear to final silence. On the page the word is frozen like a 'labrada estalactita'; when it frees itself its concept bridges the gulf 'Del silencio al grito'. But in the labyrinth of the ear sound patterns confuse meanings and the mind is side-tracked into senseless games: 'lamenta la mente. / De menta demente . . .'.

This chaos distorts the cry which language was to express so that it goes unheard, 'grito / Desoído'. There is only one escape—the way of innocence and silence: 'Para hablar aprende a callar.' Language, as poets and mystics alike learn through anguish, is at best a distortion of the absolute in whatever terms its intuition is felt.

'Aspiración' and 'Espiración' are held together as complementary pieces by a loose web of antithetical developments of a few common themes, and by a formal similarity which seems almost whimsical. Both have three parts, the first two consisting of two five-line stanzas of hendecasyllables interspersed in 'Aspiración' with seven-syllable lines. The third section of both is in unrhymed sonnet form and both start with lines which contain an almost identical word-play. In brief, 'Aspiración' finds the poet divorced from outer reality, aware of memory as the only link with existence on this or any other plane. Memory is his defence against 'la hora y su resaca,' and it alone asserts the reality of physical existence, be it his or another's: 'Tu cuerpo es la memoria de mis huesos.' The 'sonnet' opens with an amalgam of earlier themes of shade and sun: 'Sombra del sol / Solombra segadora.' The burden of vitality which memory bears descends now upon the words in which this assertion is expressed. The ear is carried by alliteration and assonance, *s*, *n*, and *a* sounds in the first quatrain, *m*, *n*, and *a*, in the second. Words are coined in order that sound may carry a meaning in as valid a way as does sense: 'Mas la memoria desmembrada nada / Desde los nacederos de su nada . . . .' Plays on words ('nada [i.e., it swims] contra la nada'), paradox ('Sentido sin sentido'), daring images ('Pentecostés palabra sin palabras'), and more alliteration ('Lengua de fuego fosforece el agua') all accumulate until the climactic interplay of sound and sense of the last tercet:

> Sentido sin sentido No pensado
> Pensar que transfigura la memoria
> El resto es un manojo de centellas.

The reader is left dazzled by impossible imagery and bewildered by paradox, but aware that the poem offers an affirmation of some lasting element in the human spirit.

'Espiración' is the descent from this peak. Its first part picks up motifs from 'Aspiración'—the white shadows of the day, and the existence of memory—but the image has changed. Memory is now a 'torre hendida, / Pausa vacía entre dos claridades'. The city has become disembodied, and the outer world invisible. Does memory provide a defence? '¿En tu memoria / Serán mis huesos tiempo incandescente?' The image of death dominates the second section, death in its macabre, skeletal manifestation. There is no defence against physical decay, and all that love leaves is a 'trazo negro de la quemadura . . . en lo blanco de los huesos'. The 'sonnet' plays with the shade–sun paradox of its partner. The order is reversed—'Sombra de sol' to 'Sol de sombra'—and the sound of 'segadora' is kept, though a new image is superimposed: 'Solombra cegadora'. This reinforces the theme of blind eyes which occurred in the first part of 'Aspiración' and again in its sonnet, but now the poet insists upon the reverse concept. Though sun and shade blind the natural vision (i.e. death cuts down physical life), there is an inner vision which remains: 'Mis ojos han de ver lo nunca visto. . . El revés de lo visto y de la vista.'

The same word-games (alliteration, assonance, etc.) bring to the second quatrain the flavour of a burlesque funeral ceremony: '(Los laúdes del laúdano de loas . . .)', and the last tercet ends in an irony of verbal play which makes the cryptic last line capable of a paradoxical doubling of interpretation:

> Lo nunca visto nunca dicho nunca
> Es lo ya dicho el nunca del retruécano
> Vivo me ves y muerto no has de verme

Thus another level of the power of words has been explored, namely irony, in which plays on words can not only call to mind varieties of associative meanings, but can also introduce an atmosphere of polyvalency which sets the poem in a context of ambiguity. This combination of surprising images with verbal experimentation and irony sums up, I suggest, the surrealist mode as Paz used it. That is to say that he was not by conviction a Surrealist, and could use their techniques with the pinch of objectivity which the ambiguity of this poem suggests. Yet he was well aware of the pertinence of their tenets and literary methods, and used this mode as it suited his bent. Precisely for this reason it is possible to discuss a surrealist mode within the works of a poet who could never by reason of his eclecticism be pigeon-holed as a Surrealist.

The Image

The Surrealists wished to revitalize an alienated world by the spontaneous activity of the imagination. They saw violence and shock as effective ways to recreate in the adult the immediacy and totality of vision given to him as a child but later lost by all but certain 'âmes privilégiées'. The way to this lies through the visual and emotional shock of imagery which calls upon the intuitive world of the imagination. By juxtaposing two distant elements a new element is created, and the world is transformed, becomes more than real, as the image flashes a new light upon the disparities it has fused together. The result is often a 'beauté convulsive', which gives a violent shock to a mind imprisoned in old concepts and conditioned to respond intellectually to its surroundings. Thus surrealism literally causes a revolution in our perceptivity, and an acceptance of imagery which brings to light connections of which the perceiver has been sluggishly unaware. Lautréamont's famous image of 'la recontre fortuite sur une table de dissection d'une machine à coudre et d'un parapluie', links literary surrealism realism to the art of Miró, Magritte, Dali, and the world of the ready-mades.

This use of the startling image to transform reality is abundant in those volumes of Paz already mentioned. Sometimes creation of an atmosphere is an end in itself, and images in weird and troubling combinations disturb the acceptance of outer reality. *¿Aguila o sol?* provides so many examples of such imagery that one chosen at random may be considered representative. 'Lecho de helechos' communicates a mood of mystic expectancy by means of a Daliesque landscape. The poet stands at the end of the world, before him a landscape of immense, sleeping, but still sparkling eyes, and there stares at him 'tu mirada última—la mirada que pierde cielo'. Shining scales of glances cover the beach, and a liquid gold wave is receding. The life-force gazing at him becomes a lunar drumskin, a piece of star on the edge of a crater, and the poet seems to hold up reality with the magnetism of his eyes: 'Te sostienen en vilo mis ojos, como la luna a la marea encendida. A tus pies la espuma degollada canta el canto de la noche que empieza'.

The violent fusion of disparate objects can have more troubling effects, as in 'Entrada en materia', the first poem in *Salamandra*. The mood of suffering and alienation which is conveyed by imagery of city life seems to suggest that the 'materia' of the title is an objective correlative for the underworld of the myth of birth and rebirth. The hero must be withdrawn from his normal sphere, his worth tested against forces both alien and dangerous, in order to emerge into the new consciousness to which he is heir. The initiate, in other words, must earn his right to knowledge of ancient truths by pain and frustration on a physical or a spiritual level.

Like the initiate, the poet stands to gain greater awareness of human and ultra-human truths, but at a price—the price he must pay himself, when he stands as a stranger in his land, faced with an alien society and unacceptable values. The city is Paz's waste land in 'Entrada en materia', and the poem dwells on the paradox of man's spiritual and physical beauty caught in a labyrinth of concrete which echoes the inhumanity of the modern civilized world.

The opening image of this poem is hard and cold, the repeated *r* and *i* sounds of the first line sharp and cruel—'Piedras de ira fría'. The city is bitter and claustrophobic, full of tall houses with saltpetre lips: 'casas podridas en el saco del invierno'. This technique of personification grows more horrible as the human attributes become more shocking:

> Noche de innumerables tetas
> y una sola boca carnicera . . .

The neon lights are decorated with 'guirnaldas de dientes', they blink with 'El guiño obsceno de los números', and in the destroyed night the city becomes synonymous with 'Gatos en celo y pánico de monos'. But inhuman though time and place may be, there is still

> El sagrario del cuerpo
> El arca del espíritu
> Los labios de la herida

The last image (which ends the poem in the first edition) evokes in the reader's mind the triple concept of poet-sufferer-speaker which appeared already in the much more direct image of 'Fuente', and which will reappear in the poignant image of 'Cosante':

> Con la lengua cortada canta
> Sangre sobre la piedra
> El ruiseñor en la muralla

The atmosphere grows more threatening as the invisible tide of fear overtakes 'torres ceñudas . . . sonámbulos palacios . . . graves moles', and brings in evil:

> El mal promiscuo el mal sin nombre
> Todos los nombres del mal
> El mal que tiene todos los nombres. . .

The city becomes a grotesque female figure:

> Entre tus muslos un reloj da la hora
> Demasiado tarde
> Demasiado pronto
> En tu cama de siglos fornican los relojes. . .

Time and place are out of season, and the poet's ears ring with the senseless sounds of the city and the tick of clocks which defeat language.

The moon with its connotations of mystery and magic rises, but is defeated too; it falls 'como un borracho' and is defiled by the 'perros callejeros', by a convoy of trucks, by a cat, and 'Los carniceros se lavan las manos / En el agua de la luna'. The chime of a clock leads to a labyrinthine play on the words 'hora' and 'ahora', as the poet senses himself at a point in time where there is no place for him. He is unable to grasp the immediacy of the moment, yet finds himself trapped in the passage of minutes and hours.

The poem's focus turns to the figure of the poet again, and to Paz's constant preoccupation with language, condemned by 'la conciencia y sus pulpos escribanos' to perpetual inadequacy:

> El tribunal condena lo que escribo
> El tribunal condena lo que callo . . .

To the poet who is caught between the limitations of time and reason, words seem only to construct their own incoherence:

> Una ciudad inmensa y sin sentido
> Un monumento grandioso incoherente
> Babel babel minúscula . . .

But the alternative is silence which 'no es fácil y además no puedo', and furthermore there is a mysticism in the whole process by which things are given their names. Names and nouns interpret the outer world: 'Ejes / anchas espaldas de este mundo'; provide a bulwark against time: 'Lomos que cargan sin esfuerzo al tiempo'; and lead beyond materialism to spiritual regions, though the entry is perilous: 'Puerta puerta condenada'. This concept opens the final moment when the poet fights through the contradictions of temporality and reality to the paradox of the name, which interprets the object by defining its existence, yet in definition proves its own inadequacies. Thus the hold upon outer reality is never secure. Bound in subjectivity, man cannot escape the intangibility of what surrounds him:

> Los nombres no son nombres
> No dicen lo que dicen. . .

Civilization closes around him with 'Piedra sangre esperma / Ira ciudad relojes / Pánico risa Pánico.'

There is an emergence from the labyrinth, however, as Paz sees the poet's task:

> Yo he de decir lo que dicen
> El sagario del cuerpo
> El arca del espíritu

The essence of man is a spiritual one, as the images of ciborium and ark make clear, and it will survive, but the pain by which this survival is assured is what is remembered of this poem. Man is seen within the urban society which the civilized world has developed and so highly values, and in which he is crushed and almost annihilated. This inhuman process is expressed by dehumanized imagery made more impressive by the surrealist technique of a startling conjunction of ideas and objects. Thus, inanimate things grow wings and roots, they become alive, but with terrifying attributes—'Garras dientes / Tienen ojos y uñas uñas uñas'. The city is alive with clocks as man is enmeshed in time, but the image shocks: 'Entre tus muslos un reloj da la hora.' It brings to mind at once the concepts of flesh, prostitution, and temporality. Or to pick another example at random, conscience is pictured presiding over a tribunal table with octopus clerks around him.

The moon images show this process in which the world of spirituality and beauty is abused by the crass materialism of today. The moon in Paz's work is often connected with the female principle, as is so often the case in mythology. It also traditionally connotes chastity, mystery, distance from human commerce; and a long line of poetical antecedents condition us in our awareness of its potential symbolism. All the more impressive then, the contrast between the conditioned reaction to the moon and the unsavoury opening simile, and the even blunter punch of the *o*, *e*, and *b* sounds of the fifth line:

> Como un enfermo desangrado se levanta
> La luna
> Sobre las altas azoteas
> La luna
> Como un borracho cae de bruces. . .

The harsh *c* continues through the moon metaphors—perros callejero', un convoy de camiones', 'un gato cruza'—and reaches its climax in the brutality of the butchers who wash their hands in moonlight:

> Los carniceros se lavan las manos
> En el agua de la luna. . .

The poet's horror at the ugly facts of existence in a modern world thus is communicated through a surrealist vision of personified objects (the night, the city, the moon) which are alive with the grotesque and fearful characteristics of human or animal life. Style and content are at one in this nightmare sensation of the human being in a world which reduces him to the level of the inhuman—an equation produced precisely by the personification mentioned above. To transmit anguish Paz engages sight, or rather imagination, in a series of contorted transformations of the 'real' to the 'super-real'. That which is seen and recognized is magically changed by its being related to some distant but otherwise perfectly recognizable facet of reality. Thus 'night' given 'countless nipples' begins a chain of associated ideas which leads beyond the real into the depths of the unconscious mind. This unconscious is where lie hidden or half-hidden the nameless fears and atavistic taboos which so well communicate Paz's feeling of alienation both from exterior reality and from the source of poetic inspiration.

Salamandra provides other and different examples of a surrealist use of the image as reconciler of conscious and subconscious levels of reality. A whimsical scene like that of 'Peatón' is also based upon the emergence of the fantasy world into daylight, here literal, not metaphorical, daylight. The process is objectified and drily told in the third person: a man walks along minding his own business, is stopped by a red light, and looks up. Above the grey roofs 'plateado / Entre los pardos pájaros, / Un pescado volaba'. The light changes and he crosses the street, trying to pick up the chain of thought he has lost:

> Se preguntó al cruzar la calle
> En qué estaba pensando.

The technique of depersonalization in 'Augurios' covers deeply felt emotions, and the disfiguration of the images in this poem correlates with the pain of the poet, out of harmony with the civilization around him. All that he sees tends to the distortion of generosity and love, and to the palliation of the masses: 'Una filantropía que despena', an easy materialism whose comfort anaesthetizes emotion. The weird opening image objectifies the annulment of heroism and love in the bottling of the Cid's daughters:

> Al natural, en cápsulas, abiertas
> O cerradas, ya desalmadas,
> Elvira y doñ Sol . . .

To communicate the feeling that humanity is being dulled out of suffering and thus out of awareness, Paz uses a string of images which surprise by their content or their juxtaposition. There is a sedative against everything:

> Contra las erosiones . . .
> Crisis, poetas solitarios auto-
> Críticas, purgas, cismas, putschs, eclipses . . .

The city dehumanizes to the point of ridicule—'Pulgas / Vestidas a la moda'—and Nature herself has been degraded—'En las playas mariscos erotómanos'. Mankind is hell-bent on escaping any kind of sensation but the hedonistic: 'Cura de sueñ, orgasmos por teléfono. / Arcoiris portátiles . . .' The ultimate philanthropy will be that which does away with pain. The poet has no need to enter the poem directly, for the deliberate dislocation of the image has carried the experience of nausea and foreboding which it is the purpose of the poem to communicate. The surrealist mode itself induces the anguish which is the real subject of the poem.

The Double

One motif in Paz's poetry is most suitably discussed in the context of the surrealist mode, even though it is universal to literature. The theme of the double became characteristic of surrealist aesthetics, though it can certainly not be claimed as their prerogative. Folklore and occultism provide many stories of apparitions which are identical to still-living human beings, and the idea of a second self pervades the most sophisticated as well as the most naïve levels of literature. Because of their faith in the subconscious functions of the human mind as transformers of reality, the Surrealists were attracted by the practices and particularly the philosophy of alchemy. In this, to be sure, they picked up the earlier addiction of such nineteenth-century thinkers and writers as Victor Hugo and Gérard de Nerval, with their interest in magic and the occult. It was the spiritual content of alchemy which fascinated them, what Jung describes as '—the transcendent function, the transformation of personality through the blending and fusion of the noble with the base components, of the differentiated with the inferior functions, of the conscious with the unconscious'. Surrealist poetry often expresses a haunting consciousness of the duality of the human psyche, which allows any facet of man's activity to be called into question or set in a higher frame of reference by his other self. Breton and his colleagues sought deliberately to evoke this other self, as Paz's own words on Breton point out: 'Decir es la actividad más alta: revelar lo escondido, despertar la palabra enterrada, suscitar la aparición de nuestro doble, crear a ese otro que somos y al que nunca dejamos de ser del todo'.

Paz's conception of the double is basic to his poetic vision, and his prose writings repeat the fact again and again: 'La poesía no dice: yo soy tú; dice: mi yo eres tú. La imagen poética es la otredad'. Using only the evidence of his poetry, one becomes aware of the polyvalency of the image of the double for Paz. It acts as an objective correlative for his epistemological uncertainties, for his awareness of the plurality lying behind seemingly simple appearances, and for his vision of the poet who suffers in order to redeem.

In the early *Puerta condenada*, (1938–46) included in the second section, 'Calamidades y milagros', of *Libertad bajo palabra*, the young poet returns time and again to a discourse with his other self, as he explores the seeming certainties of reality and finds the emptiness beneath. It is as though the use of a poetic dialectic is the first step towards the paradox of the later works in which preoccupations are similar, but expression so different. 'Pregunta' opens with a direct appeal to spiritual forces which recall Alberti's angels:

> Déjame, sí, déjame, dios o ángel, demonio.
> Déjame a solas, turba angélica,
> solo conmigo, con mi multitud.

The poet stands beside one who resembles himself, who contains all opposites, who embraces and wounds, who 'me odia porque yo soy el mismo'. Then Paz apostrophizes this 'aborrecible hermano mío', trying to harmonize his consciousness of all the infinite possiblities of the human spirit with the time-corroded being of every day:

> ¿es el tuyo, tu ser, hecho de horas
> y voraces minutos?

The next strophe has a Machado-like ring; the poet returns to a solitary questioning of the inexplicable facts of human existence, body and soul united to form what Paz sees as 'una sola y viva sombra'. An earlier generation of poets echoes in the next three lines—do we dream our own existence to defy time, and are we merely the self we dream ourselves to be?

> ¿Y somos esa imagen que soñamos,
> sueños al tiempo hurtados,
> sueños del tiempo por burlar al tiempo?

Alone, the poet works through layers of appearances to reach the essence of his personality. He passes beneath words, deceiving externals, and the illusions of temporal reality, only to find his very existence disappearing before his eyes, like a mirror which reflects another mirror-image to eternity:

> me voy borrando todo,
> me voy haciendo un vago signo sobre el agua,
> espejo en un espejo.

'La caída', in the same volume, is another cry of existential anguish. The essence of the poet's despair is time, which threatens all existence, returning life to non-life in an inexorable, silent process. The poet sees himself

> En el abismo de mi ser nativo,
> en mi nada primer, me desvivo:
> yo mismo frente a mí, ya devorado.

Ultimately only reason offers him cold comfort, and 'la inefable / y helada intimidad de su vacío'.

The double, who acts as a mirror-image showing the poet truths at which he can otherwise only guess, appears again in 'Los crepúsculos de la ciudad', a series of sonnets also in *Puerta condenada*. Again the poet is imprisoned in time's destructiveness, and sees no salvation or solace:

> Vuelvo el rostro: no soy sino la estela
> de mí mismo, la ausencia que deserto,
> el eco del silencio de mi grito.

In these poems the double bears witness to the poet of the anguish and hopelessness of existence. Epistemological doubt and a sense of time draw the poet into a labyrinth from which he does not find escape, and in which his only companion is an *alter ego* doomed to the same fate as himself. This poet has found no transcendence; he has desperately sought the way to rebirth, but so far with no success. He has rejected traditional religion, the myths of older civilizations have no strength to give him, and so far he has not found for himself any personal release from the temporal world which haunts him. The existential torment of this spirit is a true initiatory rite.

In *¿Aguila o sol?* there are two curious pieces which deal with the poet's awareness of a splintering of his personality. In neither case is the second self defined simply as a double; both poems depart from complex

conceptions and move through layers of introspection to give at the last some
notion of the ambiguity of the human psyche. Thus these prose poems
objectify the exploration of the subconscious which was the guiding principle
of surrealism. The narrator faces the dark impulses of his mind by
personifying them, in slightly different ways which are parallel
manifestations of the same process. This process is basically one of
integration, since recognizing the *alter ego* in its various guises is the first step
towards unifying the divided self. And this alone can produce the balance of
conscious and subconscious urges which is needed to combat the alienating
business of existence in a modern world.

    'Antes de dormir' is a monologue directed by the poet at the
invisible being whom he feels sharing and influencing his existence. This
being is a disquieting one, since it seems to escape the limits of the rational
and set up an atavistic base of prejudices, 'muralla circular que defiende dos
o tres certidumbres'. The unseen presence looks through the narrator's eyes,
and its gaze awakens an answering animism in the objects round about. But
such demands are too strong, and the narrator threatens to get rid of this
other self for ever. Of course he cannot, and the monologue evolves into self-
justification in an attempt to integrate these complementary parts of the
personality. The outer self, the narrator, must face the world and its
exigencies. The inner self withdraws from such pressures and has to be
coaxed and persuaded to re-emerge. In times of introspection, its presence is
felt again, evidence of a spiritual life which submerges but does not
disappear: 'penetras por la hendidura de la tristeza o por la brecha de la
alegría, te sirves del sueño y de la vigilia, del espejo y del muro, del beso y de
la lágrima.' When physical life ends and the useless battle against time is
over, the inner self will be in sole possession of the field. The narrator's
ultimate confession is that life has given him only the awareness of his inner
self—'solo te tengo a ti'. But there may be an endless chain of such
dependence upon an inner presence. It may not be so simple to reach the
absolute: '. . . a mí también me ha desvelado la posibilidad de que tú seas de
otro, que a su vez sería de otro, hasta no acabar nunca . . . No, si tu eres otro:
¿quién seria yo?' Thus essentially both selves depend upon each other for
validity. The conscious self cannot be considered authentic and the inner self
as the shadow; nor can the life of the spirit provide total justification for the
outer person who must face the world. Both share the same roots ('tú
también tuviste una infancia solitaria y ardiente'), and although the conscious
mind may often mistake the nature of subconscious urges, the integration of
both levels is needed for inner harmony: 'no te siento como el que fui sino
como el que voy a ser, como el que está siendo.' The narrator probes and
questions, trying to move from this insight to categoric certainty—'¿Quién

eres?' But cajolement and vilification both fail. The interminable dialogue in which one is always silent is that of life. Only full acceptance of self, and sleep, can interrupt this one-sided dialectic: 'No me mires: cierra los ojos, para que yo también pueda cerrarlos. Todavía no puedo acostumbrarme a tu mirada sin ojos.'

The second prose poem, 'Carta a dos desconocidas', is different in degree though not in kind. The shadow self is here intuited as feminie, which seems to relate it with other obvious expressions of Paz's search for the *anima* principle, 'Piedra de sol', for example. The narrator speaks to this female presence which comes to him with greatest poignancy at moments of desperation when he feels both the horror of material emptiness and the anguish of existence: '. . . el invisible precipicio que en ocasiones se abre frente a mí, la gran boca maternal de la ausencia . . . todo, en fin, lo que me enseña que no soy sino una ausencia que se despeña, me revelaba . . . tu presencia.' The encounter becomes a triangle when the second 'desconocida,' perhaps the personification of loved womanhood, appears. The narrator is led to her by his companion, and 'soy para ella lo que tú fuiste para mí.' Yet the pursuit of the beloved is essentially that of the 'presencia'. Thus in woman the narrator is seeking that shadow self, the *anima*, which he needs to complete his being. Physical love can unite him with another body, but not with the wholeness which he is looking for. True life will come 'Si alguna vez acabo de caer, allá, del otro lado del caer. . .'. And this life, perhaps, is only another way of disguising death. The *anima* may after all return to give wholeness to his being in the moment when death ends all fragmentation: 'Pero acaso todo esto no sea sino una vieja manera de llamar a la muerte. La muerte que nació conmigo y que me ha dejado para habitar otro cuerpo.' The appeal of both pieces is for an integration of the self to face the exigencies of life and the urges of the subconscious. Both follow the path of self-discovery into the recesses of the mind. Both recognize fragmentations of the personality which demand exploration and expression before inner order and balance can be regained. Such were, among others, the impulses behind surrealism, for, to quoto Breton, surrealism 'tend a la récupération totale de notre force psychique par un moyen qui est la descente vertigineuse en nous, l'illumination systématique des lieux cachés et l'obscurcissement progressif des autres lieux'.

In 1950, at Avignon, Paz wrote 'Fuente', a poem which appeared in *La estación violenta*. The image of the double is used, along with a suffering image, but with a difference which shows Paz moving towards an escape from the sense of time of the earlier poems into a mythological interpretation of poetic inspiration. The poet is the sacrificial victim who is destroyed in the battle with hostile powers, but by his death frees the spirit of poetry and redeems the alien world. The moment of the poem is noon, and the atmosphere is one of expectancy. Like several other poems of the same volume, the lines are long and the rhythm rolling and powerful. The poet senses a presence, a promise of some transcendental happening in which time will shatter and reveal some deeper meaning. But the promise seems false and the expectancy cheated. No easy certainty dispels his questioning, though he persists until the old wounds heal, the scars almost disappear, and the meaning of the moment seems lost. Yet there is a transcendence, in very special terms. There is a privileged being who rises from his own delirium, wounded, yet

> . . . de su frente hendida brota un último pájaro.
> Es el doble de sí mismo,
> el joven que cada cien años vuelve a decir unas
> palabras, siempre las mismas. . .

The sacrifice must be made, Christ-like, but redemption—for Paz, poetry—remains:

> En el centro de la plaza la rota cabeza del poeta es
> una fuente.
> La fuente canta para todos.

This mysterious potentiality of the double to reveal truths of a spiritual nature haunts even the simplest of Paz's poems which contain this motif. 'La calle' of *Puerta condenada* recalls 'Aquí' of *Salamandra*, although the earlier work has much of the despair of the poems from the same volume discussed above. In both poems the setting is a street where the poet becomes aware of another presence, a shadow self in 'La calle', in 'Aquí' an echo of his own footsteps in a street, 'Donde / Sólo es real la nieble'. In *Ladera Este* one short poem recalls Breton's poem 'Rideau, rideau', and the earlier *Picture of Dorian Gray*, with an even more macabre twist. The mask-face has hidden the real self from the world until

> Su cara
> Hoy tiene las arrugas de esa cara.
> Sus arrugas no tienen cara.

To end this discussion of the double in Paz's surrealist mode, a quotation from one of the major poems of *Ladera Este*, 'Cuento de dos jardines', is particularly apt. I have tried to show how Paz's obvious kinship with surrealism belongs to a definite period and expresses a definite state of mind. In the latest poems both the state of mind and the expression are transcended in poems where paradox leads to the threshold of mysticism. The undifferentiated vision of such poems transforms also Paz's use of the motif of the double. The rebirth so painfully sought brings with it the amalgamation of the ego and the alter ego in a more highly developed consciousness, and this, I believe, is what lies behind these lines:

> Nadie acaba en sí mismo.
> Un todo cada uno
> En otro todo,
> En otro uno:
> Constelaciones.

Surrealism provided Paz with a style peculiarly suited to the chaos which in the cosmological myths precedes creation and form, and in the poet's psychological reference expresses the alienation from mankind and from himself which must be suffered in order to be transcended. It is a double trauma, or more exactly is expressed as such, since the poet and the man are homologous. The question is one of focus: Paz sometimes emphasizes the common nature of man as experienced by himself, at others he dwells upon his predicament as writer. Then the general chaos becomes the plight of the creative artist seeking form and expression in a world without paradigms. In the over-all view of his work surrealism seems to fulfil for Paz at one stage what paradox will do at another. That is, surrealism with its emphasis on integrating the conscious and the subconscious, the 'real' and the 'super-real', provides a dialectic which leads to unity or, in Hegelian terms, through thesis and antithesis to synthesis. It is not that the process is neatly laid out each time as this generalization might imply. The synthesis, like the mythic rebirth, is not always achieved, and the experiences communicated by the poems mark stages within this pattern which must be suffered in their own terms. Yet the final vision is the same, however expressed, whether as Jungian individuation, or Buddhist union with the One Mind, or Breton's 'point sublime', living centre of the world's unity.

JASON WILSON

Mentalist Poetics, the Quest, 'Fiesta' and Other Motifs

I have commented on Paz's use of the word *espiritual*; it could be translated as 'mental with a spiritual glow'. This points to Paz's intension: poetry is not for him the mere writing of a poem, but an event, a faith that borders on the religious experience. Poetry involves salvation and grants meaning. This is a mentalist concept in that the activity of mind in language, especially the writing and reading of poetry, is a symbolic process that opens out a symbolising consciousness. The aim is the activating of the full potentialities of the mind: poetry is faithful to this process. In 1924 André Breton defined surrealism as revelation of 'le fonctionnement réel de la pensée' (the real functioning of thought). This relevation must start from a critical and analytical act, for what we normally isolate as thought is a mere parody, a disguise, a crust over the immensities of human potential. To let language 'live' would be to recover its symbolic resonances. In surrealism the poet's role is to 'ressaisir la vitalité concrète, que les habitudes logiques de la pensée sont pour lui faire perdre' (to recapture the concrete vitality, that the logical habits of thought have almost made him lose). This justifies surrealism's attacks on 'reason', 'logic' and 'common sense' as reductive and sterilising.

This mentalist poetics can be traced to Breton's oft-quoted 'certain point de l'esprit' (certain point of the mind) where contradictions cease, a 'mental' (ideal?) place, that 'monde mental à la Genèse' (mental world in Genesis) at the heart of the surrealist concern.

From *Octavio Paz: A study of his poetics* by Jason Wilson, © 1979 by Cambridge University Press.

To have liberty is to *experience* this release from a language dead to the whole person, with his body, and his dreams. Paz criticises Lévi-Strauss for not allowing a liberty 'deeper' than economic, material or sexual conditionings, 'hay que penetrar en una esfera en que el espíritu opera con mayor libertad' (we must penetrate into a sphere in which the spirit operates with greater freedom). But to penetrate so far, conventional reality, morality and language-use must be rejected. Paz accepts the concept of the 'Romantic outsider', a position glimpsed in Luis Cernuda's poetry. Paz describes:

> el descubrimiento de un espíritu que se conoce a sí mismo y se afronta, el rigor de una pasión lúcida, una libertad que es simultáneamente rebelión contra el mundo y aceptación de su fatalidad personal.

> the discovery of a mind that knows itself and faces itself, the rigour of a lucid passion, a liberty that is simultaneously rebellion against the world and acceptance of personal fatality.

Spiritual liberty is the name for the celestial vision at the centre of Paz's poetics: 'la imagen celeste es visión de libertad: levitación, disolución del yo. La luz frente a la piedra' (The celestial image is a vision of liberty; levitation, dissolution of the ego. Light confronts stone). The antinomy of light and stone expresses that of liberty and its limitations; light and life against insensitivity, gravity and death. All of Paz's poetry spreads out in waves from this tension; for 'spirit' only exists in terms of its repression, as a relationship. Any other word, like 'being' or 'desire' (for the same area) would also imply this dynamic concept of truth.

In the relationship between liberty and poetry, the perception and experience of the spirit is liberty, is language purged and washed of its fixed associations, freed from dead metaphor. As early as 1939 Paz experienced poetry as liberating: 'El milagro poético, la única creación del hombre, la única operación que, en verdad, lo libera' (The poetic miracle, man's only creation, the only operation that in truth liberates him). The title of Paz's collection *Libertad bajo palabra* expresses a dual act: first, the word in the poem liberates language; second, language in the poem liberates the reader. The poem writes 'innocence' where there was 'sin', and 'liberty' where there was 'authority'. Paz's faith is that 'El hembre es libre, deseo e imaginación son sus alas, el cielo está al alcance de la mano' (Man is free, desire and imagination are his wings, the sky [heaven] is within reach). 'Within reach'; poetry is a liberating, sensuous experience, for it liberates desire. Thus poetry's inner, spiritual and experiential liberty is extra-aesthetic; it affects the whole man. Liberty is an elusive possibility given epiphanic reality through the poem. Here also is the seed of utopian poetics; the momentary glimpse of this liberty is projected into a society living this liberty as daily experience.

So art is not 'artistic' but 'inner liberation'. Writing about Marcel Duchamp, Paz defines this:

> Para los antiguos como para Duchamp y los surrealistas el arte es un medio de liberación, contemplación o conocimiento, una aventura o una pasión. El arte no es una categoría aparte de la vida.

> For the ancients as for Duchamp and the surrealists art is a means of liberation, contemplation or knowledge, an adventure or a passion. Art is not a category separate from life.

Real art alters consciousness and modifies life: *Corazón* (Heart), Paz's emblem for Breton, symbolises his own poetics: the heart is passion, life, experience, temporality and mystery. It is a fragile hope. Paz's poem 'El desconocido' relates the poet's bitter search after his meaning, like 'un fantasma que buscara un cuerpo' (a ghost that seeks a body) but finds nothing. Written in 1942, the poem embodies Paz's quest and anticipates that vision promised (codified) by surrealism:

> Pero su corazón aún abre las alas
> como un águila roja en el desierto.
> But his heart still opens its wings like a red eagle in the desert.

The heart is hope in the spiritual desert.

The Quest

One way of identifying Paz's attitude and surrealist poetics is through a latent metaphor underpinning all his writing. André Breton alchemically called himself a 'chercheur d'or' (seeker of gold), where base matter (life) is transformed into spirit (gold). Life becomes enriched by the action of poetry.

This quest for intensified life never ends, is never satisfied. Man finds nothing, there is no gold (only fool's gold?). For Paz, life is not static, and we live in time. He emphasises the open, the flowing.

With the notion of quest, we also articulate that of journey; poetry is a process of discovery, an adventure, an exploration. These notions have been common currency at least since Baudelaire. The poet seeks (*buscar*) the unknown; he rarely finds (*encontrar*). Because the voyage is perpetual motion (only death is rest), verbs like *entrar* (enter), *ir* (go), *penetrar* (penetrate), *descender* (descend), *seguir* (follow), *avanzar* (advance), *cruzar* (cross), *atravesar* (cross), *andar* (walk), *caminar* (walk), *correr* (run), *internar* (penetrate), *hundirse* (sink), *perforar* (perforate), condition the poetry. It would be tedious to list the occurrences.

Because poetry is a quest, verbs like *nombrar* (name) and especially *inventar* (invent) mirror the intention. The whole process is an adventure. In 1952 Breton defined surrealism as 'aventure spirituelle' (spiritual adventure); also in 1952 Paz called poetry 'aventura espiritual'. In 1951 Paz signed Breton's manifesto claiming surrealism as an 'adventure'.

The sense of the quest is utopian, based on the intuition that man is more than he seems to be or has been historically. Breton sought 'la récupération des pouvoirs originels de l'esprit' (recuperation of the original powers of the spirit) or a wholeness that had once existed. 'Recuperation' posits a Golden-Age and a fall. Paz seized on this and entitled his passionate obituary 'André Breton o la búsqueda del comienzo' (André Breton or the search for the beginning); surrealism attempted to return to the 'beginnings' to find out 'where it all went wrong'. Surrealism's 'passionate quest' is awareness of a universal nostalgia, and it became a 'método de búsqueda interior' (method of interior search) where each man had to penetrate inside himself to his lost or forgotten or repressed self.

Paz wrote that Breton's quest was 'la reconquista de un reino perdido: la palabra del principio, el hombre anterior a los hombres y las civilizaciones' (the reconquest of a lost kingdom: the word of the beginning, man before men and civilisations). Earlier, Paz had defined poetry as 'búsqueda del hombre perdido' (search for lost man); as early as 1942 he wrote that 'buscamos en vano al hombre perdido, al hombre inocente' (we seek in vain the lost man, innocent man). Paz roots this nostalgia in the tradition of rebellion of the Romantic poets, a 'búsqueda de la mitad perdida, descenso a esa región que nos comunica con lo otro' (search for the lost half, descent to that region that links us with the other). Paz and Breton belong to the same family.

'Encuentro' (Encounter), a long tripartite poem written in 1940, and excised in the 1968 edition of *Libertad bajo palabra*, deals with a fleeting 'encounter'. The poem opens with the poet in everyday reality; he hears 'music' and is transposed to another plane of experience:

> En la estancia contigua sonó la música . . .
> Y me quedé desnudo y sin pasado.
In the room next door the music sounded . . . and I
remained naked and without past.

Naked, without past or name, the poet communes with his real self; this is
not union with God, but an experience beyond attributes, beyond 'words and
signs'. He descends to the rock where he finds a 'new Adam dreaming', born
among his ruins. Here is pre-lapsarian man, Adam asleep and immanent in
twentieth-century man. *Ruins* are Paz's name for culture and history. The
poet senses a possibility of 'rebirth':

> Toco tu destrucción,
> tu verde renacer entre mis ruinas:
I touch your destruction, your green rebirth between my
ruins.

The poet touches this lost self, but there is no permanence in this region, the
rebirth is momentary only: 'Oh fugitivo encuentro, mortal beso' (Oh fugitive
encounter, mortal kiss). The kiss, sensual union, is the kiss of death. In spite
of nature's 'invading, daily innocence', in spite of the new Adam, there is evil;
and evil is time, Chronos, death. Man communes briefly; otherwise he is
outside, an indifferent, unalterable nature. In 1940, the problem of time and
death has not been resolved: there are experiences, but no meaningful
pattern, no timeless aesthetic moment.

A later prose poem is also entitled 'Encuentro'; but the mood is
contemporary, assured; sentimentality and naivety are cast aside. The text
allegorises the impossibility of a real encounter. The narrator watches
himself 'leave' himself; sees his real self desert him. He realises that it is
impossible to grasp this other self, so elusive is it: 'Quise alcanzarlo, pero él
apresuraba su marcha exactamente con el mismo ritmo con que yo aceleraba
la mía, de modo que la distancia que nos separaba permanecía inalterable' (I
wanted to reach him, but he hurried his steps with exactly the same rhythm
with which I accelerated mine, such that the distance that separated us
remained the same). The quest for self never ends. There is no certainty for
man is a temporal being; the (other) self maintains its distance. This text,
with its dynamic, ironic view of illumination, with a savage sense of humour
rare in Paz, plays with the philosophical problem of identity ('who am I?',
'How many I's are there?'). It ends on a note of confusion: 'En el camino,
tuve esta duda que todavía me desvela: ¿si no fuera él, sino yo. . .?' (On the
road, I had this doubt that still keeps me awake: and if it were not him, but

myself?). By 1951 Paz is the 'hardened' Romantic; irony has replaced naivety; but, as in many of Paz's poems, this poem articulates 'ideas' not experiences; it deals with mental life. Between the two poems, lies surrealism; the first is a yearning in weak language, soft with cliché; the second a 'cautionary tale' about the elusiveness of self.

The failure to 'encounter' is redeemed by the timeless moment; by ecstasy. Paz's much praised *Piedra de sol* fuses the *buscar/encontrar* antinomy; it is a clear quest poem, a groping through the world-as-woman's-body for points or moments of contact where the phrases 'busco a tientas' (I search gropingly) and 'busco un instante' (I seek a moment) reveal the intention and structure. This has been noted by most critics. We shall return to this 'synthesis' poem.

Because the journey–quest is an inner one, undertaken by the imagination in symbols and exteriorised into poems, the poet does not see, but *invents*. To 'in-vent' (with distant associations of wind, breath and inspiration) is not to coin neologisms but to drag up to light; to restore language's original purity through the critical, selective and surgical act of writing where language is released from the 'chains' of convention, its karma, and allowed to be. *Inventar* occurs seven times in the poem 'Libertad bajo palabra' which ends on this note of faith: 'Contra el silencio y el bullicio invento la Palabra, libertad que se inventa y me inventa cada día' (Against silence and bustle I invent the Word, a liberty that invents itself and invents me every day). Poetry, which is freed language, speaks the real 'me'. Words, made autonomous, living beings freed by the poet, create the poet by releasing his being, dulled and made opaque by cliché and culture.

True reality is desire, is invention:

> Deseada
> > La realidad se desea
> Se inventa un cuerpo de centella
> Desired, reality desires itself, it invents for itself a body of
> sparks.

This 'body of sparks' is the poem, which transforms abject conventional reality by releasing desire (how crucial Cernuda seems here). Desire is the only truth: 'Sólo se completa cuando sale de sí y se inventa' (It only becomes complete when it goes out of itself and invents itself).

We fall back on the surrealist apologist and critic J. H. Matthews who affirms: 'Paz is faithful to surrealism in considering poetry as a means to enlarge self-knowledge, to advance persistently man's search for true identity.

'Fiesta' Poetics

I will show how subtly Paz infuses a Mexican custom with metaphysical resonances central to his poetics. An obvious reality of Mexican cultural-social life, the *fiesta*, in the middle forties assumed symbolic proportions for Paz. In *El laberinto de la soledad*, written during his 'surrealist' days in Paris, Paz describes the *fiesta*. It is a popular art-form; an explosion of energy in an otherwise repressed people. The cyclical recurrence of the *fiesta* implies things sacred where time 'deja de ser sucesión y vuelve a ser lo que fue, y es, originariamente: un presente en donde pasado y futuro al fin se reconcilian' (stops being succession and becomes what it is again and is originally: a present in which past and future at last are reconciled). The *fiesta* is another name for the timeless moment. Through the *fiesta* Mexican man breaks down his wall of solitude and communicates with others and himself. Then Paz shifts from description to poetics. The *fiesta* inaugurates an enchanted world ruled by 'surprise', that central aesthetic element underlined by Apollinaire and taken up by the surrealists. Anything can happen: what does is poetry, spontaneously lived. The *fiesta* demotes authority, 'gobiernan los niños y los locos' (children and madmen govern), surrealism's moral the *fiesta* 'nos aligeramos de nuestra carga de tiempo y razón' (we lighten our load of time and reason). Reason, common sense, morality, convention are all discarded; poetry rules: 'A través de la fiesta la sociedad se libera de las normas que se ha impuesto' (Through the *fiesta* society liberates itself from the norms which it has imposed on itself). *Fiesta* is liberation. It is 'revolt', a sudden immersion in 'pure life', a 'return', a 'recreation' and a 'participation'.

For a moment repressive society is revoked, in a return to those dionysiac orgies where desire, not law, ruled. Paz reads the Mexican *fiesta* as a survival of a life-attitude embodied in poetics, in surrealism, in living poetry. In 1969 he defined man's inner needs as 'nostalgia for *fiestas*'; a nostalgia for myth, for the eternal return of the present, for ritual and ceremonies. The *fiesta* is the reincorporation of the pleasure principle. The same nostalgia haunted Rimbaud, who sought the key to the 'ancien festin' (ancient feast) where he might regain his appetite; Rubén Darío was 'triste de fiestas' (sad of *fiestas*); and surrealism's optimistic vision tended towards the *fête*, a perennial utopian dream. Most tellingly, Breton laments that there 'se perd de plus en plus le sens de la fête' (the sense of the feast is increasingly lost to us).

The notion of *fiesta* spills into that of the poem. Paz suggests that 'el poema es fiesta' (the poem is a feast) the poem is a participatory ceremony, a rite. If art is the new *sagesse*, then it will be both spiritual and communal, like a *fiesta*. (This new spiritual art heralds the end of the *obra* through its momentary 'incarnation'). In the lived poem—*fiesta*: 'La época que comienza acabará por fin con las "obras" y disolverá la contemplación en el acto' (The epoch that begins will end with 'works' and will dissolve contemplation in the act). This is the West's only hope, art as sacred happening, as collective act: 'la encarnación del poema en la vida colectiva: la fiesta' (the incarnation of the poem in collective life: the *fiesta*). Here again is the dream: 'la poesía puede ser vivida por todos: el arte de la fiesta aguarda su resurrección' (poetry can be lived by all: the art of the feast awaits its resurrection). It was restated in 1972: 'our time suffers from hunger and thirst—for *fiestas* and rites', a spiritual hunger. The *fiesta* is decidedly a spiritual, mental art. Paz's shift from Mexican rite to metaphysic is self-evident.

The Mexican revolution failed, for example, through being too narrowly 'political'. No 'vital order' was created which might coordinate a world vision of a just, free society. But Paz is utopian, in that his 'society' would be rooted in myth, outside evil and history, obeying a poetic wisdom. In 1954 Paz writes: 'El mundo se ordenará conforme a los valores de la poesía—libertad y comunión, o caerá' (The world will order itself according to the values of poetry, liberty and communion, or it will fall). As N. O. Brown states: 'To be awake is to participate carnally and not in fantasy, in the feast, the great communion.

Another prototypical utopia for Paz was the Spain of 1937. This vision stood for more than the writer's congress, more than his poems (mostly uncollected), more than his work for the exiles in Mexico. Paz said in an interview about the Spanish civil war, 'descubrí entonces una posibilidad para el hombre y advertí que allí se perdía algo cuya reconquista quizá exigiría siglos: la tradición revolucionaria no marxista' (I discovered then a possibility for man, and perceived that there something was being lost whose reconquest would perhaps demand centuries: the non-marxist revolutionary tradition). Paz had glimpsed a society which was not gripped in a life-denying ideology.

He saw a 'new man', a society open to 'transcendence'. He saw faces expressing a 'hopeful desperation' which he never forgot—'su recuerdo no me abandona' (its memory never leaves me). The dream of hope at the source of Paz's poetics was here rooted in concrete, historical experience. Writing about the poet Antonio Machado, Paz recreates this vision in terms of a we where contradictions ceased and 'liberty [was] incarnate'. Above all, it was a concrete experience, like lived poetry: 'Casi podíamos palpar el contenido, hoy inasible, de palabras como libertad y pueblo, esperanza y revolución. . . el sabor de la palabra fraternidad' (we could almost touch the content, today ingraspable, of words like liberty and people, hope and revolution. . . the taste of the word fraternity). Dead and numbed concepts lived again; against the forces of repression rose spontaneity, naturalness, something that 'will not die'. The failure of this dream, rather than embittering him, rather than making hope a cynical joke, allowed Paz to internalise this experience, to incorporate it into his poetic dream and to sense a similar vision in the 'brotherhood' of poetry and surrealism.

For Paz, politics and power are the enemy ('la lengua hinchada de política' (tongue swollen with politics), for they are abstract: 'la benévola jeta de piedra de cartón del Jefe, del Conductor, fetiche del siglo . . . las divinidades sin rostro, abstractas' (the benevolent papier mâché face of the Chief, the Leader, the century's fetish, the faceless abstract divinities). In 1938 Paz wrote a eulogistic, almost euphoric 'defence' of Pablo Neruda's 'experiential' marxism. By 1942 he was accusing Neruda of being contaminated with politics, and attacking political poetry as otiose; Paz argued that he preferred a good speech by Lenin to a 'dead' poem by Mayakovsky. Neruda's 'vanity' sickened Paz and symbolized his deviance from traditional revolutionary theory in favour of a 'visionary' poetics.

At the same time, Paz doubts the value of merely writing poetry. He asks the crucial question: 'No sería mejor transformar la vida en poesía que hacer poesía con la vida?' (Wouldn't it be better to transform life into poetry than to make poetry with life?); and he reiterates the vision of a universal, live poetry with man freed of gods and masters. He cites Blake and Lautréamont in support, and awaits the day when 'la poesía entra en acción' (poetry enters into action). By 1965 he accepts this vision as a chimera, but a necessary ambition, and repeats that it is the question of all questions. This ideal, frustrated by actuality, is based on the inner organisation of the poem in relation to the 'communing' reader. This is surrealism. Breton's 'comportement lyrique' heralds the end of the poem, where the reader is transformed into the poet, and where the dream is of opening the door out of the poet's shaky house to find oneself 'on his feet in life'. For Paz this dream too is surrealism: 'le surréalisme est la tentative désespérée de la poésie pour s'incarner dans l'histoire. C'est pour cela que son sort est lié à celui de l'homme même' (surrealism is poetry's desperate attempt to incarnate itself in history. That is why its lot is tied to that of man himself). Paz's disillusion with politics only temporarily blurred his vision; his contact with the surrealists, that brotherhood who lived a utopia of open friendship, enabled him to 'believe' again.

In 1939, reviewing Emilio Prados' poetry, Paz wrote that the best poetry was a 'life-style'. By 1944 the desire to incorporate poetry into life, to live poetry, becomes his central dream:

> soñé en un mundo en donde la palabra engendraría
> y el mismo sueño habría sido abolido
> porque querer y obrar serían como la flor y el fruto.

I dreamed of a world where the word will engender and the very dream would have been abolished, because wanting and doing would be like a flower and fruit.

But this early poem remains pessimistic; 'communion' is a vain desire, and the poem ends with the poet's despair at the atrocities of history. Like all despair, it stems from a frustrated vision: that the word could take root and flower. By 1948, in his celebrated 'Himno entre ruinas', the vision overpowers the 'nightmares' of history and ends on the utopian hope of 'palabras que son flores que son frutos que son actos' (words that are flowers that are fruits that are acts). This would be the process that would restore meaning and truth; a poem-act that ushers in a change in consciousness. Paz's text 'Eralaán' describes how man could live the intensities of the poem; where language would consist of beautiful objects, conversations would be exchanges of gifts, life would be 'un insólito brotar de imágenes que cristalizan en actos' (a strange sprouting of images that crystallise in acts) and poetry would be 'al alcance de todos los paseantes' (within reach of all who pass). Again the poet is unable to sustain the vision and falls back into 'this' reality.

The tension between this reality and the vision is formally evoked again, as in 'Himno entre ruinas', through italics and lower case in the poem 'Un poeta' (a poet). This 'poet' posits a perfect society where knowledge, dreaming and action are one. He writes: 'La poesía ha puesto fuego a todos los poemas. Se acabaron las palabras, se acabaron las imágenes. Abolida la distancia entre el hombre y la cosa, nombrar es crear, e imaginar, nacer' (Poetry has set fire to all poems. Words have finished, images have finished. Abolished the distance between man and thing, to name is to create and to imagine is to be born). This is the millennial dream where the poem gives birth to 'real' language in which the word is the thing it names and not mere arbitrary convention. The text 'Hacia el poema' (Towards the poem) symbolises this 'future' poem that actual written poetry prophesies. It is the same vision, with the same tensions. When history sleeps, it talks in our nightmares; when history 'awakes' it stops being a nightmare and 'la imagen se hace acto, acontece el poema: la poesía entra en acción' (the image becomes act, the poem happens: poetry enters into action). Real poetry for Paz is a lived act. This is the dreamed-of Golden Age again 'en la que pensamiento y palabra, fruto y labio, deseo y acto son sinónimos' (in which thought and word, fruit and lips, desire and act are synonymous). Roland Barthes calls this the 'dreamed-of language whose freshness, by a kind of ideal anticipation, might portray the perfection of some Adamic world where language would no longer be alienated'. Northrop Frye sees this 'vision' as the central myth of art, 'the end of social effort, the innocent world of fulfilled desires, the free human society'. Behind these lines lies William Blake; a Blake recuperated by the surrealists and Paz.

Adamic man, innocence, nostalgia and unity: these are the Romantic-surrealist constants veining Paz's *obra*. The Golden Age for Paz is an immutable model that lies between nature and history, deep in every man. And this golden-age quality must be restored:

> los dos se desnudaron y se amaron
> por defender nuestra porción eterna
> nuestra ración de tiempo y paraíso,
> tocar nuestra raíz y recobrarnos,
> recobrar nuestra herencia arrebatada
> por ladrones de vida hace mil siglos

the two stripped naked and made love to defend our eternal portion, our ration of time and paradise, to touch our root and recover ourselves, to recover our heritage snatched by thieves of life a thousand years ago.

This is a clear poetics; life has been *stolen*, and at the dawn of time man lost his roots. Paz wants to start again; wants to return to the 'beginning'. This can be related to Breton's cry that 'Tout paradis n'est pas perdu' (All paradise has not been lost) and his paradoxical awareness of this 'croyance irraisonnée' (unreasonable belief) which mocks his belief in an Edenic future even as he pursues it. For Breton and Paz, it is woman who leads man back:

> Derrière toi
> Lançant ses derniers feux sombres entre tes jambes
> Le sol du paradis perdu

Behind you throwing its last dark fires between your legs the ground of lost paradise.

The myth of purity and innocence is confronted with the anguish of contamination. Breton's fanatical anti-Christianity is grounded in this conflict. For Paz, man's way back to innocence is through poetry which is innocent (where language is 'purified'): 'con la poesía el poeta recobra la inocencia, recuerda el paraíso perdido' (with poetry the poet recovers innocence, remembers lost paradise). This is also Paul Eluard's dream: 'La force absolue de la poésie purifiera les hommes' (The absolute force of poetry will purify men). It leads us to Paz's serious pun: 'Inocencia y no ciencia' (Innocence and not science). This innocence is natural wisdom and is antithetical to culture and learning. Paz lauds 'noble ignorance' he boasts that

> No sé nada
> Sé lo que sobra No lo que basta
> La ignorancia es ardua como la belleza
> un día sabré menos y abriré los ojos
> I don't know anything. I know what is superfluous, not what suffices. Ignorance is arduous like beauty; one day I will know less and will open my eyes.

Poetry de-schools, unlearns, teaches innocence and re-writes language; it is a 'fiesta de ignorancia' (a feast of ignorance).

The child is the archetype for this 'song of innocence'. The child is a *natural* poet, a discoverer, free and open to ventures into the unexpected and the unknown; he embodies a magical attitude to reality. Childhood is another name for paradise lost, with poetry as 'childhood recovered at will'.

In Paz's poem 'Soliloquio de medianoche' (Midnight soliloquy), the insomniac poet reflects on his 'buried infancy', irremediably lost:

> Inocencia salvaje domesticada con palabras, preceptos con
>   anteojos,
> agua pura, espejo para el árbol y la nube,
> que tantas virtuosas almas enturbiaron.
> Wild innocence domesticated with words, precepts with glasses, pure water, mirror for tree and cloud, that so many virtuous souls have muddied.

The adults' 'dirty' language with their abstract concepts, cultural artificialities and castrating morality: these are the weapons that an 'unpoetic' society employs against the poet. To the child, reality is not 'fixed' and 'dead', but in a perpetual state of metamorphosis where 'las cosas cambiaban su figura por otra' (things changed their figure for something else), where nature *talks*:

> Sobre su verde tallo una flor roja me hablaba
> y sólo yo entendía su cifrado lenguaje;
> On its green stem a red flower talked to me and only I
> understood its cyphered language;

The 'magic word of childhood' opens all doors and reality obeys the child's inner desires. But inevitably and painfully the adult world triumphs:

> Infancia, fruto comido por los años,
> barca de papel abandonada en el légamo una tarde de
> lluvia
> Infancy, fruit eaten by the years, paper boat abandoned in
> the mud one rainy afternoon.

Mud and corruption symbolise the way the adult's world alienates the child from the poet. There is an echo of Rimbaud's farewell to childhood; the sad child launching a frail boat in a cold black puddle. But for a litany of memories, nothing remains of that magic, a 'sepulcro tapiado' (a covered tomb). Prudence, the summa of adult values, condemns the poet to sterility and loneliness.

A symbol for Paz of childhood's natural wisdom and spiritual permanence is the fig tree. Paz's emotional identification with the *higuera* in the Mixcoac garden of his childhood found a strange correspondence and confirmation in that Buddha sat under a *ficus religiosa* when he was illumined. As a symbol, it spreads across his *obra*; we note that same process from experiential reality to spiritual emblem typical of Paz.

The prose poem 'La higuera' describes the fig tree as the child's only comfort; it called him and he penetrated its centre, experiencing an intense 'plentitude'. But his special pleasure was to climb this tree, 'mi cabeza sobresalía entre las grandes hojas, picoteada de pájaros, coronada de vaticinios' (my head stuck out among the great leaves, pecked at by birds, crowned with prophecies). From up there the child envisioned the world as a promise; and though the same tree still invites him, the poet is unsure whether to chop it down with an axe or to dance with it. This fig tree is a mental event: 'La higuera aquella volverá esta noche' (That fig tree will return tonight). It is a religious, maternal, sexual and natural symbol, but its richness is rooted in experience.

Another analogy for the magic of childhood and paradise is the garden, Baudelaire's 'vert paradis des amours enfantins' (green paradise of childhood loves). The garden is the magical enclosed space of childhood. Paz's suppressed poem 'El jardín' is a projection of the poet's mind and his luxuriant inner world, with its 'alta delicia inmóvil' and its 'quieto universo' and its 'parada hermosura sin orillas' (its high immobile delight, its quiet universe, its still beauty without shores). The poet 'drinks from this source' and it survives in him.

The later text 'Jardín con niñn' (Garden with child) evokes, during a bout of insomnia, a green intact garden that defies time and that, like the pines, is 'siempre de pie, sin cambiar nunca de postura' (always standing, without ever changing posture). The poet lists its natural delights and calls it a 'sacred site', the 'gloria entrevista, compartida' (glimpsed, shared glory) of childhood. He relives its moments of discovery; the purity of his vision made all the more bitter by the present moment of the adult poet writing 'estos cuantos adioses al borde del precipicio' (these few goodbyes at the edge of the precipice). The precipice is the fall into adulthood. Only poetry leads back.

In the poem 'Cuento de dos jardines' (Tale of two gardens), the poet remembers his Mixcoac garden, and sees the 'other side of being' only to realise that 'después no hubo jardines' (after there were no gardens). Yet his garden is always there in his mind: 'No hay más jardines que los que llevamos dentro' (There are no more gardens other than those we carry inside). The same process from physical reality to mental symbol is inherent in the very nature of the word.

The dream is the emblem of the poetic society; for during the dream desire is released. This is a constant in surrealism, the attempt to integrate waking and dreaming into a liberating synthesis. Dreams must be lived.

Tracing the role of the dream chronologically in Paz's poetry leads to the problem of expression and meaning. His early poem 'Monólogo' (Monologue) poses a technical problem. The 'dark current of dreams' rises up from a 'mar sonámbulo, ciego' (a blind, somnambulist sea). This 'blind' source points to a split between lucidity and what the dream is saying. The poem 'Nocturno' predicates the same split: '¿Cómo decir, oh sueño, tu silencio en voces?' (How to say, O dream, your silence in voices?). The poet finds no words adequately to evoke the dream; it slips through. The poet complains 'Quedo distante de los sueños' (I remain distant from the dreams); and there is no balance between dreaming as escapism and compensation, and dreaming as nightmare.

By 1937 he glimpses, in the suppressed poem 'Al sueñ' (To the dream), written while in Madrid, that the dream is also a liberation:

> El sueño nos penetra,
> rompe todos los lazos,
> The dream penetrates us, breaks all the bonds.

The dream strips away appearances and reveals the real person by revealing desire: 'somos nuestros deseos' (we are our desires). And through the dream the new man is born out of the annihilated self. The poem ends on a paradox about truth's experiential thrill, for the dream gives a 'death' that is more life than life, where 'death' is only the death of the social or false self. The dream becomes a manifestation of the spirit, an archetype of the perfect society, for it undermines the ego.

The poem 'Noche de resurrecciones' (1939; Night of resurrections), severely abridged in its later versions, hints in its title at a dream-salvation. The dream 'grows' inside man and raises its fiery 'maravilla' (marvel) where the body's resurrection is glimpsed. The dream leads man back to his origins, his 'remote baptism' where his true self is born.

But the tension between empirical reality and the dream continued. In the poem 'El muro' (The wall), the wall represents the final and real limitations of man's nature, as opposed to the dream's promise of 'eternity'. The dream's

> dichas, goces, bahías de hermosuras, eternidades
> sustraídas, fluir vivo de imágenes, delicias desatadas,
>   pleamar
> happinesses, joys, bays of beauties, eternities removed,
> living flow of images, released delights, high tide

are but a 'blind' paradise because the dream has not been incorporated into waking life. This is also a poetic problem, for the dream is *mute*, and the poet's sterility and incapacity to express the dream's visions are the source of the anguish, the wall or block in his work. Until the 1940s the dreams are no more than 'brief paradises' that they are 'henchidos de presagios' (swollen with portents) is all the more painful.

'Soliloquio de medianoche' expresses this dissatisfaction. Mere dreaming divorced from the act of living is frustrating, for there is no pattern, no synthesis. Paz seeks a more real dream, real vision:

> Soñé en un mundo en donde la palabra engendraría
> y el mismo sueño habría sido abolido
> I dreamed of a world where the word would engender and
> the very dream would have been abolished

but this greater dream that foretells the end of daily dreaming is a chimera; trapped in history, man's only escape is random dreaming.

If dreams must be lived, then liberty is to become one's dream. However, by 1948, Paz has overcome this problem of 'context' of meaning; he has found a metaphysic, an integrating poetic: 'El sueño es explosivo. Estalla. Vuelve a ser sol' (The dream is explosive. It bursts. Becomes a sun again). The dream becomes daylight, the new sun. Surrealism's poetics illumined Paz's confusion and darkness.

The true life is the lived dream:

> Ni el sueño y su pueblo de imágenes rotas
> . . . Más allá de nosotros
> . . . una vida más vida nos reclama.
> Not the dream and its people of broken images. . .Beyond
> us. . .a life, more life, reclaims us.

Paz envisions the poetics of the waking dream. His dreams urge the dreamer to 'live them in broad daylight'. For the dream expresses man's inner truth: 'somos ese sueño y sólo nacimos para realizarlo (we are this dream and we are only born to realise it); not to be the dreamer but the dream itself. This dissatisfaction with the dream's gratuitous imagery reflects Paz's quest for lucidity, 'a tener conciencia de su delirio' (to be conscious of his delirium); also his (and Villaurrutia's) rejection of 'blind' automatism.

His crucial poem 'El cántaro roto' (1955; The broken jug) contrasts the fecundity of the dreamscape with the aridity of the Mexican landscape. There seems no way of uniting vision with this empirical reality, except through the notion of the waking dream:

> Hay que dormir con los ojos abiertos, hay que soñar con las
>   manos,
> soñemos sueños activos de río buscando su cauce, sueños de sol
>   soñando sus mundos,
> hay que soñar en voz alta . . .
> cantar hasta que el sueño engendre y brote del costado del
>   dormido la espiga roja de la resurrección.
> We must sleep with our eyes open, we must sleep with our hands,
> let us dream active dreams of a river seeking its bed, dreams of a
> sun dreaming its worlds, we must dream aloud . . . sing until the
> dream engenders and spouts from the side of the sleeper the red
> wheat-ear of resurrection.

Dreams must be lived, must become part of our daily activity and must speak out aloud (the dream is the real language of communication). But this is prescriptive, a *must*, and not an actual experience; Paz's is a poetry of intentions, a poetics. Between 1939 and 1955 we can trace how subtly Paz has embodied an integrative poetics (of surrealism) through the notion of the lived dream (utopia) despite similar imagery (resurrection, wheat). Paz conforms to Paul Eluard's definition of the poet as the 'rêveur éveillé' drawing his poetry up from the 'sommeil vivant' (the awakened dreamer, living sleep).

Open and closed eyes

Paz's vision is articulated in a recurrent motif cutting across all his work. It is rooted in a dialectic—the open and the closed—crucial to Paz. It runs through *El laberinto de la soledad*, a critique of the 'closed' Mexican, trapped in himself and scared of opening out and revealing himself. But it also looks back to surrealism. Breton's exploration of the 'subconscious' and the dream led him to define surrealism as 'la descente vertigineuse en nous, l'illumination systématique des lieux cachés' (the vertiginous descent into ourselves, the systematic illumination of hidden places). Paul Eluard posits a utopian future when man will only have to close his eyes 'pour que s'ouvrent les portes du merveilleux' (so that the doors of the marvellous open). Many other poets exploit this closed-eye vision, from Pedro Salinas and Robert Desnos to Luis Cernuda and others. It is a visionary tradition rooted in a verbal expression.

When Paz the poet opens his eyes, he sees empirical reality as shadowy, ungraspable and empty: 'bosteza lo real sus naderías' (reality yawns its nothingnesses). When the poet looks down at Mexico in 'El cántaro roto' he sees a moonscape of bones, dust, rags and insects. The perceptive and reflective eye, pure retina without faith or vision and unable to grant sense to 'abject' reality, sees a wasteland.

Thus the poet *shuts* his eyes and looks inside himself; the surrealist proposition. He shuts his 'outer' eyes and 'opens' them inside himself. Inside he sees the real midday, the real light, and hears the real song of his ancient, buried nakedness. This is real seeing, the poet's mental lucidity. Poetry is light, and when the poet invents he sees his own creation 'que renace lentamente bajo la dominación de mis ojos' (that is reborn slowly under the domination of my eyes). The poet sees the 'evidencias del mundo / para los ojos puros' (evidences of the world for my pure eyes), for poetry purifies and restores vision, not mere sight. This is linked to Eluard's claim: 'Je devins esclave de la faculté pure de voir' (I became a slave to the pure faculty of seeing). Poetry makes the poet's eyes 'prophetic' and reveal the real self 'me vi al cerrar los ojos' (I saw myself when I closed my eyes), the self beyond reductions:

Y los sentidos palpan
la forma presentida
y ven los ojos lo que inventan

And the senses touch the intuited form, and the eyes see what
they invent.

The inner eye that sees is a device in many poems: 'tu espalda fluye
tranquila bajo mis ojos' (your back flows tranquilly under my eyes); this is not
retinal art but desire-art, vision. Paz writes:

La presencia sin más
. . . Con nuestros ojos ven lo que no ven los ojos

Nothing but presence . . . with our eyes see what our eyes do not
see.

The paradox, seeing what cannot be seen, is illusory; with desire 'liberated'
we see and we experience.

Woman is closer to this truth or insight. She is in touch with herself;
her eyes are 'puertas del más allá' (doors of the beyond). Paz unequivocally
states: 'abre los ojos el Poeta, los cierra la Mujer. Todo es' (the poet opens his
eyes, woman closes them. Everything is). She grants reality, for the act and
experience of love is the truth.

And this truth is beyond words and eyes: 'Toma mis ojos y
reviéntalos' (Take my eyes and burst them); and the truth of presence is
described thus:

Mis ojos han de ver lo nunca visto
Lo que miraron sin mirarlo nunca
El revés de lo visto y de la vista

My eyes have to see what has never been seen, what they looked
at without ever looking, the reverse of what is seen and sight.

Paz the poet sees beyond what man has earmarked as reality; but this
is done only through desire, liberating the self from this marking, this
deformation. Poetry helps because it 'cleans the doors of perception' by
stripping language of its dead, dirty 'skins'. That sight is the prime sense in
Paz is clear; from his interest in the visual arts to his visionary poetics, his aim
is to *see*. His intention is to 'dream again with his eyes closed' and, living that
dream, to become himself.

Urban wasteland

The open mind, the surrealists' 'dispoinibility', always open to chance and arbitrary experiences, responding to whatever stimuli it received without imposing any deforming schema or grid; this corresponds to Paz's poetics, to his dialectic of 'loneliness' and 'communion'. André Breton was obsessed by the 'Ouvert' (Alexandrian; Open), always striving to 'ouvrir, toujours ouvrir, à tout prix' (Jaccottet; to open, always open, at all costs). To write, for Paz, is to 'abrir las puertas condenadas' (to open sealed doors); to prise open the hardened, encapsulated ego and let fresh air and life in.

Soledad (Loneliness) shows that the root of man is his essential loneliness; the fact that only he himself can die and that his profoundest experiences are solitary and incommunicable. On another level, meditating, thinking, reading and writing are solitary acts. Each poem begins in an act of *soledad* and only from this inner laboratory of loneliness will the new poetry spring: 'Por todas partes los solitarios forzados empiezan a crear las palabras del nuevo diálogo' (Everywhere the forced solitaries begin to create the worlds of a new dialogue). The centre of Paz's psychology is man's *soledad*: 'Soledad / Única madre de los hombres' (Loneliness, man's only mother). It is this real *soledad* that forces man to communicate, talk, write, make love and transcend his solitary self.

The poet suffers this *soledad* more intensely because of his values, his insights, his lucidities, that isolate him from the mass of society and place him to one side of the time-sanctioned securities. Paz writes: 'Condenado a vivir en el subsuelo de la historia, la soledad define al poeta moderno' (Condemned to live in the subsoil of history, loneliness defines the modern poet). The poet reflects the fragmented and divided culture in his over-sensitised self. For *soledad* is being divided in two: 'Todos estamos solos, porque todos somos dos' (We are all alone, because we are all two).

The critic Ramón Xiran has shown how this theme of isolation characterises an epoch, without suggesting that 'surrealism' offered Paz a way out, a poetic. Both in *El laberinto de la soledad* and in 'Himno entre ruinas' there is a solution to loneliness, and both were written in Paris.

Two central, recurrent symbols convey the restricting and alienating sense of *soledad*: *muro* (wall) and *espejo* (mirror). Both are poetic commonplaces and reflect the poet's inability to convey the real sense of isolation. Deeper than the *theme* of *soledad* is the feeling that the poet was divorced from his capacity to write poetry; repeating other men's symbols; dead, literary symbols: the 'wall' that blocks the exit, the 'mirror' that reflects the surface self. And the 'wall' is closer to what psychologists call the 'block'; rather than accept this block nostalgically Paz seeks a poetics of self-knowledge. For only self-knowledge will reveal the wall and smash the mirror; and surrealism gave Paz the clue in its utopian dream of a poetic society that would 'echar abajo las paredes entre el hombre y el hombre' (knock down the walls between man and man).

A deeper meaning underlying Paz's use of the 'wall' is that it is *artificial*, a man-made barrier. The sense is that man has lost contact with his *natural* sources and has universalised reason, worshipped science and numbers and what is quantifiable. To Paz this is a mutilation: 'mass él cierra los poros de su alma al infinito que lo tienta ensimismado en su árida pelea' (but he shuts the pores of his soul to the infinite that tempts him, absorbed in his arid struggle).

Paz senses that the things we label reality—social, urban, 'objective' reality—are all grotesque parodies of what *is*. Paz sympathises with the Romantic rebellion against 'wasteland' culture. For culture has lost contact with its 'spiritual' roots.

Mexican reality, part of universal reality, is a deformed parody of what it should be. This is the theme of *El laberinto de la soledad* and central poems like 'Himno entre ruinas' and 'El cántaro roto'. 'Ruins' is Paz's word for contemporary culture; a 'broken' absent wholeness. Mexican culture is damned; its 'guitarras roncas', its songs that end in a curse, its shadowy substance that 'nos cierra las puertas del contacto' (hoarse guitars; close the doors of contact). This is the wasteland of 'El cántaro roto'; there are no living people, no crickets singing, only cold volcanoes, dry gulches and cacti and stones, and a vague smell of burnt seed: 'He aquí a la piedra rota, al hombre roto, a la luz rota' (Here is the broken stone, the broken man and the broken light).

But Mexican man is contemporary with all men; the grey uniform of the twentieth century is worn by all; New York, London and Moscow are no different to Mexico City; all are peopled by a 'crowd of rats', by 'domestic bipeds'. And Paz includes himself, trapped in his own inner, sunless mental labyrinth; he is sterile and empty: 'Y todo ha de parar en este chapoteo de aguas muertas' (And everything has to stop in this splashing of dead waters).

Paz rejects conventional, societal values and morality; he identifies with a surrealist *topos*. He senses the stranglehold of 'shoes', 'family ties', 'false smiles and hopes' he satirises 'money, glory, justice, power, god'; the capitalistic system is unacceptable. 'Magic money' builds its dreams on human bones; 'porque el dinero es infinito y crea desiertos infinitos' (because money is infinite and creates infinite deserts). The grand ideals are 'elocuentes vejigas ya sin nada: Dios, Cielo, Amistad, Revolución o Patria' (eloquent bladders now without anything: God, Heaven, Friendship, Revolution or Fatherland). Businessmen, politicians, *caudillos* and urban man in general have renounced the quest for a 'better' life and go to the cinema, Mass, the office and death.

All that divides man from man—laws, banks, prisons, the army, the church, teachers—must be rejected:

> major el crimen,
> los amantes suicidas, el incesto
> . . .
> el adulterio en lechos de ceniza,
> . . .
>   mejor ser lapidado
> en las plazas que dar vuelta a la noria
> que exprime la sustancia de la vida,
> cambia la eternidad en horas huecas,
> better crime, suicidal lovers, incest . . . adultery in beds of ash . . .
> better to be stoned in the squares than to turn the water wheel
> that squeezes out the substance of life, changes eternity into
> hollow hours.

The rebellion is in terms of a richer *life*, not 'abstract shit' nor 'copper coins'; it is any rebellion that is against convention, anything that restores despised 'spirituality' rather than tread round and round the wheel.

The only imperative is 'pisotear las reglas' (to trample on the rules); to step on literature, morality, reasonable women, novels, psychology, friends. The imperative is to negate: 'No: renuncio a la tarjeta de racionamiento, a la cédula de identidad, al certificado de supervivencia' (No: I renounce the ration book, identity card, the survival certificate). Paz defines modern poetry as an experience that implies 'a negation of the exterior world'. He seeks *desmesuras*, extreme actions.

The artificiality and abstractness of urban reality nauseate Paz. The city is a sterile labyrinth, hostile to poetry; it is both very real, out there, and *mental*; the city as symbol of rational consciousness. Again the outer city reflects the inner and vice versa.

Other city symbols repeat this sterility: in the poem 'La calle' (The street) it is the street that alienates:

> Es una calle larga y silenciosa.
> Ando en tinieblas y tropiezo y caigo
> . . .
> Todo está oscuro y sin salida,
> y doy vueltas y vueltas en esquinas
> que dan siempre a la calle

> It is a long and silent street. I walk in darkness and stumble and
> fall. . . All is dark and without exit, and I turn and turn at corners
> that always give on to the same street.

Other images of sterile repetition include 'corridors', 'galleries', 'halls',
'alleyways', all leading nowhere.

Another set of symbols of *soledad* in the city clusters around the hotel
room; expressive of what is anonymous and transient. 'Room', bedroom,
door and *puerta condenada* amplify these connotations. These last are both
outer doors and inner doors; the doors to being that are opened by poetry.

There are many other wasteland symbols and most are
conventionally literary; some are also obvious allusions to the Mexican
landscape and convey the fusion between inner mental sterility and the outer,
real deserts of most of Mexico; recurrent words such as sand, desert,
wasteland, ash, dust, saltpetre, stone. This last—stone—is most frequent in
Paz; stone is dead matter which can also be resurrected through poetry, for
stone is a word that can defy gravity and live, a symbol. There is a word that
between 'las piedras mudas' (the mute stones) and the 'piedra [que] vive y se
incorpora' (stone [that] lives and gets up), the 'piedra partida que mana
inagotable' (cracked stone that flows inexhaustibly).

The poet negates the '*ruins*' and '*shadows*' of twentieth-century
urban culture, symbolised in a set of images—the Mexican landscape, urban
culture and its values, and the modern poetic tradition. As a cluster of
images, it is derivative and stale because Paz is still in the shadow of other
poets, unable to find his voice. The poems of this period antedate by a few
years Paz's sought-after surrealist experience, and the *mood* is dominated by
the crushing presence of T. S. Eliot's urban poetics. Paz has noted this
conjunction:

> El hombre moderno es el personaje de Eliot. Todo es ajeno él y
> él en nada se reconoce. Es la excepción . . . El hombre no es
> árbol, ni planta, ni ave. Está solo en medio de la creatión

> Modern man is Eliot's character. All is alien to him and he does
> not recognise himself in anything. He is the exception . . . Man
> is not a tree, nor plant, nor bird. He is alone in the middle of
> creation.

Paz rebels against this derivative, alienated voice. His use of negatives
reveals his values. He seeks to belong (religion), to find his roots (tree), to
overcome his loneliness.

The Way through, Life, Epiphany

At this point (the early 1940s) we leave T. S. Eliot's shadow, and we leave Paz groping for a style, and go in search of a poetics. Paz believes in redemption. For him, as for Breton (in the poem to Sade) there is a *'breach'*, the door can be unlocked. Various recurrent images point to this sensing of a way through. Terms like *herida* (wound), *llaga* (wound), *cicatriz* (scar), and *tatuaje* (tattoo) reveal this. The wound is also woman's sexual organ, a reminder that we have an origin and that we have fallen. This wound sings; it is resonant. One day it will 'open' again; and man must scratch around these badly healed wounds. The ancient goddess (obsidian butterfly) reminds the poet: 'Yo soy la herida que no cicatriza' (I am the wound that never heals); for every wound is also a fountain. This is explicit in the poem 'Mutra':

> Tras la coraza de cristal de roca busqué al hombre, palpé a tientas
>   la brecha imperceptible:
> nacemos y es un rasguño apenas la desgarradura y nunca cicatriza
>   y arde y es una estrella de luz propia,
> nunca se apaga la diminuta llaga, nunca se borra la señal de
>   sangre, por esa puerta nos vamos a lo oscuro.
> Behind the rock-crystal cuirass I looked for man, I gropingly
> touched the imperceptible breach: we are born and it is hardly a
> scratch, the tear, and it never heals up and it burns and it is a star
> of its own light, the diminutive wound never goes out, the sign
> of blood is never wiped out, through that door we go to the dark.

The rich sonorous lines lead the reader like an umbilical cord back to the dark origins: woman's sexual organs, breach, scratch, unhealed scar, the 'life door' which is the site of separation. Paz's metaphysics of union is very literal and symbolic, for this 'oscuro' is none other than Rimbaud's 'bouche d'ombre', the very source of life. Back through woman lies 'real life': 'una herida en la que bebo la sustancia perdida de la creacíon' (a wound in which I drink the lost substance of creation).

Other terms prevalent in his poetry, such as the conventional symbols of *llave* (key) and *puente* (bridge)—the key to the sealed door, the bridge over to the 'other'—also the underscore the process from breach through to communion. Expressions of and variations on *frontera* (frontier) and *orilla* (shore) substantiate this 'journey' through limitation and restrictions. But above all, poetry will be the poet's *weapon* to break down the wall; this is a violent aggressive activity (the Romantic outsider) and the poet invokes *daga* (dagger), *puñal* (dagger), *cuchillo* (knife), *navaja* (razor), *hacha* (axe), *lanza* (lance), *espada* (sword), *flecha* (arrow) as well as *garra* (claw), *uñas* (nails). Faced with the numbed body of culture, the act of writing a poem is at first a destructive act, in that its starting point is critical. This is clearly reflected in these listed terms.

But all this is only in search of a richer, more intense life. The poet despairs that 'la vraie vie est absente' (Rimbaud; the true life is absent) and he cries out 'qué sonido remoto tiene la palabra vida' (what a remote sound the word 'life' has). The poet wants to sense that he is living, and that life has a meaning.

Above all, this means facing death by stripping away false illusions, by rejecting the comforting gods and the diverse religions and ideologies, and incorporating the fact of death into life. Paz affirms 'el culto a la vida, si de verdad es profundo y total, es también culto a la muerte' (the cult to life, if it is truly profound and total, is also a cult to death). Poetry becomes this cult to life, the 'poétique vécue' is the answer: 'el decir poético, chorro de tiempo, es afirmación simultánea de la muerte y la vida' (poetic saying, stream of time, is a simultaneous affirmation of death and life). Poetry, like music, is an art in time (we read along the lines, each word effacing the next) and yet the whole act is repeatable and defies time by charging the timeless moment with presence: where desire, being and language are one: 'Nacer y morir: un instante. En ese instante somos vida y muerte, esto y aquello' (To be born and die: an instant. In this instant we are life and death, this and that). Poetry fixes the *vertiges* (as Rimbaud put it) and redeems time by recreating it.

However, nothing can be said about death except

> Todos vamos a morir
> ¿Sabemos algo más?
> We are all going to die. Do we know anything else?

and a living life is what we have and are. Yet to sense this living intensely is not easy, for life has been numbed and dulled. Paz can write lines like 'Yo estaba vivo, en busca de la vida' (I was alive, in search of life). Straightforward living is given (i.e. that we are breathing) but to experience real life, 'asir la vida' (to grab life), is arduous. The poet wants to 'give [more] life to life', for to him living should mean living the full intensity of the present (ecstasy) as a 'lúcida embriaguez', (lucid rapture), as a 'vivacidad instantánea' (instantaneous vivacity). Paz seeks an elixir: 'Qué agua de vida ha de darnos la vida' (What water of life has to give us life?).

The actual situation is that life is alienated from man, as if life 'unlives' man; Paz (deliberately?) echoes Breton in his cry 'la vida es otra, siempre allá, más lejos' (life is other, always over there, farther away). Something is very wrong with what we call life and it is the poet who suffers this 'absence'. Paz ends his prose poem 'Carta a dos desconocidas' (Letter to two unknowns; life and death are the two unknowns, both feminine in Spanish) thus: 'A la verdadera vida, a la que no es noche ni día, ni tiempo ni destiempo, a la vivacidad pura' (To true life, that which is not night or day, nor time nor untime, to pure vivacity); real life is 'pure vivacity', the centre of Paz's poetics, as the excellent critic Guillermo Sucre has shown in another context.

Vivacity, presence, the present moment: these notions point to the ontological centre of Paz's poetics, the intense experience that transcends language (culture and history) to reveal desire and being and man's inner truth in the epiphanic moment, or *instante poético*. This is Paz's answer to man's pressing, ever-present temporal limitations; what Breton called 'eternity' in the 'instant'.

As an experience that transcends Chronos the most apt analogy with the timeless moment would be the orgasm; the basic metaphor in Paz's body–spirit poetic. Erotic love is the link, the 'absolute' experience shared by poet and reader, the cypher of eternity. This orgasmic *instante* reveals desire–being, where the poet becomes the poem he has written, an *image* of what he can be, his desire temporarily liberated. However, behind the uniqueness of this 'now' or poetic presence lies a paradox: for man the arrival of a successive 'now' is trapped in time. Once again poetry points to a solution; for it redeens time and fixes the temporal flux by creating a *retour éternel*, an ever-renewable experience based on cyclical or natural time. Paz ends his book *El arco y la lira*: 'En el poema, el ser y el deseo de ser pactan por un instante, como el fruto y los labios. Poesía, momentánea reconciliación' (In the poem, being and desire for being agree for a moment, like fruit and lips. Poetry, momentary reconciliation). Hence poetics (surrealism) replaces religion and metaphysics.

The centre of Paz's poetics is *experience*: not coherence, nor even originality of thought; experience is the sensuous apprehension of the present moment intensified, and this is a common heritage, a commonplace.

Here poetics ends and the problem of writing begins, much as in 'mystical' verse where the crux is how to recreate (or invent) in language the intense experience. Many of Paz's poems deal with negative moments—also moments that clude the word—as well as dealing with the positive, ecstatic ones. These latter sustain many poems. The long 'Piedra de sol' is structured about these negative and positive *instantes* of successive time. Paz describes this as el tema central [el] de la recuperación del instante amoroso como recuperación de la verdadera libertad, 'puerta del ser' que nos lleva a la comunicación con otro cuerpo, con los demás hombres, con la naturaleza.

the central theme is that of the recuperation of the moment of love as a recuperation of true liberty, 'door of being' which leads us to communication with another body, with other men, with nature.

This poem 'recuperates' the epiphany where the moment of erotic union gives life its meaning in terms of experiential knowledge:

>   se derrumban
> por un instante inmenso y vislumbramos
> nuestra unidad perdida, el desamparo
> que es ser hombres, la gloria que es ser hombres
> y compartir el pan, el sol, la muerte,
> el olvidado asombro de estar vivos;

they collapse for an immense instant and we glimpse our lost unity, the helplessness that is being men, the glory that is being men and sharing bread, sun and death, the forgotten amazement of being alive.

The experience of this momentary *amazement* at being alive is given through erotic love and poetry.

Paz conveys the *instante* through a series of terms such as *relámpago* (lightning)—that sudden, blinding flash of light—and *chispa* and *centella* (spark); or *ola* (wave), the wave of time, rising and falling; or *mediodía* (midday), the moment of revelation with the sun casting no shadows; and many others. We will restrict ourselves to one other imagistic vein.

Vertigo, the experience of dizziness and thrill glorified by André Breton, is a figure of the fusing of 'orgasm' and the *instante poético*. Vertigo is the experience of lovers: 'los amantes se asoman al balcón del vértigo' (the lovers show up on the balcony of vertigo); the climax of their union is 'en lo alto del vértigo' (in the height of vertigo), the trampoline of vertigo (where man is thrown out of himself). To sense that one is alive is a 'vertiginosa y lúcida embriaguez' (vertiginous and lucid rapture). Vertigo can be ascribed to the inner world of the dream: 'y un mundo de vértigo y llama nace bajo la frente del que sueña' (and a world of vertigo and flame is born under the brow of him who sleeps), a variation on Breton's 'descente vertigineuse en nous'. Vertigo can also be predicated of the experience of the poem itself: as it is the dissolution of reason, of form and language itself, 'el vértigo sin forma' (formless vertigo), as in Rimbaud's poetics. 'fijar vértigos'. Vertigo is the word that describes the experience of the absolute: 'luego el vértigo: caer, perderse, ser uno con lo Otro . . . Ser todo. Ser' (then vertigo: to fall, lose oneself, be one with the other . . . Be all. Be). To give in to vertigo might even change the world:

> el mundo cambia
> si dos, vertiginosos y enlazados,
> caen sobre la yerba . . .

the world changes if two, vertiginous and entwined, fall on the grass . . .

Vertigo is the source-experience of a new religion:

> Esculpimos un Dios instantánco
> Tallamos el vértigo

We sculpt an instantaneous God, we carve vertigo.

Vertigo is the centre of Breton's poetics as well: 'Ce que j' ai connu de plus beau c'est le vertige' (What I have known that was most beautiful is vertigo); he is only moved by nature and events

> . . . qu'en function de la part de vertige
> Faite à l'homme . . .

only as a function of the amount of vertigo dealt to man.

A metaphor of vertigo and the vision granted by the *instante poélico* is provided by the notion of 'transparency'; according to Rachel Phillips this is Paz's most personal motif. Transparency is otherwise opaque matter penetrated by the vision, just as crystal is stone metamorphosed. The state of transparency is described as one of the most effective and beautiful conjunctions of opposites: a state sought by 'mystic and surrealist alike' (Cirlot). The point here is that Paz is not being 'personal', but consciously participating in a tradition. André Breton was obsessed by the 'crystallisation' of thought into poetry, which he deemed the 'total transparency' between the material and the mental. His 'praise of crystal' derives from a sense of it as the archetypal work of art, combining hardness, regularity, lustre and transparency, but formed naturally and mysteriously. Breton's poetic ideal is 'transparence' (Alexandrian); he was haunted by transparency (Audoin); this is also the basis of Eluard's poetics, where the 'idea of transparence, of the penetration of surfaces, of passing the frontiers of the real' (Matthews) is the ideal. The crystal is the surrealists' emblem, and their enemy 'c'est l'opacité' (Breton; is opacity).

Paz inherits and shares this ideal: 'el arte aspira a la transparencia' (art aspires to transparency). Transparency is the quality of all great poetry, and Paz applies it to Gorostiza, Mallarmé and Michaux. Answering a questionnaire sent by Breton and published in Breton's *L'Art magique*, Paz selects an Uccello vase for its transparency, 'on peut voir l'autre côté' (one can see the other side). Poetry transforms language's normal opacity; it creates 'bosques de árboles transparentes' (woods of transparent trees), rocks of 'entrañas transparentes' (transparent cores); poetry is a 'dialogue of transparencies'. This is the essence of the mental and visionary worlds where poetry is not a question of style or words but of vision.

> el mundo ya es visible por tu cuerpo,
> es transparente por tu transparencia,
> the world is already visible through your body, is transparent
> through your transparency.

This leads us to the central symbol of 'unity' in Paz's poetics; namely *light*. Paz is a poet who *looks*, lucidly seeking enlightenment. Light bathes his concerns; it is the light of creativity as well as mental light, and as well as the sun or the dawn revealing the world as it really is. This stress on light has its roots in Paz's ambiguous *mexicanidad* where the light of the high plateau is so 'crystal clear'. We will investigate some of these layers of meaning.

When the dream 'explodes' it becomes a 'sun'; here lies the link between light and spirit and being. The divine vision is one of light, of 'seas of light'; for the original divinity was light. Paz recalls a quartz stone shown him by the surrealist painter Wolfgang Paalen, engraved with an image of the rain god Tlaloc: Paz wrote a short poem about this:

> Tocado por la luz
> el cuarzo ya es cascada.
> Sobre sus aguas flota, niño, el dios.
> Touched by the light the quartz is already a cascade. On the
> waters floats, a child, the god.

The mineral quartz is brought to life by the light and *flows*. Light is the divine creative archetype; and, as in this short poem, its antithetical image is that of inert matter, the opposition between 'la luz frente a la piedra'; (light confronts stone). Petrification is another metaphor for ego-limitation, as David Gallagher has pointed out, and as we saw in Paz's poem on Sade. Light is a traditional symbol of the spirit, and there is also an inner, mental sun, a 'soleil spirituel'. Nerval's 'black sun'. The *word* 'sun' is not the sun that heats the earth, but the word shines.

Gaston Bachelard makes this clear by quoting from Novalis:"'Dans les espaces infinis, la lumière ne fait donc *rien*. Elle attend l'oeil. Elle attend l'âme. Elle est done la base de l'illumination spirituelle'" ('In the infinite spaces, light then does nothing. It awaits the eye. It awaits the soul. It is then the base of spiritual illumination'). Paz is rooted in this tradition of poets who give evidence of the sovereignty of light. He has his eyes open and sees the light that reveals, destroys, creates and gilds a world indifferent to man.

> como la luz ligera y sin memoria
> que brilla en cada hoja, en cada piedra,
> dora la tumba y dora la colina
> y nada la detiene ni apresura.

Like the agile and memoryless light that shines in every leaf, in every stone, gilds the tomb and gilds the hill and nothing stops it nor hurries it.

Light is an image of Eden and infinity; it inaugurates 'un reinado dichoso' (a happy kingdom); it is formless perfection.

Paz's *Semillas para un himno* is a series of poems about the paradisal world before man, inundated with light; it explores a dual theme, linking this dawn of pre-history and myth with the creative act itself in the form of the *birth* of the solar, luminous world—word. Light leads the world out of the darkness of chaos, and the word out of the dark mass of language. Here light fuses inner and outer, poet and paradise:

> Al alba busca su nombre lo naciente
> Sobre los troncos soñolientos centellea la luz
> . . .
> La luz despliega su abanico de nombres

At dawn what is born seeks its name. On the dreamy trunks the light sparkles . . . The light unfolds its fan of names.

This 'light' creates a world of surface perfections:

> La luz corre por todas partes
> Canta por las terrazas
> Hace bailar las casas

Light runs everywhere, sings on the terraces, makes the houses dance.

Creative light makes reality tangible, 'luz que madura hasta ser cuerpo' (light that matures until it is a body), and this body—light is song or poetry:

> Cierra los ojos y oye cantar la luz
> Shut your eyes and hear the light sing.

The dawn of light is the dawn of the word in poetry, and the result is language perceived sensuously. Real man, buried under a civilised mask, is a fragment of this cosmic light. Through woman this light can be recovered in the *instante* of erotic love which leaves the poet dazzled: 'Gran vasija de luz hasta los bordes benchida de su propia y poderosa sustancia' (Great vessel of light filled to its edges with its own and powerful substance).

The inner light of being, *estrella interior* (interior star), the divine light of the beginning, daylight, the light in woman, and the light of creativity are all analogues linked by the celebration of the *instante* in the title poem of the collection, which ends:

> La luz se abre en las diáfanas terrazas del mediodía
> Se interna en el bosque como una sonámbula
> Penetra en el cuerpo dormido del agua
>
> Por un instante están los nombres habitados

The light opens out in the diaphanous terraces of midday. It penetrates the wood like a sleepwalker. It penetrates the sleeping body of the water. For an instant, names are inhabited.

The critic Ramón Xirau, in a review of the book, selected unity and 'luminosity' as the central motifs of the collection, labelling it a 'diurnal' or 'daylight' poetry.

The main source of light is the sun, the heart of the sky. Paz's sun has associations with the Aztec cosmology as well as with the more mundane omnipresence of the sun in the Mexican sky. The sun 'reveals the reality of things' ambivalently, for it both regenerates and burns to destruction. Paz is well aware of the Aztec solar religion; the ancient dream was to be born again as a sun. Paz modifies this nostalgia for regeneration and incorporates it into his poetics. For Paz, behind the jade mask of the Mexicans shines a 'secret sun'; and Mexicans still dream of being suns again.

To be a sun, in Paz's terms, is to live the dream and recover the spiritual centre, for 'el sol es la vida henchida de sí' (the sun is life swollen with itself). Paz writes of the painter Rufino Tamayo: 'le bastaba descender al fondo de sí mismo para encontrar el antiguo sol, surtidor de imágenes' (it sufficed him to descend to the bottom of himself to find the ancient sun, fountain of images). The link between inner sun and descent inside returns us to the surrealist myths and metaphors. Paz describes his poetics: 'preveo un hombre-sol' (I foresee a man-sun). This man-sun will be the new man, and the experience of regeneration is described in the poem 'Piedra nativa':

> El sol lo cubre todo lo ve todo
> Y en su mirada fija nos bañamos
> Y en su pupila largamente nos quemamos
> Y en los abismos de su luz caemos
> Música despeñada
> Y ardemos y no dejamos huella

The sun covers all, sees all, and in its stare we bathe, and in its pupil for a long time we burn, and in the abysses of its light we fall, hurled down music, and we burn and leave no trace.

This sun burns away the false selves, and through its heat and passion liberates desire; this act of liberation is music or poetry or being.

The poem 'Himno entre ruinas' has the sun as its central motif. The opening stanza describes the perfect, natural world without man, a paradise lost. The sun's 'alto grito amarillo' (high yellow shout) fecundates nature. Here the sun lays its golden egg that spills over the sea; 'La luz crea templos en el mar' (The light creates temples in the sea) where the visual and symbolic meet in an image that expresses all Paz's poetics—light penetrates the water, creating shafts or columns that hint at some other, grander and natural 'sea-temple'. This same sun becomes the luminous, sweet orange of twenty-four segments through which man communes (tastes, bites) with nature and his natural self. Compared to this magnificent sun, the sun of twentieth-century man in his labyrinthine civilisation is 'un sol anémico' (an anaemic sun) and a 'sol sin crepúsculo' (a sun without twilight). Likewise the whole of the literally splendid *Semillas para un himno* is bathed in sunlight; the seed of the sun opens noiselessly; this sun is in all things as *seed*. It is poetics of hope, of potential, a seminal poetics.

JULIA A. KUSHIGIAN

Flowing Rivers and Contiguous Shores: The Poetics of Paz

Few would deny Octavio Paz's principal role in the advancement and preservation of Orientalism in Hispanic letters. Paz's interest in the Orient is both historical and anthropological, as he confirms that the Native American is of Asiatic origin, and that this Asiatic origin perhaps explains the numerous similarities between Chinese and American civilizations. His interest is also sociopolitical in nature, as Octavio Paz was ambassador to India for six years beginning in 1962 and resided during his service in New Delhi. It is, in addition, literary, as Paz began to read about the Orient in books obtained in France and continued his scholarly research of philosophies, religions, and literatures of the East (in translation) throughout his career. The result of this intellectual engagement with the East and a defining of his own culture vis-à-vis the Other is a series of critical essays, in addition to numerous collections of poetry.

There arises from the works of Octavio Paz a dialectic that complements and at times subtracts from the other source, be it poetry or essay. Paz's theory of Orientalism, then, is maintained in a constant state of flux. Let us remember Paz's analogy between movement and immobility within the relationship: "Lo esencial es que la relación no sea tranquila: el diálogo entre oscilación e inmovilidad es lo que infunde *vida* a la cultura y da *forma* a la vida" ("The essential thing is for the relationship not to be a

From *Orientalism in the Hispanic Literary Tradition: In Dialogue with Borges, Paz, and Sarduy* by Julia A. Kushigian, © 1991 by University of New Mexico Press.

tranquil one: the dialogue between oscillation and immobility is what gives a culture *life* and life *form*"). This movement and combination of elements will be shown to represent Paz's search for the metaphysical meaning of poetic image, erotic love, and the sacred being, giving evidence that East and West blend, are contiguous, separate, and then reflect each other. One need only refer to the first title (the title in the superior position over the names of the author and the collection) of *Ladera Este* to comprehend the interrelationship of the East and West in Octavio Paz's work: "las dos orillas" (the two shores). Manuel Durán, among other critics, has noted the significance of the pervasive image of "la otra orilla" (the other shore) in Paz's poetry as a symbol of the momentary fusion of opposites. While la otra orilla is a highly significant image in Octavio Paz's poetry, las dos orillas is a more satisfying and profound representation of Hispanic Orientalism. La otra orilla does imply the existence of an opposite shore, but its focus is directed to the Other, which is reinforced by Paz's surrealist perspective. Las dos orillas implies the confluence of opposing elements and emphasizes their continuity and contiguity in time and space. Rather than situating the image in a topology that is binary, the image of the two shores, arrived at through one shore's relationship to the other, suggests the blending and separation of opposites. The symbolic orilla implies the Buddhist concept of the symbolic leap to the other shore, providing us with a graphic and metaphorical representation of the touching of the two sides. The water of the river flows rhythmically between the two shores, washing up on both, as its current flows and perpetually merges with that of the other shore. Sarduy employs the geometric image of the Möbius strip to envision the blending of oppositions in Hispanic Orientalism; similarly, Paz appears to subscribe to a figure represented by the river that stretches indefinitely, its body being in constant communication with both shores.

I will attempt to elucidate Paz's Orientalist construct through a dialogue created between his essays and his poetry. This is a significant approach in that many authors and critics, including Carlos Fuentes, have concluded that Paz's essays and poetry are inseparable because they are united philosophically. Poetry, on the one hand, normally presents a single-sided image in that it speaks unequivocally with the voice of the poet. That is to say, there might arise doubt, conflicts, and polemics in the poem, questioning nature, love, and life, but they are still presented from the single mind of the poet. The voice of the poet is a native one in that it is unaffected and unencumbered, the most direct communication that can be sustained with the reader. It cannot enter the minds or convey the angst of a variety of protagonists because it speaks through an incontrovertible and singular view. Language is normally present to the poet from within, in the work it does to bring about an effect, through images, musicality, and so on, in the reader. It cannot, because of its timeless quality, be present to the poet from without as a culturally, historically, and socially limited linguistic reality. Poetic style is monologic in nature. The prose writer may distance himself from speech, but the poet cannot.

While it would appear, then, that internal dialogization of discourse is not used in poetic discourse, it does seem that Paz makes use of the many double-voiced images that are dialogized in his Orientalist poetry. These images suggest a dialogue with, and a questioning of, the East that breaks down the images of oneself and the Other, destroying the closed, fixed image we have of both. The instability of the relationship is evident because we can hear another's voice in a word or phrase given. It may even be the voice of the poet transformed momentarily into another, bringing to life a strangeness or exoticism in the poem. In order to avoid alienating the reader, Paz includes in the Joaquín Mortiz edition a list of terms to clarify allusions and make concepts less exclusionary and distant, encouraging the reader to approach the Other. Moreover, this blending, separation, and further blending with the Other represents Paz's view of Hispanic Orientalism both linguistically through dialogue with the East, and aesthetically through the spatial relationships of the words that are imitative of Oriental poetry, philosophy, and art.

Spatial relationships on the page, key to the understanding of the haiku form of poetry, in addition to the physical folding of pages and the paper selected for printing, combine to superimpose one linguistic, aesthetic system over a distinct literary and cultural system. This is the case with the poem "Blanco," which, as Paz's note in *Ladera Este* explains, could not be reproduced as in the original edition whose typography and binding underscored not so much the presence of the text but the space that supported it. In the original, boxed edition the poem is read as it is unfolded, so that space and time disperse with the fixed image, calling the reader in to decipher the mandala. As this act is not possible in the mass-marketed edition of *Ladera Este*, the poet offers instead six possible readings of his poem, incorporating distinctions by columns, parts, or placement on the page. Superimpositions such as these of cultural and linguistic systems open a dialogue and force an interaction of values, ideas, and images that are symbols of one's destiny.

One rather natural image that presents itself in the analysis of Orientalism in Paz's work is that of the garden. "Quite frequently it is through these unheralded, simple images that we are introduced to the most startling literary theories. Paz relates the essence of an essay written by Donald Keene that signals the salient characteristics of one example of art from both Eastern and Western cultures: Ryoanji's garden and the Sistine chapel. The difference between the two is that the Sistine chapel is presented as something complete and perfect so that it keeps us at a distance. The garden of Ryoanji (like all Buddhist contemplative gardens) brings us into its design: "hecho a piedras irregulares sobre un espacio monocromo, nos invita a rehacerlo y nos abre las puertas de la participación" (made with irregular stones over a monochrome space, it invites us to recreate it and opens the doors to participation). Paz then draws together the worlds of literature and art: "poemas, cuadros: objetos verbales o visuales que simultáneamente se ofrecen a la contemplación y la acción imaginativa del lector o del espectador" (poems, paintings: verbal or visual objects that simultaneously are offered to the contemplation and to the imaginative activity of the reader or the spectator). This wilful denial of the finishing act, as Paz refers to this obvious imperfection, appears to reinforce the fragility of life in the flowing from one experience/interpretation to another. The meditation on the stones represents one method of interior liberation through spirituality and through imperfection, which implies a constant movement toward the state of perfection (on the other shore).

Poetry remains for Paz a spiritual exercise, another method of interior liberation, because each poem is unique and contains the vital elements of all poetry, just as each stone in the garden bears something of all stones. Each poem, then, is in dialogic relationship to other poems. The language of the poet is infused with multivoiced images, at times opposing, then reinforcing and questioning the potentiality of the representation. The Western literary word is viewed in light of the Eastern image, and is seen therefore through that image, which leads ultimately to knowledge of the self. The cultures and languages interanimate each other, renewing and unifying these images that stylistically had been held at a distance before.

The image of the garden flourishes in the collection of poetry titled *Ladera Este* (1962–1968). The poems that best convey the Eastern concept of garden and the images of imperfection, liberation, and contemplation are "Concierto en el jardín (Concert in the garden); "Lo idéntico" (One and the same); "Viento entero" (Wind from all compass points); and "Cuento de dos jardines" (Fable of two gardens). "Concierto en el jardín" and "Lo idéntico" demonstrate the blending of opposites commonly found in Tantric and Mahayana Buddhism. "Concierto en el jardín" also displays influence from haiku poetry," and more distinctly from José Juan Tablada, who, according to Paz, was probably the first Latin American Orientalist of merit. This stanza—

Se abre, flor doble, el mundo:
Tristeza de haber venido,
Alegría de estar aquí
(The world, a double blossom, opens:
sadness of having come,
joy of being here)

—recalls the blending of opposing emotions whose search for the state of perfection takes the action back to the center from which perfection may be attained through the void, or nirvana. The last verse of the poem, "Ando perdido en mi propio centro" (I walk lost in my own center), reinforces the concept of perpetual, unfinished movement in search of the perfection of the state of being, or possibly the perfection of language. "Viento entero" unites Paz's themes of erotic love and spirituality, where opposites such as beauty and violence are joined with the metaphysical theme of the timelessness of existence. In this long and complex union of dissonant notes we find a symbolic mention of the garden:

> *Dos o tres pájaros*
>
> *Inventan un jardín*
>
> (Two or three birds
>
> invent a garden).

Once the poet has removed from language its customary associations, the dynamic quality of language transforms each poem into a new object. The impreciseness of the number of birds, in juxtaposition to the exact date and the announcement of the arrival of spring, is coupled with the concept of creating or inventing the garden and rearranging the stones with every renewed glance.

Similarly, the garden as theme surfaces in "Cuento de dos jardines," written during Paz's sea voyage between Bombay and the Canary Islands. "Cuento de dos jardines" symbolizes prophetically the feeling of drifting between las dos orillas and the vertiginous blending of opposites. In the remembering, even the gardens flow ("fluyen los jardines"), unfolding one memory over the other. The two gardens are remembrances of real gardens in Paz's life: the Western garden is from Mixcoac where Paz spent his childhood, and the Eastern garden is one in India where Paz remarried. The poet beings the mythic voyage between gardens with that which brings to mind Bachelard's phenomenological approach to the memory of roads and houses:

> *Una casa, un jardín,*
> > *No son lugares:*
> *Giran, van y vienen.*
> > *Sus apariciones*
> *Abren en el espacio*
> > *Otro espacio,*
> *Otro tiempo en el tiempo.*
> (A house, a garden,
> > Are no places:
> They spin, come and go.
> > Their apparitions
> Unfold in space
> > Other space
> Other time within time.)

The garden becomes a poetic image in which the reader is asked to participate, opening up to a spatialization of time and memory where the image spins around (collides with?), goes to, and comes back from the Other. This movement is emphasized also by the graphic spatialization of words on the page, indicated by the typography and enhanced by punctuation, that have the eyes spin (like prayer wheels) and move in a backward and forward motion. Its space is another, as we are removed from the familiar and taken to another space or possibly another series of spaces, each one echoing the one that precedes it or the one that follows; and this holds true again for time. The negation of the passage of time, central to the Hindu experience (standing in direct opposition to the Western concept of linear time and progress), is illuminated in the phrase "El presente es perpetuo" (The present is motionless) from "Viento entero," and reinforces the possibility of many "times." The questioning of time in its linear or circular combinations interjects an element of relativity and becoming in contrast to the stagnancy of an immovable image. The poet is connected through a dialogic opening to other traditions and cultures, seeking to defeat limitable linguistic boundaries that distinguish the cultures in evidence. Their thoughts are valued, even if their linguistic systems cannot be shared. Sarduy bridges the gap between Eastern thought and Western images through cultural displacement, but Paz achieves the same effect through the genre of poetry, making the world "real" through the word.

In the essay *El mono gramático* (The monkey grammarian), which recreates a trip down a metaphorical road toward creation, the theory of time is further elaborated, complementing poetic reasoning. The grammarian monkey, Hanumãn, is said to jump from India to Ceylon in one bound: "Es la visión de Hanumãn al saltar (géiser) del valle al pico del monte o al precipitarse (aerolito) desde el astro hasta el fondo del mar: la visión vertiginosa y transversal que revela al universo no como una sucesión, un movimiento, sino como una asamblea de espacios y tiempos, una quietud" ("This is the vision of Hanumãn as he leaps [a geyser] from the valley to the mountaintop or as he plunges [a meteorite] from the star to the bottom of the sea: The dizzying oblique vision that reveals the universe not as a succession, a movement, but as an assemblage of spaces and times, a repose"). The poetic images of the garden respond to the concept of an assembly of spaces and times, because in Paz's vision of poetry one image is the echo of another, and therefore: "No hay fin y tampoco hay principio: todo es centro. Ni antes ni después, ni adelante ni atrás, ni afuera ni adentro: todo está en todo" ("There is no end and no beginning: everything is center. Neither before nor after, neither in front of nor behind, neither inside nor outside: everything is in everything"). The poem "Cuento de dos jardines" continues the search for the complete center:

> *Un jardín no es un lugar:*
> *Por un sendero de arena rojiza*
> > *Entramos*
> *En una gota de agua,*
> > *Bebemos en su centro*
> *Verdes claridades*
> > (A garden is no place:
> By a footpath of russet sand
> > We enter
> a water-drop,
> > We drink at its centre
> Green clarities).

The drop of water that contains something of all drops is a center, that is, a center from which we drink in search of Perfect Knowledge. The first specific garden to which we are introduced is the garden of Mixcoac, the garden from Paz's childhood, that was about to "collapse." Negative images abound in that comparisons are drawn between a boat run aground and the poet's grandfather. Mexico is characterized as a land of darkness:

> > *El galope negro del aguacero*
> *Cubre todo el llano.*
> > *Llueve sobre lavas.*
> *México: sobre la piedra ensangrentada*
> > *Danza el agua.*

                              (The black gallop of downpour
Covers all the plain.
                              Rains on the lava.
Mexico: over the bloodstained stone
                              Dances the water.)

The colon after the identifying term, Mexico, appears to establish a wall or
a mask from behind which Mexico has not been able to stray throughout its
history. The lament is felt in very personal expressions, including the
prophetic phrase that apparently announces the end to gardens and the
future solace they may provide:

> *Sed, tedio, tolvaneras:*
> *Impalpables epifantas del viento.*
> *Los pinos me enseñaron a hablar solo.*
> *En aquel jardín aprendí a despedirme.*
>
> *Después no hubo jardines.*
>
>   (Thirst, tedium, sandstorms:
> Impalpable epiphanies of wind.
> The pines taught me to talk to myself.
> In that garden I learned to say good-bye.
> Afterwards there were no gardens.)

The next garden mentioned, the garden of India, is introduced
immediately after the announcement of no more gardens, which is to say that
within the same space of the poet's two metaphysical moments of awareness,
where he is invited in the second instance to the Beginning (the
capitalization reinforces the recognition of the moment), there are no other
such moments. Life is conceived of as proliferation and repetition in time
and space (this concept of repetition and multiplicity is also seen by
Susnigdha Dey in her study on the influence of India on Paz's poetry). A play
of reflections, repetitions, and echoes of light and sound follows:

> *Un día,*
> *Como si regresara,*
> *No a mi casa:*
> *Al comienzo del Comienzo,*
> *Llegué a una claridad,*
> *Ancha,*
> *Construida*
> *Para los juegos pasionales de la luz y el agua.*

<blockquote>
(One day,
As if I were returning,
Not to my house:
But to the beginning of Beginning,
I reached a clarity.
Wide-open,
Built
For the impassioned play of light and water.)
</blockquote>

The following verse, "Dispersiones, alianzas" (Dispersions, alliances) brings to mind the rhythmical separation and union in the cosmological perception of the universe in ancient China, which is conceived of as a cyclical combination of two rhythms—yin and yang. In cosmological terms, the woman symbolizes the elements, for example, water, and man symbolizes light, among other positive elements. Woman and man are the subjects of the passionate games, the dispersal and the union of the opposing forces of which the poet speaks. These are important manifestations of liberation and, ultimately, samsara, or rebirth.

The nim tree is the focal point of the garden of India, because, on the one hand, as Paz concludes in *El mono gramático*, trees repeat trees, perhaps visually and biologically, and on the other, it may symbolize the sacred tree beneath which Siddhartha Gautama, the founder of Buddhism, achieved enlightenment. It is at the foot of the nim tree where Paz learns: "Negarse es crecer" ("And self-denial is growth"), which is a form of enlightenment. With respect to Buddhist and Hindu doctrine and their parallels as presented by Paz in more than one collection of essays, it is curious that Octavio Paz at times will not distinguish among the three fundamental religious philosophical positions in India, referring to at once the entire country, "La India," but on other occasions will go to great lengths to stress their distinctions, as in, for example, the differences between Tantric Buddhism and Tantric Hinduism. In *Corriente alterna* Paz refers to negation as one of the principal features of Indian thought in both the Hindu and the Buddhist branches of Tantrism. To summarize, even superficially, India through its practices and religious sentiments negates change, and therefore negates the passage of time. The path to liberation is achieved through a negation of the empirical world. Nagarjuna, one of the Greater Vehicle philosophers, held that reality is essentially empty, or void. Therefore, it is reasonable to conclude, as Paz does: "La India ha inventado la liberación por la negación y ha convertido a ésta en la madre sin nombre de todos los seres vivos. . . . El hindú ejerce la negación como un método interior: no pretende salvar al mundo sino destruir en sí mismo al mundo" ("India has invented liberation by way of negation and made it the nameless mother of all living creatures. . . . The Hindu practices negation as an inner method: his goal is not to save the world but to destroy the world within himself").

With the theory of negation in mind, two other references Paz makes to the garden become more expressive:

> *Un jardín no es un lugar:*
> > *Es un tránsito,*
> *Una pasión:*
> > *No sabemos hacia donde vamos,*
> *Transcurrir es suficiente,*
> > *Transcurrir es quedarse.*
> (A garden is no place:
> > It is a transition,
> A passion:
> > We know not where we go,
> To elapse is enough,
> > To elapse is to remain.)

If reality is a void, then the garden is not a place but rather a transition, a movement like the movement between the forces of the cosmos, or the movement between opposing forces presenting a nontranquil relationship. I believe this is what Paz means by "transcurrir es suficiente" ("to elapse is enough"). At a later point the poet realizes:

> *El jardín se ha quedado atrás.*
> > *¿Atrás o adelante?*
> *No hay más jardines que los que llevamos dentro.*
> *¿Qué nos espera en la otra orilla?*
> > *Pasión es tránsito:*
> *La otra orilla está aquí,*
> > *Luz en el aire sin orillas:*
> *Prajnaparamita,*
> > *Nuestra Señora de la Otra Orilla*
> (The garden has been left behind.
> > Behind or ahead?
> There are no gardens save those we carry within us.
> What awaits us on the other shore?
> > Passion is transition:
> The other shore is here,
> > Light in the shoreless air:

Prajnaparamita,
> Our Lady of the Other Shore).

The blending of the girl the poet meets into Mother India in the first instance, then into *prajnaparamita*, or Perfect Knowledge, the other shore, and then into "Nuestra Señora de la Otra Orilla" reinforces the blending of the East and West in Octavio Paz. As Borges recalls the image of Allah, asking direct participation in order to liberate him from transgression, Paz invokes the presence of prajnaparamita to liberate the bounded image of perfection, whether it reflect absence of sin or the void. The insertion of prajnaparamita is similar to the introduction of another language or socioideological system into a dialogue of intersecting "languages," disclosing the heteroglot nature of Hispanic Orientalism. Paz conjures a very strong image when he calls up the presence of prajnaparamita, translating the restricted bodily image into a dialogue or colliding of images. It is significant that the figure of prajnaparamita becomes Our Lady of the Other Shore, a female image that embodies the metaphysical search for the Other with whom the poet may fuse or become one. The sense of the erotic goes beyond the corporeal and is satisfied metaphysically when it searches for the other Shore. What do we wait for? The closed, single image is dead; we have already begun down the path of becoming. In effect, "the other shore is here," as Paz concludes in the poem. The dialogue with the Other renders a powerful fusion of two supreme philosophical symbols in one, impelling the birth of the new, the greater, the more complete.

The internal dialogization in "Cuento de dos jardines," which in one instance is made obvious through the plaintive questions posed, is in evidence in much of Paz's poetry even though it normally is excluded from the poetic genre. The persistent dialogue with the East allows the images to join but they are never restricted by absolute fusion, because even though the images are brought closer through dialogue, the stylized word is necessarily distanced, as the poet speaks from within. That is to say, the poet significantly takes responsibility not only for the ideas, the images presented, but also for the language at work in all of its aspects and nuances. But even though the full weight of the language is always felt, it can be said that Paz is in dialogue with the Other rather than simply reproducing it. The images (prajnaparamita, Nuestra Señora de la Otra Orilla, etc.) interanimate each other so that Paz's language moves to reflect a worldview or global image in itself.

The image of the garden does not represent a place but rather a state of being that we carry inside, which would appear to symbolize the blending of the two opposing forces into one, then one into nothing. The East is transfigured into the West, and the architecture that is ready to topple over is mixed with the architecture without weight. In the resolution of the self/Other, East/West, the elements fuse and the distinctions are erased, absorbed, momentarily one into the other. In this manner Paz brings to a close "Cuento de dos jardines": "Los signos se borran: yo miro la claridad" ("The signs are blotted out: I stare into clarity").

The short poem titled "Efectos del bautismo" (The effects of baptism) brings a smile or produces laughter at every reading:

> *El joven Hassan,*
> *Por casarse con una cristiana,*
> *Se bautizó.*
> >   *El cura,*
> *Como a un vikingo,*
> *Lo llamó Erik.*
> >   *Ahora*
> *Tiene dos nombres*
> *Y una sola mujer.*
> (Young Hassan,
> in order to marry a Christian,
> was baptized.
> >   The priest
> named him Erik,
> as though he were a Viking.
> >   Now
> he has two names
> and only one wife.)

Baptism, among other rites, prepares us to reach the other shore, leaving behind what we were so that we may join the Other. Paz expands on the intention of these rites:

> *Pocos realizan la experiencia del salto, a pesar de que el bautismo, la comunión, los sacramentos y otros ritos de iniciación o de tránsito están destinados a prepararnos para esa experiencia. Todos ellos tienen en común el cambiarnos, el hacernos "otros". De ahí que consistan en darnos un nuevo nombre, indicando así que ya somos otros: acabamos de nacer o de renacer. El rito reproduce la experiencia mística de la "otra orilla" tanto como el hecho capital de la vida humana: nuestro nacimiento, que exige previamente la muerte del feto. Y quizá nuestros actos más significativos y profundos no sean sino la repetición de este*

morir del feto que renace en criatura. En suma, el "salto mortal", la
experiencia de la "otra orilla", implica un cambio de naturaleza: es un
morir y un nacer.

(Few attain the experience of the leap, in spite of the fact that
baptism, communion, the sacraments, and other rites of
initiation or passage are intended to prepare us for that
experience. They all aim to change us, to make us "others." Thus
we are given a new name, to indicate that now we are others: we
have just been born or reborn. The rite reproduces the mystical
experience of the "other shore" as well as the capital event of
human life: our birth, which requires the previous death of the
fetus. And perhaps our deepest and most meaningful acts are
merely the repetition of this death of the fetus that is reborn as
an infant. In short, the "mortal leap," the experience of the
"other shore," implies a change of nature: it is a dying and a
being born.)

Baptism, then, pushes us outside of ourselves in search of the other shore,
and, in effect, in search of the self. What sweeps us to the other shore
culminates in an act of unity, of reconciling the self with oneself and of
communing with the self. Although Paz emphasizes in *Conjunciones y*
disyunciones the contradictory components of the smile, as opposed to loud
laughter (in terms of the participation of others), both smiling and laughing
fuse the self with the Other. Ramón Xirau, in his study on Octavio Paz, notes
that in *Ladera Este* Paz introduces a sense of irony in his short epigrammatic
poems. In Buddhism and Hinduism life is viewed in terms of oppositions of
polarities that are resolved through their fusion. The "uncrowning" of
Hassan, giving him another name and thereby forcing upon him another
cultural system, brings him closer and makes him familiar to us. Through
irony the blending that takes place in the object is ridiculed and examined
openly, unframing the fear that normally compels us to keep our distance
when coming into contact with the Other. In this poem, the hero Hassan is
free to improvise, to put on a mask (to use a familiar metaphor in Paz).

   The mask in "Máscaras mexicanas" from *Laberinto de la soledad*
(Mexican masks in Labyrinth of solitude) signifies a distancing in that the
mask hides the nature of the user, thereby allowing the user to assume any
identity, any destiny, by not opening up to others and revealing a true nature
and destiny. The theme of the mask is perhaps the most complex theme of
folk culture. The mask, based on a peculiar interrelation of reality and image,
unites joy and negation—joy in change and metamorphoses and negation of
uniformity, similarity, and even conformity to oneself. The fusion of

opposites is symbolic of our duality and opens itself to the element of laughter. Paz conceives of the smile as a sign of our duality that allows for laughter and even making fun of oneself, because we perpetually represent the self and the Other. As the concludes in *Conjunciones y disyunciones*: "Ambos, el chiste y el poema, son expresiones del principio de placer, victorioso por un instante del principio de realidad" ("Both the joke and the poem are expressions of the pleasure principle, which for a moment, wins out over the reality principle"). The idiom of laughter cannot be used for destructive purposes; it triumphs over death and oppression, manifesting the unyielding character of the human psyche while signaling the future.

The fusion of contraries (at times polarities in the branch of Tantric thought) is the basis of the stream of religious thought in Hinduism and Buddhism, and it is only through this relationship that the terms make sense. Paz employs India as an example: "La India acentúa los extremos: la casta exagera el vínculo social; el ascetismo exalta el aislamiento. El hindú oscila siempre entre estos dos polos" ("India creates extremes: the caste system exaggerates the social bond; asceticism exalts the isolation of the individual. The Hindu continually oscillates between these two poles"). Both Hinduism and Buddhism, at least in their Tantric forms, predicate the achievement of liberation in this life through the fusion of opposing elements: feminine and masculine; light and darkness; life and death; the material and the spiritual; the sexual act and the aesthetic act, that is, body and no-body, which simply symbolizes any binary pair composed of opposing elements. Buddhism and Hinduism exemplify this binary system in India, because even though Buddhism almost completely disappeared from India in the eleventh century, crushed by the Muslim invasion, it is kept alive today through its architecture and through the efforts of the many Tibetan monks and other natives of Tibet who have been living in exile in India since the Chinese invasion of their country. Liberation, realizing the void, is possible here and now according to the practices in both Buddhism and Hinduism, and this is achieved through the absorption or fusion of contrasting elements. This is what the Orient, or India in particular, offers to Octavio Paz and his critical approach to Orientalism in Latin America.

The reconciliation of a binary, oppositional structure is curiously evident in Paz's statements on the Orient as well as in the structure itself of *Ladera Este*. We notice that beginning with page 64 of the Joaquín Mortiz edition, Paz has opposed/juxtaposed poems of Western theme with those of Eastern theme. The poems of Western theme are titled "Intermitencias del Oeste" and represent intermissions, breaks in the presentation of the Orient to reaffirm the presence of the West, so that we are not tempted to isolate the East and consider it alone, thereby negating the constructs of

Orientalism. Some critics refer to these binary structures as paradoxes of the East. In my mind, this minimizes the polarity and the visual expressiveness of the opposition of East and West, because paradoxes hinge on the "seemingly" contradictory nature of a statement that may in fact be true. The question of truth does not enter into the debate on Hispanic Orientalism, or into the oppositional structure defining East and West. One term is not more "true" or "valid" than the other. This is in accordance with the premise "cuerpo/no-cuerpo" (body/no-body), which does not represent the affirmation and negation of the same concept, but rather the possibility of an opposition of terms. Dialogical relationships, after all, are infused with these concrete semantic expressions, but they are not reducible to oppositional structures because they have their own specificity.

"Viento entero" is an example of a poem that combines binary oppositional statements contrasting East and West, through an inquiry into Oriental philosophies that are compatible with the metaphysics of Octavio Paz. "Viento entero" begins:

> *El presente es perpetuo*
> *Los montes son de hueso y son de nieve*
> *Están aquí desde el principio*
> *El viento acaba de nacer*
> > *Sin edad*
> *Como la luz y como el polvo*
> (The present is motionless
> The mountains are of bone and of snow
> They have been here since the beginning
> The wind has just been born
> > ageless
> as the light and the dust)."

We are once again in India and the allusions are to Hindu philosophy, as, for example, the concept of time: "El presente es perpetuo" ("The present is motionless"). Paz sustains the theory that dialectics of opposition and fusion are evident in all civilizations and all times, but in *Conjunciones y disyunciones* he makes use generally of India and China in opposition to the West for the following reason: "Me serviré de ejemplos extraídos de Occidente, India y China por esta razón: creo que la civilización india es el otro polo de la de Occidente, la *otra versión del mundo indoeuropeo*. La relación entre India y Occidente es la de una oposición dentro de un sistema. La relación de ambos con el Extremo Oriente (China, Japón, Corea y Tibet) es la relación entre dos sistemas distintos. Así en el caso de estas reflexiones, los ejemplos chinos no son ni convergentes ni divergentes: son excéntricos. (¿Cuál es el otro polo del mundo de China y Japón? Tal vez la América precolombina)" ("I shall use examples taken from the West, from India, and from China, since I believe that Indian civilization is the other pole of that of the West, the other version of the Indo-European world. The relationship between India and the West is that of an opposition within a system. The relationship of both with the Far East [China, Japan, Korea, and Tibet] is a relationship between two different systems. Chinese examples in these reflections are thus neither convergent nor divergent: they are eccentric. [What is the other pole of the world of China and Japan? Perhaps it is pre-Columbian America]").

As Paz has always been open to European literary renovations of language and structure, so will he remain open to literary and metaphysical experiences from India. He will not necessarily exclude the Far East from his contemplation of the binary structure, because he believes that perhaps pre-Columbian America may be used as a departure point from which to oppose Latin America and the Far East in an oppositional framework. In *Ladera Este* (East slope), in contrast to his perception of time in *Piedra de sol* (Sun stone) as total or circular (incorporating symbolism of time from Aztec legends), Paz redevelops a sense of the negation of time that is germane to Hindu philosophy. The perfection of ritual performed continuously, the reversability of terms that allows anything to be itself and its contradiction simultaneously, and the perception of the person's eternal soul existing forever through reincarnation, reinforce the Hindu concept that denies change and the qualifying of the past, present, or future moments. The desire not to change, as experienced in the Hindu segment of Indian civilization, encourages the poet to refer to the present as perpetual; just as air, light, and dust are envisioned in an ageless state. Paz, curiously, makes reference to the mountains that have existed since the beginning, but because of the corporeal reference to bones, this can be understood as man, who is (through reincarnation) there in the beginning and in the present; there is no change, just as the fresh snow is absorbed into that which came before it, blending into one. Paz reminds us, in his essay "Naturaleza, Abstracción, Tiempo" (Nature, abstraction, time) from the collection *Corriente alterna*, that: "La naturaleza no conoce la historia pero en sus formas viven todos los estilos del pasado, el presente y el porvenir" ("Nature has no history, but its forms are the living embodiment of all the styles of the past, present, and future"). Although the Hindu approaches to the Truth are many, they are not negative in form as in Buddhism, whose ultimate aim is nirvana, the establishing of the void. But they both have parallel representations in Indian life of the negation of history, which is to say the negation of time through the perception of change as the manifestation of the impermanence of life.

Paz summarizes the criticism of time in India:

> *Desde el principio la India se propuso abolir la historia por la crítica del*
> *tiempo y la pluralidad de sociedades y comunidades históricas por el*
> *régimen de castas. La infinita movilidad de la historia real se*
> *transforma en una fantasmagoría centellante y vertiginosa en la que los*
> *hombres y los dioses giran hasta fundirse en una suerte de nebulosa*
> *atemporal; el mundo abigarrado del acontecer desemboca o, mejor dicho,*
> *regresa a una regió neutra y vacía, la en que el ser y la nada se*
> *reabsorben. Budismo y brahmanismo niegan a la historia. Para los dos*
> *el cambio, lejos de ser una manifestación positiva de la energía, es el*
> *reino ilusorio de la impermanencia. Frente a la heterogenidad [sic] de*
> *los grupos étnicos—cada uno con una lengua, una tradición, un sistema*
> *de parentesco y un culto particulares—la civilización india adopta una*
> *solución contraria: no la disolución sino el reconocimiento de cada*
> *particularidad y su integración en un sistema más amplio. La crítica del*
> *tiempo y el régimen de castas son los dos polos complementarios y*
> *antagonistas del sistema indio. Por medio de ambos la India se propone*
> *la abolición de la historia.*

(From the beginning, India set out to abolish history by means of the critique of time and to abolish the plurality of historical societies and communities by means of the caste system. The infinite mobility of real history turns into a shimmering and dizzying phantasmagoria in which men and gods whirl about until they merge in a sort of atemporal nebulosity; the varied world of events leads, or rather returns, to a neutral and empty region, in which being and nothingness are reabsorbed. Buddhism and Brahmanism negate history. For both, change, far from being a positive manifestation of energy, is the illusory realm of *impermanence*. Faced with the heterogeneity of ethnic groups—each with its own language, tradition, kinship system, and mode of worship—Indian civilization adopts an opposite solution: not the dissolution but the recognition of each particularity and its integration into a broader system. The critique of time and the caste system are the two complementary and antagonistic poles of the Indian system. By means of both, India aims at the abolition of history.)

The desire to abolish history and to concentrate on the instant rather than on the totality of being permeates Paz's "Viento entero" through his understanding of Indian thought. Through language, Paz seeks to make sense of the all-important image or moment, as opposed to understanding an entire history.

The culturally charged moment Paz has chosen to examine is one bursting with oppositional statements. The "Príncipes en harapos" (Princes in tattered clothes) stand on the shore of the river and "Rezan orinan meditan" ("Pray pee meditate"), which would appear in Western thought to be an unholy combination of licit and illicit acts but should rather be appreciated as the prerequisite for Tantric ritual. Tantrism abandons generally acknowledged morality and proposes instead a total experience that is carnal and spiritual at the same time. From the mixture of human flesh and excrement, the foul and impure are mixed, purified, burnt, and then eaten during one of the violent rituals of the Tantric banquet. Ritual is an important function of eroticism also: "What is normally considered wrong and seductive (for the sweet fruits tend to get forbidden, though, of course, not *all* sweet fruits) is performed under controlled conditions, in the course of a ritual occasion. For instance, sexual intercourse was used as a controlled means of symbolizing the non-dual mystical experience: for the fleshy union and ecstasy bring about, for the moment at any rate, a merging of two beings." The erotic experience begins when the poet meets, in Paris, "Una muchacha real/Entre las casas y las gentes espectrales" ("A real girl/among wraithlike houses and people"). Cultural displacement is in evidence, as images of the marketplace at Kabul blend with that of a neighborhood in Paris, and then alternate with those of northern India, western Pakistan, and Afghanistan, later returning to Latin America with references to Santo Domingo and Mexico respectively: "En Santo Domingo mueren nuestros hermanos/Si hubiera parque no estarían ustedes aquí" ("Our brothers are dying in Santo Domingo/'If we had munitions/You people would not be here'"). The juxtaposition of cultural and historical references of the East and West underscores Paz's Orientalist principles, in that he achieves rhetorically in his work an approximate duplication of Oriental philosophic and theoretical practice, which involves opposition, absorption, fusion, and opposition ad infinitum, maintaining the relationship in a constant state of flux while integrating it into an ever-broadening system.

Opposition comprises the physical description of the woman with whom the poet is in love: "Si el agua es fuego/Llama/En el centro de la hora redonda" ("If water is fire/flame/dazzled/in the center of the spherical hour"). The erotic quality of the siting of the woman on a red quilt is enhanced by nature's touching of the loved one: "El sol se ha dormido entre tus pechos" ("The sun has fallen asleep between your breasts"), for just as nature discredits time, the lovers will also ignore time, in an erotic embrace. The idea that for Octavio Paz poetry is a revelation of love (eroticism), the sacred, and the poetic image is supported by Saúl Yurkievich's statement: "En Paz poética y erótica se abrazan y confunden como la pareja primordial" (In Paz the poetic and erotic embrace and are entangled like the primordial couple). It should be remembered that the doctrine of Eros is fundamentally a doctrine of salvation. Anders Nygren stresses the similarities between the ideas grouped around the Eros motif and those around the ancient mysteries, such as the belief in the transmigration of souls. The "mystical-ecstatic" way of salvation, in addition to asceticism, unites the theory of Eros to Oriental doctrines, reconciling in this manner both philosophies. The sense of desire, of longing for what one does not have, leads the poet to seek satisfaction in a higher state.

Paz will also recall the Orient to reinterpret a theme that would support his vision of the material and poetic world. The act of copulation unites opposing elements—man/woman, samsara/nirvana, existence/void, and so on—according to Tantric ritual, and even seeks to reconcile the opposing elements within each one of us (e.g., in each man there is something of the woman and vice versa). According to Manuel Durán, the addition of historical elements is an intended effect that reinforces Paz's poetic intuitions. The poet's pleasure is curiously hindered by descriptions of human suffering, as examples are derived from the countries of Santo Domingo, Mexico, and also from instances of Muslim cruelty, blending death and violent tragedy with eroticism in very close proximity. Even the erotic moment that presents the union of the two lovers—

> *Abajo*
> > *El desfiladero caliente*
> *La ola que se dilata y se rompe*
> > > *Tus piernas abiertas*
> *El salto blanco*
> *La espuma de nuestros cupos abandonados*
> (Down there
> > the hot canyon
> the wave that stretches and breaks
> > > your legs apart
> the plunging whiteness
> the foam of our bodies abandoned)

—is tinged by the sight on the other side of the river: "En la barcaza el batelero estrangulaba pollos" ("The boatman/on the barge was strangling chickens"). This is followed by a description of India:

El país es una mano abierta
Sus líneas
Signos de un alfabeto roto
(The countryside is an open hand
its lines
marks of a broken alphabet).

These signs of a broken alphabet also symbolize language in Paz's theory of poetry. Paz speaks in *El arco y la lira* of the poetic process or poetic creation as beginning with a violent act of language. The poet begins by uprooting the word, taking from it the accustomed connections so that each term then becomes unique, completely new. It would appear that Paz is conveying in "Viento entero" the concept that time is fragmented as well as language. The beginning is achieved again in "El mismo día que comienza" (The same day is beginning), so that the linear passage of time through Hindu theory is denied.

I would like to close this examination of those poems from *Ladera Este* that best exemplify Orientalism in Octavio Paz with the poem "Blanco" (1967). "Blanco" is probably the most complex of poems in the collection and is assuredly the most frequently analyzed, so I will limit myself to an analysis of its structure. "Blanco" offers the possibility of various readings, as Paz himself suggests in the notes that precede the poem in the Joaquín Mortiz edition. What is most curious is the juxtaposition of columns that blend into one, and then become two again on four distinct occasions. The column on the left is an erotic poem divided into four moments that correspond to the four traditional elements, according to Paz. The column on the right is composed of four variations on sensation, perception, imagination, and understanding. The advancing moment of change from two columns to one, et cetera, is seen by Guillermo Sucre as the preparation of an amorous order. Curiously enough, in the second section of double columns there is no capitalization of letters or punctuation, and the eye tends to flow from the boldfaced type of the column on the left to the italics of the column on the right, as they are separated only by the blank space in the middle. The third section of double columns begins a technique of visually joining the two columns by eliminating the wall between them, so that wherever the verse of the left-hand column finishes, the verse of the right-hand column begins, regardless of symmetry or thematic divisions. It is as if two voices were heard in dialogue, or at the very least, another person's voice in the poet's word. The inserted voices objectify reality and are to a certain degree parodical in their opposition. The physical presentation of the poem reinforces the Oriental concept of fusion of fragments or opposites, both philosophically and graphically, in endless succession (not impeded by punctuation), as in the theory of reincarnation. As was stated earlier, the original edition of "Blanco" was boxed and read by unfolding the paper on which it was printed. As the poem unfolded, the variations of typeface became evident, with contrasting red and black columns, resulting in a sort of "typographic mandala." Rachel Phillips, in her study of Octavio Paz's poetry, examines the sections that characterize the double columns, underscoring the flowing-river motif. This motif is applicable to our greater satisfaction in the third and fourth sections, where one verse visually appears to flow into the other. The rhythm is eventually altered to return the columns to the presentation given in the beginning, of separate columns and capitalized letters as warranted by context.

Paz has selected an epigraph from the *Hevajra Tantra* that portends the tone of "Blanco": "By passion the world is bound, by passion too it is released." I believe that the prominence of passion in this reference regards both spiritual and corporeal passion. In this sense the language of the *Hevajra Tantra* is allegorical, in that it designates both sexual and spiritual attributes to the words employed. It appears that Paz on many occasions applies Oriental philosophy as the double of his poetic universe. In this instance the quote from the *Hevajra Tantra*, which incorporates the basic precepts of Tantrism, represents the impetus for Paz's poetic creation—the imbalance of forces in the universe that leads to an annulment of opposites without ever destroying the opposing elements. Opposites fuse and then separate in the perpetual rhythm of the universe, and as there is always a struggle between the opposition and affinity of the two elements, there will always be an imbalance of strengths in this ideal relation. The limited autonomy that arises from the imbalance is called liberty or creation. Therefore, indirectly, creativity is a product of the duality of nature and the impulse to fuse opposite forces. Paz exploits the structure of the Tantric language, which is a system of pluralities: "El lenguaje tántrico es un lenguaje poético y de ahí que sus significados scan siempre plurales. Además, tiene la propiedad de emitir significados que son, diría, reversibles. La reversibilidad implica que cada palabra o cosa puede convertirse en su contrario y después, o simultáneamente, volver a ser ella misma. El supuesto básico del tantrismo es la abolición de los contrarios—sin suprimirlos; ese postulado lo lleva a otro: la movilidad de los significados, el continuo vaivén de los signos y sus sentidos" ("The language of the *Tantras* is a poetic language and its meanings are always multiple. It also has a quality that I would call reversibility: each word can be converted into its contrary and later, or simultaneously, turn into itself again. The basic premise of Tantrism is the abolition of contraries—without suppressing them. This postulate brings on another: the mobility of the meanings, the continuous shifting of the signs and their meanings"). Passion then is the core through which energy flows, and which is alternately bound and released in the perpetual imbalance of opposing actions.

The fusion of opposites in addition to the Hindu concept of the negation and the discontinuity of time are themes developed throughout "Blanco." The poem begins with the beginning, but not so much to signal the arrival at a point in time, as to speak of its potential:

> *el comienzo*
>   *el cimiento*
> *la simiente*
>   *latente*
> *la palabra en la punta de la lengua*
> *inaudita*   *inaudible*
>   *impar*
> *grávida*   *nula*
>   *sin edad*
> (a stirring
>   a steering
> a seedling
>   sleeping
> a word at the tip of the tongue
> unheard   unhearable
>   matchless
> fertile   barren
>   ageless).

The beginning, origin, and seed are similar because they have not yet realized their potential, they are undiscovered for the moment. The beginning is the essence of a future visibility, an openendedness in contact with the unfinished, but it has not been placed in opposition to another point in time and should not be considered as an introduction to a linear perception of time. The pregnant potential of this unspoken word on the tip of the tongue echoes the latent quality of the seed and the beginning. Here Paz refers directly to time (as if to erase doubts), and reminds us that the word is ageless. The word has no temporal reference because it is new, reborn with each occasion of its use.

In the first section of double columns, the flame is a purifying one that enhances the erotic union of the lovers, while it explores the senses in the second section:

en el muro la sombra del fuego
en el fuego tu sombra y la mía

el fuego te desata y te anuda
Pan Grial Ascua
            Muchacha
tú ríes—desnuda
En los jardines de la llama
(on the wall the shadow of the fire
in the fire your shadow and mine

the fire unlaces and fastens you
Ember Bread Grail
            Girl
you laugh—naked
in the gardens of the flame).

llama rodeada de leones
leona en el circo de las llamas
ánima entre las sensaciones

frutos de luces de bengala
los sentidos se abren
en la noche magnética

flame encircled by lions
lioness in the circus of the flames
soul among sensations

fruits of the fireworks
the senses open
in the magnetic night

The reflection of language is infused with the erotic ("*ánima entre las sensaciones*" ["*soul among sensations*"]), and, to paraphrase Guillermo Sucre, the erotic would appear to explain the poetic process in evidence ("en el fuego tu sombra y la mía" ["your shadow and mine in the fire"]). Indeed, the subsequent imbalance liberates the poet momentarily to perform an ontological search for metaphysical identity—"En el pecho de México caído./Polvo soy de aquellos lodos./Río de sangre,/Río de historias" ("dropped on the chest of Mexico./I am the dust of that silt./River of blood,/river of histories")—which after the next section of two columns followed by one, is reduced to violence. The transition is then completed (between the silences) from pain to violent reaction that is cognizant of its futility: "Te golpeo cielo/Tierra te golpeo" ("sky I beat you,/land I beat you"). The center single column, whose theme is the passage of the word from silence to silence, demonstrates that the oppositional structure, which is so evident in the play of the erotic, is equally significant in the poetic creation:

                No y Sí
Juntos
        Dos sílabas enamoradas
    Si el mundo es real
              La palabra es irreal
    Si es real la palabra
            El mundo
    Es la grieta el resplandor el remolino
No

Las desapariciones y las apariciones

                                                        Sí

El árbol de los nombres

                                  Real irreal

                  (No and Yes

together

                two syllables in love

If the world is real

                                  the word is unreal

If the word is real

                                  the world

is the cleft the splendor the whirl

No

disappearances and appearances

                                                  Yes

the tree of names

                        Real unreal).

The acknowledged self ("I am the dust of that silt") sees itself through its own eyes, not simply through the eyes of another, from a distanced plane.

Poetry for Paz is no longer a high-distanced genre whereby the individual is a finished and completed being, completed by the gaze of the Other. The "I" is no longer the sum of its characteristics on the surface as seen by others. The "I" possesses the ability to be exposed, guessed at, and deciphered. There is not a single and unified view that would hold inevitably true for the individual. Poetry, through this novelization of the genre, becomes dialogized, open to an ever-evolving reality, an openended present. The fusion of opposites ("no/yes," "real/unreal," "disappearances/ appearances") that takes place in this evolving reality emphasizes one of the tasks of "Blanco," which is to negate the analytical logic of language. As stated earlier, Chinese civilization has conceived of the cosmos as an order composed of a dual rhythm—union, separation, union—of two opposites. It is here, in the imbalance of these components of the oppositional structure, that a limited autonomy is achieved, and for the poet Paz this means a type of liberation—creation. It is here also that the void acquires a positive meaning. Words are liberated from their meaning, torn from their previous roots to be renewed. The world is a metaphor for the body, granting life and establishing reality, and its seeds are words that flourish through this liberation: "El mundo/. . . Da realidad a la mirada" ("The world/ . . . brings reality to seeing").

Orientalism in Octavio Paz's work is a mixture of exhaustive study, of philosophy and literature read in translation in Europe, and of personal experience resulting from a prolonged stay in India. While his texts are not intended to replace Oriental philosophical canon, nor do they claim to be philosophical texts, they do introduce Eastern concepts that are compatible with Paz's premises about poetry and literature in general. To summarize these theories, we refer first to the Taoist concept of yin and yang, which through its duality and prospect for unity demonstrates that the body is the archetype for the cosmic order. This supports the Tantric principle that understands the body to be the double of the universe, which in turn is a manifestation of the body of the Buddha. The Tantric texts provide the liberating creative force necessary for the next step, which would be the union of writing with the cosmos: "Estos textos están regidos por la misma necesidad psicológica y artística que llevó a nuestros poetas barrocos a construirse un idioma dentro del idioma españstica la misma que inspira al lenguaje de Joyce y al de los surrealistas: la concepción de la escritura como el doble del cosmos" ("These texts are governed by the same psychological and artistic necessity that caused our Baroque poets to build a language of their own within the Spanish language, the same necessity that inspired the language of Joyce and the Surrealists: the conception of writing as the double of the cosmos").

Writing for Paz is grounded in openness, in a dialogue with the Other. The dialogized image in his poetry is inserted through a dramatic unease created by a questioning of issues as conflictive as the search for the meaning of life, the erotic, and the sacred being. The dialogized image projects itself linguistically as the aesthetic object of the poet's work and is also evident graphically in the spatial separations comprehended by typography, folded pages, exotic papers, and imaging. In Paz's work dialogue dissects the closed, fixed image of the Other, calling rather for a nontranquil relationship formed when opposites fuse, separate, and fuse in an antithetical movement. As in India, a recognition of each particularity is achieved, propelling the integration into a broader system. Then, in another view, the struggle between the opposition and affinity of two elements duplicates for Paz the rhythmical separation and union in the cosmological perception of the universe from ancient China. Poetry for Octavio Paz is open to an ever-evolving reality, an openended present supported by his defining of the universe in an extraordinary example through Orientalism.

DJELAL KADIR

Arborescent Paz, Interlineal Poetry

> La experiencia de la literatura es
> esencialmente la experiencia del otro.
> - O. Paz, *Pasión crítica*

"The other constitutes us," notes Octavio Paz. And the allegory of the reading lesson in the Borges of our previous chapter teaches us that to pretend to appropriate the other into our own image spells an eradication of otherness that inevitably translates into our own undoing.

As we have seen, Borges's allegory labors on the slippery ground of irony. Irony is, by definition, the double-edged instrument of otherness, the partitive device that sunders monisms and shatters the univocal into alterior multiplicity, into sundry resonances and altercations. Socrates domesticated irony's instrumentality into a pedagogical tool, and his disciple Plato sanctioned its possibilities by conferring philosophical highmindedness on irony's ends. Borges made a vocation of disporting with such sanctimony, recouping irony's potential for multifariousness from the philosopher's sobriety and the self-privileging orthodoxy of the metaphysician. And this is why for the steadfast ideologues and witless monodists of his time, Borges has proved as unsavory as Socrates did for the Sophists of his own epoch. Irony has always exacerbated otherness, and the other has been recapitulated into sameness, into less threatening, though deadly, oneness, most often

From *The Other Writing:Postcolonial Essays in Latin America's Writing Culture* by Djelal Kadir, © 1993 by Purdue Research Foundation.

through the expatiating sacrifice of the *eiron*. Borges, of course, made a habit of baiting the pharisees of his time, and he did so with a mischievousness that bordered on perversity. In a time and within a continent wracked by immeasurable human suffering, Borges's tenacious adherence to a detached aesthetic and its anachronistic proclamations has led many to indict his political ethics as abhorrent and led many others to view him as politically irrelevant, if not pernicious. Borges may well deserve such condemnation. But be that as it may, political oddities and ethical curiosities of a given epoch are no less instructive or any less reflective of the heterodoxies of that era and its local narratives.

Octavio Paz, though some fifteen years younger, may be Borges's most signaled contemporary (Borges was a "late bloomer," Paz brilliantly precocious). He may have been, as well, his most singular antagonist; not necessarily because the two held diametrically opposed views on literature and politics but precisely because of the relative absence of such polar contrariety. Borges himself often dramatized the uncanny coincidence, the ironic congruity between diametrical extremes and between those espousing such convictions (e.g., "The Theologians"). Paz has always cautioned against the dangers of unyielding adherence, even to the principle of nonadherence. Whereas Paz has managed, or at least has made a career-long attempt, to negotiate the capricious inconstancies of such a paradox. Borges, cannily perceptive of the paradoxical human predicaments he so often dramatized in scribal allegories, suffered an insurmountable blockage when it came to the transference of that allegorical insight to his own life practice. And, while he saw clearly that unbending agnosticism could itself constitute a religion, just as the most consummate ironist could be duped at some indeterminate turn by irony's implacable métier, he remained steadfast in his studied nonconformity, albeit to his own professions. At the end of the day, he proved no less pharisaic in his own constancy than the pharisees he unrelentingly taunted with glee, or at least with the twisted mask of a gleeful mannerism and the facade of unperturbable chivalrousness.

Writing, in the final analysis (on the hypothetical assumption that such finality could obtain), is a human activity, and the easiest way to sound foolish might be to claim any one human activity as tantamount to life. Like other mortals, writers must demonstrate or betray a humanity larger than their own activity or professions, lest they reductively delimit their own lives to the minimalism of a function or role within the script of an absurd theater authored and directed by some inscrutable and incomprehensible Scriptor. Our most extreme absurdists, our most Faustian modernists, like our most Stoic comedians of postmodernity, scream—mockingly, in earnest, or with irony—against such functional minimalism as a human fate. We are agons, whether in pathos or in derision. And the agonist's vocation, whether Luciferian or Hudibrastic, aspires for more than the acts and actions of that vocation, moved as such a vocation is by the necessity of insufficiency, by the desire (hedonistic or pious) that reaches beyond selfsatisfaction and that is by definition unsatisfiable.

For more than half a century now, Octavio Paz, as poetic agon and as iconoclastic Jeremiah, has mediated for us that other space which lies between (and often belies) our acts and our humanity, between our actions and inhumanity. He has tried to chart the course of alternating currents that energize and liberate, that authorize and enslave. All the while, he has allowed for a permeability in the edifications of his own discourse, for a transparency in his own mask(s), for a contradiction to his own dictum, for yet one more otherness to his multiple oneness. Thus when he writes, "the other constitutes us," by the nature of that constitution we are to understand not a finished result but an interminable process that proscribes our finishing ourselves off in the self-satisfaction of our attainment, in the self-privilege of our precognition, in the self-righteousness of our ideas, in the narcissism of our reflection(s), or in the echo of our own words:

> Words turn into reflections, shadows and fog in rags. The "other" flutters and the landscape evaporates: we are before the sheet of paper, the table, the window anew. We perceive, almost as a sensation, our mortality. The experience of literature is, essentially, the experience of the other: the experience of the other that we are, the experience of the other that are the others, and the supreme experience: the other, the woman. But in all these experiences throbs, hidden, the *other* experience: the experience of death, the knowledge of ourselves to be mortal.

We would be irredeemably remiss were we to understand the otherness Paz articulates simply in terms of a schematic reduction, of a dichotomous I and thou, of an existential binary and its illusionary optativity of either/or, or in terms of the historical progressivists' (whether metaphysical or materialist) dialectic of a now and a then. The intimations of our mortality are not reducible to an antiphonous duet intoned as the dirge of being and nothingness. Our mortifications are daily, but they are no more unrelenting than our sempiternal superventions. It is through the indomitable impulse of immortality and its scribal acts (supremely exemplified by Paz as writer and eloquently instantiated by Paz in the writing)—it is through this impulse and its attendant acts of insurrection that "we perceive, almost as a sensation," the certitude of our mortality. Yes, we are mortal as historical beings, says Paz, but our history is constituted by the perennial other, the countercurrent impetus of immortality. And if death as other constitutes us in turn, death is only made possible by virtue of life. For Paz, of course, death is not just an end line, a matter of eventual ultimacy, but an institutional warrant to be overcome through ruse, subversion, laughter, and critical verve in our cultural and political lives. Referring to the particular history of his own region, a reference that obviously has great potential and undeniable precedent for generalizability, Paz writes: "Our history is infested with strongmen, just as the waters of the Mexican Gulf with sharks, and our intellectual history with heretic-burning canons, with decapitating Jacobins, and Marxists with a jail warden's vocation." The abdication of critical and self-critical heterodoxy to the orthodox monody of any ideology implies necessarily a capitulation to a mortality whose death in life, as history demonstrates, becomes fatal by contagion or by the deliberate transference of one's own death sentence unto the other. And the fatality of that projection is not merely a risk but all too often a ghastly reality of human disappearances, torture chambers, and mass graves.

Nor is Paz cavalier when it comes to the politics of gender. His reference to "the supreme experience" of the other as embodied in woman is not the flippant gesture of a chauvinist. Rather, it epitomizes Paz's urgent concern for difference, a concern that would have us be ever-mindful of the incommensurability of equality and identity. To fall into the latter in pursuit of the first translates into another form of capitulation of difference, into an abdication of otherness and the fateful aggravation of conditions one seeks to redress. Some two decades ago, in September 1970, Paz articulated as much in an interview with Rita Guibert at Cambridge University, where, at the time, he held the Simón Bolívar Chair of Latin American Literature:

> . . . equality doesn't mean identity, homogeneity . . . what distinguishes us is what unites us. We ought to conceive of society as an association of complementary opposites, the chief opposition being between masculine and feminine. I'll go further: I think that from the interplay of masculine and feminine a new and hitherto undreamed-of culture and creativity might arise. . . . When a society presents the masculine as its sole archetype, violence and distortion results . . . women have had to adapt themselves to this model; by masculinizing herself, woman has become deformed . . . Western civilization should be feminized. . . . Our men should be more feminine and our women more masculine. . . . The true revolution would consist of women imposing masculine and feminine archetypes on society, and men seeing ourselves in them.

Difference, then, is the indispensable requisite that enlivens otherness—the necessary other, not necessarily of one's own truth but of one's necessity. In the history of Western culture, within and against which Paz often writes, such difference is a radical desire, suspect because it tends to question the historical impulse for sameness and identity, for homogenization and self-privileging, but a difference desired, nonetheless, because it may be the only deterrent to the centripetal impulse of territoriality and usurpation of the necessary other. Paz's is a scene of instruction from which we are to come away with a "poetic generosity," and by "poetic" we should understand not an idealized abstraction but an experiential mode of everyday living and the array of its pragmatic entailments. We are enjoined to dwell poetically, not merely within a philosophical dwelling as prescribed by Martin Heidegger in his discussion of Hölderlin but with a self-critical capacity and a disposition beyond nostalgia (enablements countermanded by Heidegger's own historical, experiential life, *pace* his philosophical wisdom). Paz, then, would have us live a life, as he himself has exemplified, that critically opens up to difference, alterity, and the indispensable other.

Within the multiple alterities that constitute Paz himself, one cannot miss a continuity between political engagement and poetic practice. The critical differentiation that obtains in one carries into the other. In fact, Paz would more than likely look askance upon such schematization that would have the poet juxtaposed with the political man. "Yes," he would allow, "I am same and I am different." But we would have to understand that this is a constancy of "same" founded on otherness, on a vocation dedicated to life-enhancing criticism and difference, to the insurrectionist acts of immortality these make possible. In keeping with this monitory appreciation, Paz's poetry must be read in the spirit of a differential poetics that it makes possible by assuming such enabling conditions for its edifice and edification. Paz's scene of instruction, then, is a site of writing whose declared necessity makes it not a primal but an ever-alterior scene of transgression, a self-transgression that opens a breach in its fortitude, that parts its waters to allow a passage to the other within and to the other who might venture in from without. On this writing scene, we encounter a poetry whose verses point to the diversity between the furrows they occupy on the face of the page, between the masked facades of their impagination. And in this sense, too, Paz not only writes such poetry, but, as reader, he also teaches us to read accordingly. In a note he wrote on 12 April 1972 on the occasion of an art exhibition by the painter Adja Yunkers in Cambridge, Massachusetts, Paz lays out the alterior but simultaneous ways of the creative process, whether in painting or writing, or, inextricably, in reading. Paz's note is entitled "La invitación del espacio" and is deliberately echoic of another poet of spatial and ideological transgression whose *sententia* Paz cites in his commentary—"si l'on obéit à l'invitation de ce grand espace blanc" (Stéphane Mallarmé):

> Two attitudes: to re-cover the canvas, the wall, or the page with lines, colors, signs—configurations of our language; to discover in their nakedness lines, colors, signs—configurations of an other language. To tattoo space with our visions and obsessions; to heed what the empty wall says, to read the blank sheet of paper.

But the creative artist, writer, or reader faces a paradoxical predicament in the sheer plenitude that belies the nakedness of wall, the emptiness of canvas, or the blankness of page that threatens to overwhelm with the abundance of possibilities. As Paz himself has often demonstrated, most dramatically in his simultaneously plural *Blanco*, the two options he posits here become incrementally compounded with their own and with each other's otherness in the execution. The first, re-covery(ing), proves a palimpsestuous act whose transparencies betray indelible opacities of otherness with inalienable claims to simultaneous coexistence; and, the second, discovery, becomes at once an encounter with "configurations of an other language" *and* a confrontation with the critical reflection, an inverted mirror image of our countenance in the *vultus mercurialis* of the would-be blankness. The multifariousness in each of these options endures yet another compounding in the dilatory realization that the two options cannot be exercised in turn or discretely. A mutual implication in their alterities bedevils their duplicity into yet an other "in/mediation" and critical heterodoxy. The critical mediation, the discriminating intrusion, comprises necessarily a selectivity, a negotiated and provisional election. And the process itself chastens us in compensation for the inevitable curtailments of our critical mediations. In this sense, the artist's, writer's, reader's enterprise becomes a "*via negativa*." "But," notes Paz, "the via negativa is not passive. Criticism is a creative operation, the negation is active. An inversion of values: less becomes more".

In this economy of compensation where one must yield in order to harvest a yield, "asceticism, negation, criticism: all of these terms could be deceiving. The critical-creative operation assumes, alternatively, the form of convocation and of provocation. Convocation is a receptive disposition in the face of space; provocation is a transgression: a breach, a violation of space. Convocation and provocation are attitudes that insinuate themselves in the dialogue between contemplating and making". Let us hasten to bracket the alternative quality of Paz's pro-/con-vocation, for, in practice, these are not "alternative forms" but indivisibly enmeshed alterities. They are spatially superimposed and entwined, temporally simultaneous and comingled, as Paz's own work often illustrates. These are operations that function as fused coefficients, just as the horizons of critical subject and object of criticism fuse in the performance of "contemplation" and "making."

Contemplation is performative, and "making" is no less a contemplative exercise. Just so, "convocation" has no fewer provocative entailments. And within this myriad arena of contending otherness, acts of painting, writing, reading, and acts of political engagement become critical acts, that is, acts that mediate and differentiate. They are all implicated engagements of a poetic constellation, all committed to a *poesis*, a performance that *makes for* a particular social and cultural dwelling. Where does this dwelling occur? On what ground(s) does its dweller come to reside? What articulates dwelling into community? What poetic economy, that is, what "house rules," legitimate those binding articulations? These are critical questions whose responses require critical performance; which means, of course, that one cannot come to rest on a particular response that does not entail the germination of yet another coefficient, yet another act, yet one more alterity to compound the plurality of the heterocosm. To halt on a given response more than provisionally would be to arrest creative impulse, to petrify political will, to exchange poetic dwelling for ideological dungeon, to subsume otherness into oneness in fatal narcissism, to cannibalize the living in order to apprehend life.

Octavio Paz's career has been a relentless struggle and constant admonition against such monism, a moral struggle carried on through political actions, through his diagnoses of his country's history, and through his poetry. A rebel by vocation, Paz has always been wary of revolutions and revolutionaries because of their inexorable penchant for falling into the monisms of self-justifying ideology. He has not winced from pointing to the history of Mexico's own revolution as a supreme example. His disdain for its institutionalization into a one-party system with an imperial presidency is as unremitting as his condemnation of what he refers to as "Stalinisms," whether of the left or of the right, whether in the satrapism of our "civilized" institutions or in the petty Caesarism of the Caribbean and of Central and South America. He has censured such terrorisms, whether perpetrated by the state or by the individual self-righteous, with equal vehemence.

The fall into such institutional or individual acts of immediation means reducing our historical existence to single-minded obsession, into a-historical abstraction of a metaphysics that dehumanizes and converts human dwelling from life-enhancing performance to deadening and deadly deformation: "If it is history and not metaphysics that defines the human, we shall have to displace the word *to be* [*ser*] from the center of our preoccupations and replace it with the word *between* [*entre*]". Paz's poetic persona and its moral force dwell, as he would have us do, in the interstices of this ambiguous threshold and its heterodox mediations. To "dwell poetically," then, means to dwell nomadically. "To be" [*ser*] must derive from an ontology of exception. Community, even an academic one, ought to imply the communing of differential alterities, its members bound by supple articulations, its economy responsive to the supple diversities of plurality, its cultural and political ecology resilient enough not only to withstand but also to engender a heterology capable of infusing orthodoxy's scleroses with heterodox vitality.

Ser [to be] is a sterile copula, *entre* [between] a prepositional convocation, but no less a provocative injunction whose imperative verbal urgency invites entry of/into the other. *A Tree Within*, Paz's latest poetic collection, figures a passionate and compassionate invitation to partake of a tree of life, to dwell in the midst of a poetic genealogy, to commute between root and branch, between verse and obverse, in a commuting that commutes sentences of monomaniac judgment, and interdicts the dicta of a fixed idea, that banishes the claims of arborescent taxonomy and the inflexible order of its scansion tables. Paz's arbor is a dwelling to be entered and not an elemental tree by which to decline and parse historical existence and poetic filiation into the taxidermy of a prosaic grammar or a prosodic system. Divided into five parts. *A Tree Within* proffers a quintessential branching, an indexical handful ("un manojo") that reaches out with prolific roots from the seminal syllabary ("sílabas semillas") of its convocatory "Proema." The five parts of the volume are appropriately entitled "Sheaf" ("Gavilla"). "The Open Hand" ("La mano abierta"), "A Sun More Alive" ("Un sol más vivo"), "Seen and Said" ("Visto y dicho"), and "A Tree Within" ("Arbol adentro"), which includes the title poem. A germinal progression marks this titular unfolding, unmistakably, culminating in the fraternal credo of eros and solidarity of the final poem's declarative "Coda." This last poem, perhaps the finest in the collection, is fittingly entitled "Letter of Testimony" ("Carta de creencia").

Between proem and coda, Paz negotiates an intricate communion, an elaborate conversation with the dramatic personae of his poetic itinerary and its itinerant dwelling: Roman Jakobson, Matsuo Basho, Sor Juana lnés de la Cruz, Hsieh Lin-Yün, Kostas Papaioannou, Alberto Lacerda, Marcel Duchamp, San Juan de la Cruz, José Lezama Lima, John Donne, Joan Miró, Roberto Sebastian Matta, Chuang Tzu, and, among others, the myriad prosopopoeia that is Octavio Paz. It is a motley crew with which to take to sea, and its motliness is symptomatic of the multifarious syllabary that mans the poet's crossing: "se embarca en un barco de / papel y atraviesa, / durante cuarenta noches y cuarenta días, el mar de / la angustia nocturna y el pedregal de la angustia / diurna" ("boards a paper boat and crosses, / for forty nights and forty days, the night-sorrow sea and the day- / sorrow desert"). Casting off unto the lapidary and nocturnal wilderness of the white page, the poet's paper vessel must convey "the migrations of millions of verbs, wings and claws, seeds and hands; / the nouns, bony and full of roots, planted in the waves of language" ("las migraciones de miríadas de verbos, alas / y garras, semillas y manos; / los substantivos óseos y llenos de raíces, planta- / das en las ondulaciones del lenguaje").

Like its alluded scriptural prototype, Paz's is at once a spiritual and a historical, that is to say, a poetic pilgrimage that *makes* and *re-makes* its way within the echoic wilderness of spectral solitudes and between way stations of otherness, a passage through "la idolatría al yo y la execración al yo y la / disipación del yo; / la degollación de los epítetos, el entierro de los / espejos" ("the idolatry of the self and the desecration of the self and the dissipa- / tion of the self; / the beheading of epithets, the burial of mirrors"). There is a persistent and eerie other-worldliness to the worldly itinerary of this pilgrimage, a haunting precognition that any *ars vivendi*, as we have noted in Paz earlier, serves as perspicuity into our mortality, into life's inevitable other; art's insurrectionist acts shade into preparatory essay for an *ars moriendi*. The collection's final poem, "Carta de creencia" ("Letter of Testimony"), to which I have already referred, broaches the subject explicitly. Here it becomes clearer than ever that for Paz the art of life is an amatory art, an erotic commitment to the fullest extent. In the end, the question becomes "El arte de amar / ¿es el arte de morir?" ("The art of love /—is it the art of dying?").

But to return to the "Proem" for a moment longer, we have there an insistent interment and vertiginous descent that hauntingly searches for the genealogical ascendancy of life's poetic dwelling, its versicles sifting down like particles of sand onto the desert-page, its restless resting place. The inward arborescence enciphered in the title, "A Tree Within," has at once a descendental rather than a transcendental trajectory. Thus, the triple "vertigo" of the proem's first couplet, each in affiliation with body, fortune, and death, that lead one, shut-eyed, to the edge of the precipice and to the early morning stroll in subaquatic gardens. Poetry as life, clearly, must embrace life's spectral other side: "A veces la poesía es el vértigo de los cuerpos y el / vértigo de la dicha y el vértigo de la muerte; / el paseo con los ojos cerrados al borde del despe- / ñadero y la verbena en los jardines submarinos" ("At times poetry is the vertigo of bodies and the vertigo of fortune and / the vertigo of death; / the walk with eyes closed along the edge of the cliff, and the verbena / in submarine gardens" [Weinberger mistranslates "dicha" as "speech." I return the term to its original "fortune"]). At the end of this proemial overture and submersion, what remains is the unseen, the unheard, and the unspoken in life that now, in art, must comprise the rest of the book's commemorative multitude, which is comprised, in turn, by the parentheses of eros and an other life (or other lives) that bracket its genealogy. This is an eros of solidarity, an eros fraternally proffered rather than self-directed: "el amor a lo nunca visto y el amor a lo nunca oído / y el amor a lo nunca dicho: el amor al amor" ("love of the never seen, and love of the never heard / and love of the never said: love of love" [so thoroughly has Weinberger botched this coda of the "Proem" that I choose to ignore his rendering altogether here]). And this love disseminates itself in the italicized "*sílabas semillas*" scattered from the Proem's invocation into and between the verse furrows of the book's subsequent pages.

A spectral symmetry haunts in the ensuing syllabary that germinates from this seeding. As with the "Proem," the focus in the poems of this collection also falls on the liminal, on the wilderness of *entre* rather than on the domestic hegemony of *ser*. Take the first poem, for example. It is dedicated to Paz's friend Roman Jakobson and was occasioned by the distinguished linguist's death in 1982. As an elegiac apostrophe, it addresses the activities that consumed Jakobson's peripatetic life, activities so intimately reflected in Paz's own. The poem meditates on the harvest of a long career that chose poetic dwelling as its vocation, a meditation on what remains after all is said and done. The poem is entitled "Decir: Hacer" ("To Say: To Do" [In the Weinberger translation not only is the title excised and substituted by the poem's first line, but the original poem, *en face*, is also stripped of its original title and given its first verse as heading!]). The prosody is intricate, and it keeps its semantic vigil through the doubled period—the colon—that hinges the verbal infinitives in the title. This simple punctuation mark would obviously mean much more than its conventional usage as convocatory aperture to exemplum, citation, or ratio to the signaled linguist Jakobson. At Jakobson's wake, one could say, Paz transforms the colon into a prosodic Jacob's ladder, a column on which he articulates the limbs and verbal extremities of a poetic edifice. It becomes quite clear that in this bipartite poem poetic vigil is tantamount to bifrontal wakefulness, an alert watch that turns on dia-critical hinges, now to the declarative inter-dictions of "decir," now to the conversative inter-actions of "hacer," to weave both terms into the watchful prosopopoeia of poetry's own masks. The anaphoric insistence and incremental repetition of the initial quartet yield their dialectical oscillation between alterities, at least provisionally, to the precarious constitution of poetry itself:

Entre lo que veo y digo,
entre lo que digo y callo,
entre lo que callo y sueño,
entre lo que sueño y olvido,
la poesía.

("Between what I see and what I say, / between what I say and what I keep silent, / between what I keep silent and what I dream,/ between what I dream and what I forget: / poetry".)

Provisional and precarious are characterizations that inevitably describe poetry's predicament in which the quatrain reaches its caesura; and poetry's interstitial genesis occupies a most fleeting position. Its locus proves a slippery ground on which poetry slides, slipping from the stanzaic shuttle of alterities that constitute it into the liminal betweenness of the predicates:

    Se desliza
  entre el sí y el no:
        dice
  lo que callo,
      calla
  lo que digo,
      sueña
  lo que olvido.
     No es un decir:
  es un hacer.
     Es un hacer
  que es un decir.
      La poesía
  se dice y se oye:
      es real.
  Y apenas digo
    es real,
  se disipa.
     ¿Así es más real?

("It slips / between yes and no, / says / what I keep silent, / keeps silent / what I say, / dreams / what I forget. / It is not speech / it is an act. / It is an act / of speech. / Poetry / speaks and listens: / it is real. / And as soon as I say / *it is real,* / it vanishes. / Is it then more real?")

The form of the poem itself follows the slippage, with the squared block of the initial quartet sliding into a ladder or step formation. The interactive terms of *hacer* ("to act") slide to the right of the margin; the declarative variants of *decir* ("to speak") hang plumb to the left. The poem, then, forms a stepladder that leads to dissolution and to the ontological querying of poetry's own reality at the foot of the poem's part one—"¿Así es más real?" ("Is it then more real?").

Dispelled as predicative declaration, as "saying/doing," in the dissipation of its reality, poetry re-turns, as it always does, in the second part of the poem to shuttle, once again, between alterities and, thus, to weave and unweave its graphic syllabary, its seminal inscription in the eye of the page and in the page of the eye:

> Idea palpable,
> > palabra
> impalpable:
> > la poesía
> va y viene
> > entre lo que es
> y lo que no es.
> > Teje reflejos
> y los desteje.
> > La poesía
> siembra ojos en la página,
> siembra palabras en los ojos.

("Tangible idea, / intangible word: / poetry / comes and goes / between what is / and what is not. / It weaves / and unweaves reflections. / Poetry / scatters eyes on a page / scatters words on our eyes".)

Like our social commitments and political engagements, then, poetry is beheld but not arrested; it is beholding but not beholden. And poetry's own dwelling is in poetic intervals, on interlineal throughways, through nomadic way stations. Poetry's composition occurs as *poesis*, as "making" that traverses the composures of diction, a traversal through opaque verse and that opacity's ob-verse—white space—where poetic making ("hacer") and declarative deed ("decir") conjugate and converse as interlineal versification. But here, too, the resultant poem cannot, ought not, succumb to a static self-composure, to a self-identity, to the spectral narcissism of *ser* as ontological copula that binds and petrifies. True to poetry's vocation as a transgressive interaction, the poem must become an occasion for poetic dwelling as heterodox nomadism. In this sense, there is an uncanny and unmistakable consonance between poetry as occasion and occasional poetry in *A Tree Within*. For Paz's collection consists primarily of *vers de circonstance*, occasioned for the most part by the most implacable reminder of our fleeting nature, our inexorable nomadism, our mortality. *A Tree Within* is an extended elegy to poetry and poets, to poetic dwelling and its interstitial habitation between othernesses of temporality and poetic careers. This genealogy, this family tree, then, resonates as a multifarious conversation with and among limbs, members, radicals of a nomadic tribe ("gavilla" means this, too). *A Tree Within* becomes an occasion of communing in which poets (and readers) hear from one another, but they do so neither in echo, nor in spectral reflection. They remain, indeed, other to themselves as they do to each other, and nowhere is Paz more obvious and emphatic on this differential intermediation than in his elegiac apostrophe to the Cuban poet José Lezama Lima. "Refutación de los espejos" ("Refutation of Mirrors") is the title of the poem that commemorates Lezama's passing through the looking glass of Lezama's own words, emphatically intercalated into Paz's poem through italicization:

> Ya entraste en *el espejo que camina hacia nosotros*,
> el espejo vacío de la poesía,
> *contradicción de las contradicciones*, ya estás en la
> casa de las semejanzas,
> ya eres, a los pies del Uno, sin cesar de ser otro,
> idéntico a tí mismo.

("You have now entered *the mirror that comes towards us*, / the empty mirror of poetry, / *contradiction of contradictions*, you are already in the / house of similitudes, / already at the feet of the One, you are, without ceasing to be other, / identical to yourself" [My translation; the poem has mysteriously been rendered a spectre altogether, alas, in the book's life in English.])

Paradoxical doxologist of the paradoxical, Lezama, perhaps more than any other contemporary of Paz, elevated the vocation of poetic dwelling to exquisite proliferation of alterities. America's "Poet Unbound," and unbounded, Lezama exemplified for Paz the poetic possibilities of shattering all mirrors and loosing the myriad crystal fragments to pursue their magnetic constellations. His *Fragmentos a su Imán* reached Paz in xeroxed manuscript form just after Lezama's death. In Lezama's poetry, Paz finds an undeniable instance of freedom from the hubris of specular appropriation and mimetic representation, a freedom from narcissistic reflection that in poetry translates into deadening self-seizure and in politics into deadly ideology:

> Los espejos repiten el mundo pero tus ojos lo
> cambian: tus ojos son la crítica de los espejos: creo en
> tus ojos.

("Mirrors reproduce the world but your eyes / transform it: your
eyes are the critique of mirrors: I believe / in your eyes.")

This is the unorthodox belief, an investment in *critical* speculation
rather than in reflection's dogmatic proprietariness, that has guided Paz's
mediations and crossings from otherness to otherness, a vocation of building
invisible bridges that breach intangible and interminable facets: "*Un puente,
un gran puente, no se le ve*" ("A bridge, a great bridge, is not visible")—
Lezama's words that Octavio Paz had read fifty years earlier and now
incorporates into his commemorative poem. These are words Paz clearly
took to heart and, as he confesses:

> Desde entonces cruzo puentes que van de aquí
> a allá, de nunca a siempre,
> desde entonces, ingeniero de aire, construyo el
> puente inacabable entre lo inaudible y lo invisible.

("Since then, I cross bridges that go from here / to there, from
never to always, / since then, engineer of the air, I construct the
/ interminable bridge between the unheard of and the invisible.")

And yet, as the fourth part of this five-part collection attests (it is
entitled "Visto y Dicho"—"Seen and Said"), Paz's long career has been as
much an exploration of visibilities—on canvas, stone, and screen, in museum
and in archaeological monument—as it has been of language and its audible
cadenza. Language and image and the graphic conjugation of the two form
the lapidary elements that shore up the poet's bridges in the air, his poetic
vocation of agon and Luciferian jester fading between mutabilities of
apparitions and disappearances. Or, as Paz's apostrophe to Lezama reads:

> Tü dices que *lo lúdico es lo agónico* y yo digo que
> lo lüdico es lo lücido y por eso,
>   en este juego de las apariciones y las desapariciones
> que jugamos sobre la tierra,
>   en este ensayo general del Fin del Mundo que es
> nuestro siglo, te veo . . .

("You say that t*he ludic is the agonic* and I say that / the ludic is the
lucid and so, / in this game of apparitions and disappear- / ances
we play on earth, / in the general rehearsal of the End of the
World that is / our century, I see you . . .")

The nine poems dedicated to the visual arts in this fourth section all fade from visibility into temporality; the clausura of each punctuates a permutation, a transmigration, one could say, into fleeting apparition that dances into otherworldly diaphaneity. The climactic coda of the last of these poems draws the poet himself into its elemental house of haunted vigilance, where he goes on painting his poem in simultaneity with the painter's wakeful watch in the painting:

> hay que construir sobre este espacio inestable la
> casa de la mirada,
> la casa de aire y de agua donde la música duerme,
> el fuego vela y pinta el poeta.

("we must construct the house of glances over this dubious place, / the house of air and water where music sleeps, fire keeps watch, and / the poet paints".)

The poet had already wrought his own invisibility, his own transmigration into apparition at the end of the collection's third part—"Y fui por un instante diáfano / viento que se ditiene, / gira sobre sí mismo y se disipa" ("And I was, for a moment, diaphanous, / a wind that stops, / turns on itself and is gone"). But the collection's title poem that opens the concluding part spells the poet's real *passion*. For it is here that the poet becomes consubstantial with poetry and his life becomes coincident with poetry's tree of life. Like Lezama's entry and passage through the looking glass of his words, Paz becomes at once the embodiment of the tree and its fertile ground, its radical uterine vessel and radical ("rhizomatic," as we would say in Greek) arborescence. The poet Paz and Paz the poetic persona conflate as never before. Poetic dwelling as life practice and the poem's own habitation (that "house fairer than prose," as Emily Dickinson would have it) now engage in communal convocation that beacons us to partake of the communion, for it is our partaking of it that enlivens its fire, animates its passion, and gives words to its silence. And it is here that poetry dawns, in the betweenness of our otherness, in the fugal conjugation of our alterities:

> Amanece
> en la noche del cuerpo.
> Allá adentro, en mi frente,
> el arbol habla.
> Acércate, ¿lo oyes?

("Day breaks / in the body's night. / There, within, inside my head, / the tree speaks. / Come closer—do you hear it?")

FRANCES CHILES

The Poetic Revelation

> Contra el silencio y el bullicio invento la
> Palabra, libertad que se inventa y me
> inventa cada día
> –Octavio Paz, *Libertad bajo palabra*

Readers of Paz are often struck by the fact that much of his poetry is concerned with what poetry is and how it functions (or should function) in our lives and also with how poems are made. For Paz, the poetic experience is inseparable from the act of creating and re-creating the poem: "The experience is given as naming of that which until it is named, properly lacks existence."

The primary mission of poetry in the contemporary world, Paz asserts—echoing the Surrealists—is to create "un nuevo sagrado," a new form of holiness totally unrelated to established religions which responds to our present spiritual requirements. The Surrealist conception of poetry, as with all of the arts, was founded on the belief that man should find happiness in *this* life, a notion which constituted a definitive rejection of the Christian belief in a future eternal life after death, but which at the same time retained the religious aspiration of the recovery of paradisiac unity.

While Paz would concur with Wellek and Warren that "Religion is the greater mystery, poetry the lesser," and thus poetry cannot completely fill

From *Octavio Paz: The Mythic Dimension* by Frances Chiles, © 1987 by Peter Lang Publishing, Inc. Reprinted by permission of the publisher and the author.

the void left by the loss of religion in contemporary life, he believes nonetheless that the poetic revelation at least offers hope, solace, and communion to those who are unable to accept or believe in established religions as they are presently constituted and practiced. In response to the fundamental problems of the human condition, Paz remarks, poetry does not postulate a supreme divinity external to man who requires obedience and expiation of sin. Poetry does not pass judgment on human destiny; it does not require the death of *this* life as the price of redemption, but affirms that death is contained in and inseparable from life. Instead of eternal salvation in the next world, poetry offers transient moments of revelation that enrich and transfigure our lives in the here-and-now:

> The poetic experience is an opening up of the wellsprings of being. An instant and never. An instant and forever. Instant in which we are that which we were and shall be. Being born and dying: an instant. In that instant we are life and death, this and that.

The poetic experience, like the amorous and religious ones, is a going outside ourselves, a mortal leap from this to a higher realm where we are changed and become "others" and thus recover our original condition. What distinguishes one experience from the other, or what is "privative" in each as Paz put it, is the object to which each is directed: in the erotic experience, it is union with the loved one; in the religious experience it is the union of the purified soul with God or the divine; and in the poetic and similar non-religious mystical experiences, it is the reintegration of man with his deeper self and with all that which Paz (paraphrasing Antonio Machado) terms the constitutive otherness of man's being.

The poetic experience as such is not only felt, it is said. The experience does not precede utterance but is bound up with the creative process through which it finds expression. Consequently, an analysis of the experience also involves an analysis of inspiration and the act of writing the poem.

Paz ascribes to poetic inspiration a numinous quality that is inexplicable in the empirical view of man's relation to the universe. For primitive mythmakers, as for poets of the Middle Ages, the mysterious, supernatural nature of what we now call inspiration was not in contradiction with their conception of external reality as the source of all ideas and archetypes. Hence they did not question the empirical validity of their dreams, feelings, and imagination, or the unexpected intervention of the "other voice" that collaborates in the creative process. In light of the modern literary tradition's secular vision of the universe, however, inspiration was considered a psychological problem until Surrealism negated the dualism of subject and object and affirmed the "other voice" as an integral part of man's being.

Paz's conception of what inspiration is and how it operates in the creative act differs somewhat from that of the Surrealists in that, in his view, the "other voice," like man himself, is not given; it is not something that exists outside the poet nor is it something that he extracts from within himself. "And in truth," he adds, "inspiration is not anywhere, it simply *is not*, nor is it a thing: it is an aspiration, a moving, a forward thrust: toward that which we ourselves are." The "other voice" merges with our own voice in the act of *"going beyond ourselves to the encounter of ourselves."*

Paz envisions the act of poetizing as a twofold movement of departure and return, separation and reunion. It begins with the poet in a state of "pre-meditation" or active passivity, so to speak, that allows him to detach himself from the phenomenal world and immerse himself in complete solitude and nothingness. The quotidian world and he himself cease to be what they were but a short time before. Everything, including himself, must now be created anew, but the words needed to accomplish this task have either evaporated into silence or dissolved into a gibberish of sounds, leaving him in a state of anxiety. But it is precisely while the poet is in this distressed state and at a loss for words that the second movement toward utterance and revelation begins with the sudden manifestation of inspiration; and the poet, impelled outside himself, recreates himself and the world by naming things. The silence and the stammering are replaced by the long-sought after images and missing rhythms that are transformed into a poem; and with utterance

> Now man is all that he wished to be: rock, woman, bird, the other man and the other beings. He is image, marriage of opposites, poem saying itself to itself. He is finally, the image of man being incarnated in man.

A classic example of the task of extricating the poem is "El río" (The River), another masterful poem about cities written in Geneva in 1953, and published in *La estación violenta*. The first stanza evokes the recurrent image of the solitary poet-at-work as he contemplates the wakeful city, personified here as in "Entrada en la materia," as an alien, impenetrable being which nonetheless intrudes into the poet's consciousness: "La ciudad desvelada circula por mi sangre como una abeja" (The restless city circles in my blood like a bee), forcing him to decipher its significance:

> toda la noche, uno a uno, estatua a estatua, fuente a fuente,
>   piedra a piedra, toda la noche
> sus pedazos se buscan en mi frente, toda la noche la ciudad
>   habla dormida por mi boca
> y es un discurso jadeante, un tartamudeo de aguas y piedra
>   batallando, su historia.

all night, one by one, statue by statue, fountain by fountain,/ stone by stone, the whole night long/ its shards seek one another in my forehead, all night long the/ city talks in its sleep through my mouth,/ a gasping discourse, a stammering of waters and arguing stone,/ its story.

The central metaphor of the poem, the river, refers simultaneously to the incessant, meaningless commotion of the city, to the babble of disjointed words crowding into the poet's mind that become streams of ink upon the white page, and to the silent, swift current of time whose course the poet, drawing on his psychic powers "como Buda a la orilla del río" (like Buddha on the river's edge) strives to halt even for an instant so that he might

> decir lo que dice el río, larga palabra semejante a labios,
>   larga palabra que no acaba nunca,
> decir lo que dice el tiempo en duras frases de piedra, en
>   vastos
> ademanes de mar cubriendo mundos.

say what the river says, a long word resembling lips, a long/ word that never ends,/ to say what time says in hard sentences of stone, in vast gestures/ of sea covering worlds.

The poet is unable to say what is demanding to be said; and, as we have seen, it is at this juncture that his task becomes most difficult and full of anguish: "A mitad del poema me sobrecoge siempre un gran/ desamparo,/ todo me abandona" (In mid-poem a great helplessness overtakes me,/ everything abandons me). The images of the yet unmade poem as a vast empty space ("una explanada desierta"), crumbling edifices ("terrazas devastadas, babilonias"), a sea of darkness ("un mar de sal negra), and so on, are vivid correlatives of the poet's spiritual desolation as he struggles to detach himself from the everyday world and to achieve the state of quiescence that conduces to utterance:

> detenerme, callar, cerrar los ojos hasta que brote de mis
> párpados una espiga, un surtidor de soles,
> y el alfabeto ondule largamente bajo el viento del sueño y
> la marea crezca en una ola y la ola rompa el dique,
> esperar hasta que el papel se cubra de astros y sea el poema
> un bosque de palabras enlazadas,

to stop myself, to keep quiet, to close my eyes until a green spike/ sprouts from my eyelids, a spurt of suns,/ and the alphabet wavers long under the wind of the vision and/ the tide rolls into one wave and the wave breaks the dike,/ to wait until the paper is covered with stars and the poem a/ forest of tangled words

In contrast to the somber wasteland images mentioned earlier, the recurrent organic images (seed, sun, green shoot, forest) in this context emphasize the germinating function of the imagination and imply that the completed poem itself will be a source of life.

The poet's spiritual dark night grows darker as he is unable to seize upon the word amidst the jumble of meaningless sounds; and the blood circulating silently in his veins, as well as the ink splotched page, reinforces his awareness of the city's aimless drifting and of his own life flowing unchecked downstream:

> sílabas de tiempo, letras rotas, gotas de tinta, sangre que va y
> viene y no dice nada y me lleva consigo.

syllables of time, broken letters, splotches of ink, blood that goes/ and comes and says nothing and carries me with it.

While the poetrymaking process has halted in midstream, dammed up, it would seem, by one word repeated endlessly, the poet finds himself floundering helplessly against the current. As he continues writing, however, he becomes aware of someone other than himself, "el hombre," "alguien a mi lado" (someone beside me), presumably inspiration, writing along with him. His continuing struggle to liberate the word and himself is now vividly depicted as "un combate a muerte entre inmortales" (a fight to the death between immortals), with the adversaries the creative will versus an engulfing darkness that is both physical and spiritual: "las palabras contra la noche, la noche contra la noche, nada/ ilumina el opaco combate" (the words against the night, the night against the night, nothing/ lights up the opaque combat).

In the final stanza, the poet's intense effort to bridge the distance between himself and the city, to bring the external world into alignment with his vision of another reality hidden behind outer appearances, is made more

explicit in the use of an invocatory or prayerful tone and on a grammatical
level in shifting to the subjunctive mode:

> que el agua muestre su corazón que es un racimo de espejos
>   ahogados, un árbol de cristal que el viento desarraiga
> (cada hoja del árbol vuela y centellea y se pierde en una luz
>   cruel como se pierden las palabras en la imagen del poeta)
> que el tiempo se cierre y sea su herida una cicatriz invisible,
>   apenas una delgada línea sobre la piel del mundo,
> que las palabras depongan armas y sea el poema una sola palabra
>   entretejida, un resplandor implacable que avanza,
> y sea el alma el llano después del incendio, el pecho lunar de un
>   mar petrificado que no refleja nada
> sino la extensión extendida, el espacio acostado sobre sí mismo,
>   las alas inmensas desplegadas,
> y sea todo como la llama que se esculpe y se hiela en la roca de
>   entrañas transparentes,
> duro fulgor resuelto ya en cristal y claridad pacífica.

and that the water show its heart, a cluster of drowned mirrors,/
a glass tree that the wind uproots/ (and every leaf of the tree
flutters and glints and is lost in a/ cruel light, as the words
of the poet's image are lost),/ may time thicken and its wound
be an invisible scar, scarcely/ a delicate line upon the skin
of the world,/ let the words lay down their arms and the poem
be one single/ interwoven word, an implacable radiance that
advances/ and may the soul be the blackened grass after fire,
the lunar/ breast of a sea that's turned to stone and reflects
nothing/ except splayed dimension, expansion, space lying down
upon/ itself, spread wings immense,/ and may everything be like
flame that cuts itself into and freezes/ into the rock of
diaphonous bowels,/ hard blazing resolved now in crystal,
peaceable clarity.

Although the poem is still only a possibility at this stage, we sense an
illumination of consciousness as the poet emerges from his earlier state of
darkness and desolation. Accordingly, the poem is now envisioned as "un
resplandor que avanza," and the soul in a purified state like a plain cleared of
debris and ready for planting, or the sea's calm, lunar surface—an emptiness
or nothingness which, in contrast to the earlier state, has now acquired a
positive value.

To my mind, the parallels between the various stages of the poetic experience and the mystical experience, which are present from the beginning of the poem, become most pronounced in the final verses in the use of the kind of imagery that is commonly associated with San Juan de la Cruz (e.g. "la extensión extendida, "las alas desplegadas," "la llama que se esculpe y se hiela".) Paz himself has pointed out that through a deliberate exercise of the will, the poet in the act of poetizing, like the mystic in meditation, aims at immersing himself in a state of absolute receptivity, as San Juan said, "desiring nothing"—a state in which, Paz explains, "the nothing itself becomes active, by force of the desire." Moreover, such passive states "are by no means experiences of silence and emptiness, but of positive and full moments: from the center of being flows a stream of images." Such was the poet's objective in "El río" which, as implied in the last line, he attained, as the river finally turns upstream going in a backward direction—an image in Paz that we have come to associate with a return to the original integrated state of being.

The poet's inability to verbalize his experience is attributable in part to its ineffable nature and also to the limitations and complexities of ordinary language as a medium of poetic expression. The poet's primary objective in creating the poem is to share his personal experience with others, and through the instrumentality of the poem become "another." The poem, Paz asserts, "is an original and unique creation, but it is also reading and recitation: participation. The poet creates it; the people, by recitation, re-create it." To this end, the language he uses to make the poem is the living language of the community, utilized in expressing its innermost thoughts, beliefs, and experiences, rather than a specialized poetic vocabulary.

Like many other poets and critics (Cassirer, for one), Paz believes that language, near its source, is naturally metaphorical and concrete, rather than discursive and abstract. In the creative process, the poet restores the common language to its original poetic state, which involves committing an act of "violence to language," an "up-rooting" and separating of words from their usual functions in everyday speech in order to purify and revitalize them through new connotations and relationships.

The poet's violent struggle with words, something of which we have already glimpsed in "El río" and in "Entrada en la materia," is treated extensively in ¿Aguila o sol? (Eagle or Sun?) in the long series of prose poems entitled "Trabajos del poeta" (1949) (Works of the Poet), the essence of which can be summed up in the following short poem, "Las palabras" (The Words):

Dales la vuelta,
cógelas del rabo (chillen, putas),
azótalas,
dales azúcar en la boca a las rejegas,
ínflalas, globos, pínchalas,
sórbeles sangre y tuétanos
sécalas,
cápalas,
písalas, gallo galante,
tuérceles el gaznate, cocinero,
desplúmalas,
destrípalas, toro,
buey, arrástralas,
hazlas, poeta,
haz que se traguen todas sus palabras.

Go at it again,/ fling them around,/ give it to them,/
let them bitch, the whores,/ whip them,/ put sugar in
their mouths,/ blow them up, globes, pinch them,/
suck their blood and marrow,/ dry them up,/ cut their
balls,/ cover them, cock of the walk,/ wring their
necks, cook,/ pluck them,/ rip their guts out, bull,/
drag them down, bullock,/ make them, poet,/ make them
eat their own words.

In "Solo a dos voces" (Solo for Two Voices), the last poem in *Salamandra*, the poet's confrontation with words, though less violent than the encounter described above, is no less intense. The poem is characteristically Paz as it separates the poet's consciousness into two levels of awareness or voices—an idea implicit in the punning of the title: "solo" in the sense of solitary or "all alone," as the pronominal "only one," and, in an ironical twist, as a musical composition for one voice. The other voice, as we already know, collaborates with the writer, sometimes by contradicting him; nonetheless, it should not be silenced inasmuch as all of the other voices which are and are not his own voice reveal a plurality of visions of the world. In "Solo a dos voces" one voice reveals the imaginative or mythical reality of the poem, the other presents the visible, quotidian world in which it is being written. The first voice attempts to verbalize something that eludes expression, the other, critical voice comments on the creative act.

The real setting of "Solo a dos voces" is an unnamed place—a dark, rain-drenched patio, a narrow white room; and the time is December 21 or

22, the winter solstice in the Northern hemisphere when the sun "stands still" at its farthest point south of the equator:

> Solsticio de invierno:
> Sol parado
>   Mundo errante
> Sol desterrado
>   Fijeza al rojo blanco
> La tierra blanca negra
> Dormida
> Sobre sí misma echada
> Es una piedra caída
> Ánima en pena
>   El mundo
> Peña de pena
>   El alma
> Peña entrañas de piedra
> (Cae la gota invisible
> Sobre el cemento húmedo.
> Cae también en mi cuarto.
> A la mitad del pensamiento
> Me quedo, como el sol,
> Parado
> En la mitad de mí,
> Separado.)

> Winter solstice:/ Sun stopped/ World wandering/
> Sun in exile/ Fixity at white heat/ The black
> white earth/ Asleep/ Flung on itself/ Is a
> fallen stone/ Soul in purgatory/ The world/
> Purgatorial stone/ The soul/ Stone with stony
> heart/ (The drop falls unseen/ On the wet
> cement./ It falls too in my room./ Midway
> in thought/ I stay, like the sun,/ Stopped/
> Midway in myself,/ Separated.)

As in "Himno entre ruinas," "Viento entero," and other poems, actual times and places merge to coexist with others both in and outside of history. In this instance, the Greco-Roman myths become part of the present in the evocation of the Eleusinian rituals that honor Demeter-Ceres, the Greco-Roman goddess of the fertility of the fields who, like Dionysus, god of the vine and the other divinity of earth, was especially venerated for her generosity to mankind. Demeter, we recall, was also the sorrowing mother of Persephone, "La Señora del Prado" referred to in the poem. The central part of the ritual, whose color and pageantry are captured in the following verses, re-creates her reappearance to earth each spring to restore verdancy to the fields and her death and return to the underworld at harvest time, which brings desolate winter upon the land:

> Muchachas cereales
> Ofrendan a Ceres panes y ceras;
> Muchachas trigueñas,
> Entre el pecho y los ojos
> Alzan la monda,
> Pascua de Resurrección:
> Señora del Prado,
> > Sobre tu cabeza,
> Como una corona cándida,
> La canasta del pan.

> Incandescencias del candeal,
> Muchachas, cestas de panes,
> Pan de abejas, pan de flor,
> Altar vivo los pechos,
> Sobre mesa de tierra vasos de sol:
> Como y bebo, hombre soy.

> Girls of the grain/ Offer to Ceres loaves and beeswax;/ Girls like tawny wheat,/ Between their breast and their eyes/ Lift the offering,/ At Easter-tide:/ Our Lady of the Meadow,/ On your head,/ As if crowned with candour,/ The basket of bread./ Incandescences of white bread,/ Girls, baskets of loaves,/ Rye bread and barley bread,/ Bread with a bee design, the fine white bread,/ The breasts a living altar,/ Goblets of sun on the table of earth:/ I eat and I drink, am a man.

The offering of the beeswax and the cut wheat-ear ("la monda") symbolizes both the goddess's death and her rebirth in the grain, and the bread made from it in bee-shaped figures represents her life-giving qualities. Like the young goddess they represent, the maidens in the procession become identified with the sacramental food they carry, as do all of the celebrants, including the poet, who partake of it, thus actualizing the ancient mysteries which, it was said long ago, "have not only shown us the way to live joyfully," but also have "taught us how to die with better hope."

In re-creating these rituals in the poem, we are again struck by the poet's constant concern with reconciling two opposing attitudes towards reality, the mythopoeic and the secular, expressed in different conceptions of time; and these in turn are reflected in two kinds of calendars: the one sacred or mythical, in which are inscribed certain rites and festivals based on the rhythms of the cosmos or the commemoration of archetypal events; and the other profane, in which time is measured chronometrically in hours, days, months, years. In the first, time may be repeated or reincarnated in ritual acts; in the second, time is observed merely as succession, the irreversible passing of events.

In "Solo a dos voces," as in "El río," the poet's immediate experience of these two distinct, non-verbal levels of reality, which of course are simultaneously present, is continuous with the act of expressing it in words. The poet thus attempts to synchronize the "ritual" of poetizing with the joyous planting and harvesting ritual taking place outside, though as we see, the poet's ritual and offering are not nearly so joyful or efficacious:

> (Sonaja de simientes, poema:
> Enterrar la palabra,
> El grano de fuego,
> En el cuerpo de Ceres
> Tres veces arado;
> Enterrarla en el patio,
> Horadar el cemento
> Con la gota tenaz,
> Con la gota de tinta.
> Para la diosa negra,
> Piedra dormida en la nieve,
> Dibujar un caballo de agua,
> Dibujar en la página
> Un caballo de yerba . . .)

> (Rattle of seeds, poem:/ To bury the word in
> earth,/ The kernel of fire,/ In the body of
> Ceres/ Three times ploughed;/ To bury it in
> the patio,/ Drill through the cement/ With the
> persistent drop,/ With the drop of ink./ For

> the dark goddess,/ Stone asleep in the snow,/
> To sketch a horse of water,/ To scrawl on the page/
> A horse of grass. . .)

The humid earth, the invisible, persistent drop of water in the damp patio, and the droplet of ink on the page, like the river and its corollaries in "El río," evoke the ambivalent properties of water—unceasingly regenerating the land, and also, like the sundial, silently marking the passage of time as it erodes everything in its path or flows endlessly to no end. Here, as in the earlier poem, the poet is concerned with penetrating to the heart of dead matter (the frozen earth, the humid cement, the dried-up words, and the soul, also turned to stone), and planting and nurturing within it the poetic germ.

The analogy of poetic creation to the gestational processes of nature is carried further in the comparison of the dormant, seed-containing earth to the dictionary, a spatial container or universe of inanimate words. It is worth mentioning here, perhaps, Paz's confessed penchant for reading the dictionary, especially J. Corominas's *Diccionario Crítico-Etimológico de la Lengua Castellana*, one of his favorite books and the source of the poem's epigraph: "En ninguna otra lengua occidental son tantas palabras fantasmas" (In no other occidental language are there so many ghost words . . .). The dictionary contains all of the words, but it is the work of all men, not only writers, Paz says, "to link them together so that one of those precarious associations formulates the truth about the world, a relative truth that dissolves as it is read."

Throughout the poem, the play on the sounds, rhythms, and meanings of words evokes the phantasmal, disembodied quality of words referred to in the epigraph, and also relates to what Northrop Frye terms "associative babble" or "poetic etymology," the tendency to associate words similar in sound or sense," which used to be "passed off" as genuine etymology. Though poetic etymology has been discounted, Frye maintains that an analogy between A and B may still be significant "even if the view that A is the source of B is dropped."

We find examples of these kinds of sound/sense associations, which have to do with the mentioned synchronization of the two rituals, first in the verses

> Mundo, mondo,
> Sonaja de semillas semánticas:
> Vírgenes móndigas
> (Mundicas,

Las que llevan el mundum
El día de la procesión),

Mundo mondo, clean world,/ Rattle of
semantic seeds:/ Virgin *móndigas/
Mundicas,/ Those that carry the mundum/*
The day the procession is held)

in which the sound of mundo/mondo/móndigas/mundicas/ produces an
incantatory effect, while their etymological derivations and connotations—
world, earth, purity, cleanness, pruning—allude both to the purity of the
maidens and to the seasonal rituals of pruning the vines and clearing the
fields for planting in anticipation of the earth's renewal in the spring. In a
similar manner, in the words *son*aja, *sem*illas, *sem*ánticas, the connection
between sound and sense is suggested not only in the "associative babble,"
but in genuine etymology as well. We have already seen numerous examples
of Paz's image of the poetic words as the "seed" or "sign," and here the
reference to the rattling and shaking of them suggests the imitation of the
ritual of sifting and winnowing grain, while at the same time the sonorous
rhythms produced by the assonance and the alliterative nasals and sibilants
capture something of the sounds of the festive celebration: "Voces y risas,
baile y panderos", whose purpose, perhaps, is to establish a form of the
"participation mystique" that characterizes such commemorative rituals.

The parallels become more explicit as we find the poet later in the
poem, "A solas con el diccionario" (Alone with the dictionary) shaking the
dry branch of language, and, in a manner of speaking, winnowing the seeds
from the chaff:

Palabras, muchachas, semillas,
Sonidos de guijarros
Sobre la tierra negra y blanca,
Inanimada.

Words, girls, seeds,/ The rattle of pebbles/
On the earth black and white,/ Without life.

The dictionary is envisioned as an inanimate universe with hundreds of black
words (potential seeds) lying inert upon its white pages, concealing another
elusive, invisible reality that resists utterance:

El mundo
No es tortas y pan pintado.
El diccionario
Es un mundo no dicho:
De solsticio (de invierno)
A pascua (de resurrección),
En dirección inversa
A las agujas del cuadrante,
Hay: 'sofisma, símil, selacio, salmo,
Rupestre, rosca, ripio, réprobo,
Rana, Quito, quejido,
Pulque, ponzoña, picotín, peluca . . .'
Desandar el camino,
Volver a la primera letra
En dirección inversa
Al sol,
      Hacia la piedra:
Simiente,
       Gota de energía,
Joya verde
Entre los pechos negros de la diosa.

The world/ Is not all cakes and fancy bread./
The dictionary is a world not spoken:/ From
solstice (the winter one)/ To Easter (the
resurrection)/ In a direction contrary/ To
that of the sundial-marker,/ Occur: 'spiral,
sophism, similar, selachian,/ Rocky, refuse, reprobate, quartern,/
Querulous, Quito, pulque, psalm,/
Pollywog, poison, periwig . . .'/
Retracing the road,/ Going back to the
first letter/ In a direction contrary/
To that of the sun,/ Towards the stone:/
Seed,/ Drop of energy,/ Green jewel/ Between
the dark breasts of the goddess.

The proverb "El mundo/ No es tortas y pan pintado" underlines the idea that the world, although real or given in the phenomenal sense, lacks reality—which must be created. The poet's task as maker is to arrange the words in the dictionary in such a manner that the non-verbal meaning of the universe also becomes intelligible and accessible to us through the medium of the poem.

Reading the words from the dictionary in inverse order to that of the sundial-marker expresses the poet's desire to disrupt the discursive order of language, which inhibits creativity and which, moreover, is based on a lineal conception of time, thus always pointing toward elusive futurity, and to retrace the steps back to the original incarnate word that began all creation. Though seemingly selected from the dictionary at random, the list of words suggests at least a potential unity of sound, images, and meanings which relates to the context of the poem. The connotations of some are easily determined, as in the case of "sofisma," "símil," and "salmo," for instance, which are readily linked to rhetorical language, poetry-making, and flawed reasoning. The others are more elusive, and the reader is challenged to look for possible meaningful associations that fit into this particular section of the poem. "Selacio," which refers to an order of fishes and thus could be associated with the empirical approach to classifying, ordering, and identifying things. "Rupestre," which means rocky, stony, or petrified, could be applied to the condition of the frozen, infertile land and also by analogy to the sterile condition of language. "Rosca" or spiral, evokes the cyclical patterns of the solstices, the continuous circling around a point or center, which in turn connects with "Quito", the name of the South American capital situated on the equator, the imaginary circle drawn around the earth, dividing it into the Northern and Southern hemispheres. "Ripio," "réprobo," and "rana," would appear to have little in common beyond sonority, but here again relationships can be established through their less familiar meanings. "Ripio" denotes refuse or debris, and also refers to "padding," wordiness or "filler" in a piece of writing, to which we could relate "picotín," which I interpret as a variation of "picotero," meaning "parlanchín," senseless chattering or jabbering. "Rana," to be sure, is a croaking frog, but also the term for someone adept at something or "a past master." As a noun, "réprobo" refers to one who is unprincipled or unworthy, and as an adjective, to failure, reproval, or censure, to which we could link "quejido" (querulousness) and a colloquial usage of "peluca" (severe reprimand). Finally, in a similar negative vein, "pulque" and "ponzoña" alike conjure up intoxicating, corruptive, or destructive influences.

Whether or not these, or indeed, any contextual associations are meant to be attached to these words, there seems to be intentional sound-associations through assonance and alliteration similar to what we have seen elsewhere in the poem—a kind of incantation or rhythmic "charm," as Frye put it, that expresses something nonverbal and has to do with the magical power of words. The important point made in the verses quoted above, I believe, is that words do not acquire meaning in isolation, but when they are connected together in meaningful relationships. To quote Frye again, "the poet does not define his words, but establishes their powers by placing them in a great variety of contexts."

In the poem it is clear that to the poetic imagination, alphabetizing and attaching definitions to words in a dictionary is as much a folly of the rational mind as is using the sundial as a device to measure solstices and the movement of time. Both in themselves tell us little about the world of the here-and-now in which we exist. On the other hand, by virtue of the ritual commemoration of solstices and seasons, and through the re-creation of them in poetry, we are able to regain our former rapport with the natural world. As he goes on writing "contra la corriente" (against the current)—an act of purgation—and pruning the dead branches of language, this, it seems to me, is what the poet is attempting to say in the poem, and by "saying" actualize or reproduce it as in the ritual:

> No el movimiento del círculo,
> Maestro de espejismos:
> > La quietud
> En el centro del movimiento.
> No predecir: decir.
> Mundo suspendido en la sombra,
> Mundo mondo, pulido como hueso,
> Decir es mondadura,
> Poda del árbol de los muertos.

> Not the movement of the circle,/ Master of
> mirages:/ The quietude/ At the centre of
> the movement./ Not to foretell: to tell./
> World suspended in the shadow,/ Clean world,
> clean as bone,/ Saying is a paring away,/
> A pruning of the tree of the dead.

Our vision of the world is not as it was in antiquity, yet there remains a memory, something latent perhaps in the language itself, still capable of finding its way into expression:

> (La letra no reposa en la página:
> Memoria la levanta,
> Monumento de viento.
> Y quién recuerda a la memoria,
> Quién la levanta, dónde se implanta?
> Frente de claridad, alumbramiento,
> La memoria es raíz en la tiniebla.)

(The letter does not lie still on the page:/
Memory arouses it,/ Monument of wind./ And who
is the reminder of memory,/ Who raises it, where
is it planted?/ Brow of brightness, the lightening womb,/
Memory is a root in the dark.)

The act of poetizing begins, we recall, in silence and alienation, "en el no
poder decir" (in not being able to say). Though the poet may have made a
tremendous effort to express himself, including, as we have just seen, hand to
hand combat with words, meditation, purgation of the soul, or even perusing
the dictionary, utterance often occurs spontaneously and transiently, as
described in "Semillas para un himno" (Seeds for a Psalm).

Infrecuentes
    Instantáneas
No llegan siempre en forma de palabras
Brota una espiga de unos labios
Una forma veloz abre las alas
        Imprevistas
Instantáneas
Como en la infancia cuando decíamos "ahí viene un barco
    cargado de . . ."
Y brotaba instantánea imprevista la palabra convocada
    Pez
      Álamo
        Colibrí
Y así ahora de mi frente zarpa un barco cargado de iniciales
Ávidas de encarnar en imágenes
        Instantáneas
Imprevistas cifras del mundo
La luz se abre en las terrazas del mediodía
Se interna en el bosque como una sonámbula
Penetra en el cuerpo dormido del agua

Por un instante están los nombres habitados

Seldom/ Sudden/ They do not always arrive in the form
of words/ A spike of grain bursts from some lips/
A swift form opens its wings/ Unforeseen/ Sudden/
As in early childhood when we said "here comes a ship
with a/ load of. . ."/ Fish/ Willow/ Humming-bird/
And so now from my head sails a ship with a load of

initials/ Avid for incarnation in images/ Sudden/
Unforeseen ciphers of the world/ Light opens on the
terraces of noon/ Enters the forest like a sleep-
walker/ Penetrates the sleeping body of the water/
For a moment life quickens in the names

The luminous beauty and vivacity of this poem, the title poem of a collection
of some twenty poems of similar content, typifies what M. H. Abrams called
the "vitalism" of the Romantic writers: "the celebration of that which lives,
moves, and evolves by an internal energy over whatever is lifeless, inert, and
unchanging." The images of spaciousness and the diaphanous light of the
sun at zenith are appropriate to this illuminated state of the creative act. The
poetic experience, like other epiphanic experiences, is a timeless moment
charged with revelation of the oneness of everything. And though these
fleeting moments of vision do not always present themselves in the form of
words, the poet, always receptive to their manifestation, is capable of
grasping them when they do come and embodying them in images even as
they vanish: "pez," "álamo," "colibrí"—the usual natural entities Paz
associates with physical and spiritual life.

We may also compare this idea of inhabiting objects with names
with a phenomenon peculiar to the creative process characteristic of the
"primitive" mythopoeic mentality, to which Ernst Cassirer refers as the
"hypostatization of the word," a juncture where perception is reduced to a
fixed point and the word is transformed into concrete image—the emerging
and vanishing image of a "momentary god." This expression, as Cassirer
shows, does not refer to mythico-religious entities as such, but rather to an
instantaneous mental content, the "objectification" of something that exists
only in one intense moment of experience. For this particular moment,
image and object are indissolubly merged. In mythic thinking, Cassirer
writes, "Whatever has been fixed by a name, henceforth is not only real, but
is Reality."

We find an even better example of this instantaneous, compressed
mode of perception and the "fixing" of objects or experiences with names in
"Tumba del poeta" (Tomb of the Poet). The distance or tension that exists
between the poet and the external world is exhibited in the resistant opacity
and inertia of physical objects, which he strives to overcome by naming:

Las cosas anegadas en sus nombres
Decirlas con los ojos
                              En un allá no sé donde
Clavarlas
          Lámpara lápiz retrato

                Esto que veo
                            Clavarlo
                Como un templo vivo
                                Plantarlo
                Como un árbol
                            Un dios
                Coronarlo
                            Con un nombre
                                    Inmortal

                Things drowned in their names/ To say them with the
                eyes/ In a beyond I cannot tell where/ Nail them
                down/ Lamp pencil portrait/ This that I see/ To
                nail it down/ Like a living temple/ Plant it/ Like
                a tree/ A god/ Crown it/ With a name/ Immortal

With the sudden irruption of the image into the poet's consciousness, everything—the visible and the invisible—is apprehended in its entirety; what was opaque and distant now becomes transparent and accessible; "un allá" is instantaneously transformed into "un aquí:"

                Una fracción de segundo
                                    Lámpara lápiz retrato
                En un aquí no sé donde
                                    Un nombre
                Comienza
                            Asirlo plantarlo decirlo
                Como un bosque pensante
                                    Encarnarlo
                Un linaje comienza
                                En un nombre
                Un adán
                            Como un templo vivo
                Nombre sin sombra
                                Clavado
                Como un dios
                            En este aquí sin donde
                ¡Lenguaje!
                            Acabo en su comienzo
                En esto que digo
                            Acabo

SER
    Sombra de un nombre instantáneo
NUNCA SABRE MI DESENLACE

A second's fraction/ Lamp pencil portrait/
In a here I cannot tell where/ A name/ Begins/
Seize on it, plant, say it/ Like a wood that
thinks/ Flesh it/ A lineage begins/ In a name/
An adam/ Like a living temple/ Name without
shadow/ Nailed/ Like a god/ In this here-without-where/
Speech!/ I cease in its beginning/ In this
that I say/ I cease/ TO BE/ Shadow of an intantaneous
name/ I SHALL NEVER KNOW MY BOND'S UNDOING

In Cassirer's view, utterance occurs when the tension between inner and outer reality is released by a "spark that somehow jumps across," the equivalent of which we find in Paz, I believe, in the phenomenon of inspiration which impells the poet to go beyond himself, to express in an image the reality of the objects that surround him, and to "throw" himself into being. And the idea that man himself is a process, a constant state of metamorphosis or becoming, rather than a static, given entity, is dramatically underlined in the final verses of the poem, the last written as an epitaph.

To Paz, the highest value of the poetic image is its redemptive and unifying power. "El tiempo mismo" (Time Itself) is representative of the numerous poems in which the wasteland is instantly regenerated, and in which we, too, are transfigured to become "others" by virtue of the poetic revelation.

The poem begins with the kind of depressing nocturnal scene which we have come to associate with Paz's vision of the modern city. While the natural world reposes in pre-dawn darkness and regenerates its vital forces, Mexico City is in constant motion, restlessly probing its own labyrinthine vastness:

    Es la ciudad en torno de su sombra
    Buscando siempre buscándose
    Perdida en su propia inmensidad
    Sin alcanzarse nunca
                  Ni poder salir de sí misma

    It is the city turning about in its shadow/
    Searching, always seeking itself/ Lost in

its own immensity/ Without ever finding
itself/ Nor can it escape from itself

Isolated sights, sounds, and the physical presence of the city leave their
imprint upon the poet's consciousness; but even while all of this street
activity reinforces his awareness of being alive; "¡Qué extraño es saberse
vivo!" (How strange it is to know you are alive!), nothing can alter the
awesome certainty that "Todos vamos a morir/ ¿Sabemos algo más?" (We are
all going to die/ Do we know anything else?).

Streetcars bearing evocative indigenous names (Tacuba, Tacubaya,
Xochimilco, Coyacán) depart two by two from the Zócalo, "la plaza más
grande que la noche" (the plaza that is bigger than the night), ferrying
passengers across the sprawling city to the suburbs. For the poet, the
streetcar journey is an occasion for contemplation of the dawn sky and the
tree-lined, cobblestone streets, orchards, and bougainvillae-covered walls
that managed to survive urbanization. It is in the midst of these reflections
that the poetic word suddenly emerges unbidden:

Mar de arriba

Nubes del altiplano ¿dónde está el otro mar?

Maestras de los ojos

Nubes

Arquitectos de silencio

Y de pronto sin más porque sí

La palabra

Alabastro

Esbelta transparencia no llamada

Haría música con ella

Castillos en el aire

No hiciste nada

Alabastro

Sin flor ni aroma

Tallo

Sin sangre ni savia

Blancura cortada

Garganta sólo garganta

Canto sin pies ni cabeza

The sea above/ Clouds over the high plains
Where is the other sea?/ Teachers for the eyes/
Clouds/ Architects of silence/ And suddenly

> without warning/ The word/ Alabaster/ Fleeting
> transparency unsolicited/ I would make music
> with it/ Castles in the air/ You didn't do
> anything/ Alabaster/ Without flower or fragrance/
> Without blood or sap/ A creamy whiteness/ Throat
> all throat/ Song without feet or head

In one flash of insight, the poet apprehends that although all things pass, there is continuance in time as our personal, finite time falls into harmony with the eternal rhythms of the universe:

> Hoy estoy vivo y sin nostalgia
> La noche fluye
>   La ciudad fluye
> Yo escribo sobre la página que fluye
> Transcurro con las palabras que transcurren
> Conmigo no empezó el mundo
> No ha de acabar conmigo
>   Soy
> Un latido en el río de latidos

> Today I am alive and without nostalgia/ The
> night flows/ The city flows/ I write on a
> page that flows/ I flow along with the words'
> flowing/ The world did not begin with me/
> It will not end with me/ I am but a heartbeat
> in the river of heartbeats

In "El río", we recall, the poet's inability to verbalize his experience was analogous to a struggle against the current; but here expression is achieved, and with it the consciousness of the one in the all endlessly flowing into each other. Because of this momentary revelation of the eternal in the temporal and the unity and continuity of all things, the poet is now able to perceive the ordinary external world with different eyes:

> Hoy en la tarde desde un puente
> Vi al sol entrar en las aguas del río
> Todo estaba en llamas
> Ardían las estatuas las casas los pórticos
> En los jardines pétreos racimos femeninos
> Lingotes de luz líquida

Frescura de vasijas solares
Un follaje de chispas la alameda
El agua horizontal inmóvil
Bajo los cielos y los mundos incendiados
Cada gota de agua
                    Un ojo fijo
El peso de la enorme hermosura
Sobre cada pupila abierta
Realidad suspendida
                         En el tallo del tiempo
La belleza no pesa
                    Reflejo sosegado
Tiempo y belleza son lo mismo
                         Luz y agua
Mirada que sostiene a la hermosura
Tiempo que se embelesa en la mirada
Mundo sin peso
                    Si el hombre pesa
¿No basta la hermosur?

Today in the afternoon from a bridge/ I saw the
sun enter the river/ Everything was aflame/
Statues, houses, colonnades all burning/ In the
gardens feminine clusters turned to stone/ Ingots
of liquid light/ Purity of solar vessels/ The alameda
a foliage of sparks/ The water horizontal and
immobile/ Beneath the heavens and worlds in flames/
Each drop of water/ A fixed eye/ The weight of an
enormous beauty/ Resting upon each staring eye/
Reality suspended/ On a stalk of time/ Beauty is weight-
lessness/Quiescent reflection/ Time and beauty
are one and the same/ Light and water/ Beauty sustained
by a glance/ Time enraptured in the glance/
Weightless world/ If man is weight/ Isn't beauty
alone enough?

The entire city, whose meaningless activity earlier had engendered feelings
of angst, has been redeemed by an imaginative apocalypse, and is now
envisioned as "glowing with the fires of heaven" as a radiant sun transmutes
the river, houses, trees, and statues into gold. The alchemical imagery of this
passage admirably conveys the idea of the correspondent purification and

spiritualization of the human soul and the physical world. The extended metaphor of the fixed eye of the sun as it is reflected upon the water registers simultaneously the suspension of time, a sense of wonder and beauty, and a new mode of consciousness, which is produced, as in the Romantic mode, by a "perceptual transvaluation" or "alteration of the eye." In the act of perceiving, the object seen with the physical eye is transformed by the inward eye. Behind ordinary, quotidian appearances, the poet perceives a world momentarily charged with revelation in which times past, present, and future coalesce:

>   Tal vez no pasa el tiempo
>   Pasan imágenes de tiempo
>   Si no vuelven las horas vuelven las presencias
>   En esta vida hay otra vida
>   La higuera aquella volverá esta noche
>   Esta noche regresan otras noches
>   . . .
>
>   No son las mismas horas
>   Otras
>   Son otras siempre y son la misma
>   Entran y nos expulsan de nosotros
>   Con nuestros ojos ven lo que no ven los ojos
>   Dentro del tiempo hay otro tiempo
>   Quieto
>   Sin horas ni peso ni sombra
>   Sin pasado o futuro
>   Sólo vivo
>   Como el viejo del banco
>   Unimismado idéntico perpetuo
>   Nunca lo vemos Es la transparencia

Perhaps time does not pass/ Only images of time pass/ If the hours do not return presences do/ In this life there is another life/ That fig tree will return tonight/ Tonight brings back other nights/ . . . It is not the same hours/ Others/ They are always others and the same/ They enter and force us outside ourselves/ With our eyes they see what eyes do not see/ Within time there is another time/ Quietude/ Without hours or body or shadow/ Without past or

future/ But alive/ Like the old man on the bench/
Self-contained perpetual identity/ We never see it
It is transparency

Somewhat in the manner of Eliot's "pattern of timeless moments in time," the joy and ecstasy of this moment of fulfillment calls up other such moments from the past: the fig tree in the garden of the poet's childhood home, long since destroyed, again becomes a living presence. Relinquishing selfhood and the illusions of the temporal world, the poet finds the true self, the center unbound by time and space, eternally present.

As Paz himself has pointed out, and as I have attempted to demonstrate here, such mystical revelations are particularly resistant to utterance; and it is only in rare moments of inspiration that the poet can "fix" his immediate experience with a name—thus conferring upon it not only realness but reality as well. The poetic word in this sense is the *logos*—not in terms of the usual association with logic and reason, but in the mythic sense of the light and the life, the primordial creative and redemptive power emanating from "what was said." Expression is revelation and revelation is communion.

JAIME ALAZRAKI

Octavio Paz—Poetry as Coded Silence

For Octavio Paz modern poetry is criticism: "Since *Une saison en enfer*," he has written, "our great poets have made out of the negation of poetry the highest form of poetry: their poems are criticism of the poetic experience, of language and meaning, of the poem itself. The poetic word is sustained by the negation of the word." This theme embraces much of Paz's own poetry, and silence, which accompanies this criticism of the word as a poetic theme and as a discursive meditation, is a sort of isobar which runs through the length of his entire work. It is not an isolated theme, but a long reflection spreading throughout his oeuvre. Furthermore, this reflection itself, in prose or in verse, is undertaken so that silence and its underlying meanings may be evoked. Such is the task of the poet: "Enamored of silence, the poet has no choice but to speak." In Paz this theme is a manifold image. Stated in its most elementary meaning, silence is the state before the word, the seminal point of the poem, the empty space which precedes writing: "The image is a desperate device against the silence which invades us each time we try to express the terrible experience of that which surrounds us. The poem is language in tension: in the extreme of being and in being up to the extreme. Extremes of the word and extreme words, turned in upon their own entrails, showing the reverse of speech: silence and non-meaning."

From *Octavio Paz: Homage to the Poet*, edited by Kosrof Chantikian, © 1980 by Kosrof Chantikian and KOSMOS.

147

Here his understanding of silence does not differ from the rather limited definition of Max Picard: "Not until speech comes out of silence does silence come out of pre-creation into creation, out of the prehistoric into the history of man, into close relationship with man, becoming part of man and a lawful part of speech. But speech is more than silence, because truth is first expressed concretely by speech, not by silence." Silence then, understood as a negative dimension: as non-meaning, as an opening toward the word, as the margin of the poem:

> El mundo cede y se desploma
> como metal al fuego.
> Entre mis ruinas me levanto,
> solo, desnudo, despojado,
> sobre la roca inmensa del silencio,
> como un solitario combatiente
> contra invisibles huestes
>
> (The world gives way and collapses
> like metal in fire.
> In the midst of my ruins I rise up
> alone, naked, forsaken
> on this vast rock of silence
> like a solitary fighter
> against invisible armies).

The poetic act is a struggle against silence and the poet seeks to overcome it with words: "By a path which in its own way, is negative, the poet reaches the edge of language. And this edge is called silence, blank page. A silence which is like a lake, a smooth and compact surface. Down below, submerged, words wait. And one must descend, go to the bottom, be quiet, wait. Sterility precedes inspiration, as emptiness precedes plenitude. The poetic word springs up after ages of drought":

> Dios mudo, que al silencio del hombre que pregunta
>   contestas
>   sólo con silencio que ahoga
>
> (Mute God, who to humanity's questioning silence you
>   answer
>   only with a suffocating silence).

El hombre está habitado por silencio y vacío.
¿Cómo saciar esta hambre
cómo acallar y poblar su vacío?

(Humankind is haunted by silence and emptiness.
How to satisfy this hunger,
How to ease and fill this emptiness?)

And especially in "Visitas" (Visitors) from *El girasol (Sunflower)* and in "El sitiado" (The Besieged) from *¿Águila o sol? (Eagle or Sun?):*

Del silencio brota un árbol de música.
Del árbol cuelgan todas las palabras hermosas,
que brillan, maduran, caen.

(From silence sprouts a tree of music.
From this tree hangs every beautiful word,
which shines, ripens, falls).

A mi derecha no hay nada. El silencio y la soledad extienden
sus llanuras. ¡Oh mundo por poblar, hoja en blanco!
(To my right there is nothing. Silence and solitude spread
out their plains. Oh, world to fill, blank leaf!)

But this meaning of silence as prelude to the word, as emptiness the poet must fill, already alternates from the beginning of his work with a conflicting notion: "Silence itself," Paz says in *The Bow and the Lyre*, "is inhabited by signs." In his work there appear simultaneously two very different faces of poetry: an almost absolute faith in the word—"The word is humankind itself. We are made of words. They are our only reality or at least, the only testimony of our reality. We cannot escape from language", and an equally absolute suspicion of the word—"Poetic activity is born of desperation in the face of the impotence of the word and culminates in the recognition of the omnipotence of silence." In a way, Paz's work summarizes these two moments in the history of European poetry: from the absolute sovereignty of the word to its impotence and sterility. Paz finds an answer to this apparent conflict between word and silence in Eastern thought:

The Western world is the world of "this or that"; the Eastern, of "this and that" and even of "this is that." In the most ancient Upanishad the principle of the identity of contraries is clearly asserted: "You are woman. You are man. You are boy and also girl . . ." Taoism shows the same tendencies. . . .Chuang Tzu explains the functional and relative character of contraries in this way: "There is nothing that is not this; there is nothing that is not that. Such is the doctrine of the interdependence of this and that. Life is life in relation to death. And vice versa. Affirmation is affirmation in relation to negation. And vice versa. Therefore, if one leans on this, it would have to deny that. But this possesses its affirmation and its negation and also engenders its this and its that. So the true sage puts aside the this and the that and takes refuge in Tao."

In the same chapter of *The Bow and the Lyre*, Paz quotes the *Tao Te Ching*: "The Tao that can be named / is not the eternal Tao; / The Name that can be said / is not the eternal Name"—and comments: "The condemnation of words stems from the inability of language to transcend the world of relative and interdependent contraries, of the this in relation to the that . . . All knowledge would then be reduced to knowing knowledge is impossible. Again and again the texts of Eastern tradition delight in this kind of ambiguity. The doctrine is resolved into silence." And further on: "The same thing happens in Zen Buddhism, a doctrine which is resolved in paradox and silence." Nevertheless, that worship of silence in Eastern thought (the god of the *Svetasvatara Upanishad* governs the works of silence and reveals its radiant beauty and perfection in the harmony of silence) has been transmitted through images and texts, through a language which makes from the negation of language its most powerful word. A language which nears poetry and in whose paradoxical reality Paz finds a road for his Poetry: "Chuang Tzu says that the sage 'preaches the doctrine without words.' . . . The wordless preaching to which the Chinese Philosopher alludes is not that of example but of a language which is something more than language: word which says the unsayable. Although Chuang Tzu never thought of poetry as a language capable of transcending the meaning of this and that and saying the unsayable, his reasoning cannot be separated from images, word games and other poetic forms. Poetry and thought are interwoven in Chuang Tzu to form a single fabric, a single unique material . . . The same must be said of other doctrines. Thanks to the poetic image. Taoist, Hindu and Buddhist thought become comprehensible". Paz refers to a language such that through it language is transcended in order to become presence, incommunicable image, spoken silence. Or as he puts it: A language in which "names and things fuse and are the same: poetry, realm where naming is being. The image says the unsayable. We must return to language in order to see how the image can say that which language, by its very nature, seems incapable of saying".

From his earliest poems Paz searches for a language in which "naming is being," a language which takes refuge in silence and from its transparency rediscovers the world:

> Tengo que hablaros de ella:
> de un metal encondido,
> de una hierba sedienta,
> del silencio compacto de un arbusto;
> del ímpetu invisible
> que hace crecer las cosas,
> de lo que sólo vive
> como sangre y aliento.
> Del silencio del mundo,
> del tumulto del mundo.
>
> (I must speak of her
> of a hidden metal,
> of a parched grass,
> of the dense silence of a shrub;
> of the invisible impulse
> which makes things grow,
> of that which only lives
> like blood and breath.
> Of the world's silence,
> Of the world's uproar.)

The encounter with the Word is the encounter with silence "[un] canto/cantando en el silencio deslumbrado" (a song/sung in dazzling silence)—which from its nothingness says "la plenitud de lo vivo" (the fullness of living):

> Canta, desde su sombra
> —y más, desde su nada—el alma.
> Desnudo de su nombre canta el ser,
> en el hechizo de existir suspenso,
> de su propio cantar enamorado.
> . . .
> Es el secreto mediodía.
> El alma canta, cara al cielo,

y sueña en otro canto,
sólo vibrante luz,
plenitud silenciosa de lo vivo.

(The soul, from its shadow
—and even from its nothingness—sings.
Stripped of its name, the being sings,
in the spell of suspended existence,
of its own enamored song
. . .
It is the hidden afternoon.
The soul sings, facing the sky,
and dreams of another song,
vibrant light,
silent fullness of living.)

For Paz silence and plenitude coalesce and from this fusion the word emerges as a footprint of silence. Poetry does not dwell in words from which the poem is made, but in that space carved by words: "brota del fondo del silencio / otro silencio." In his essay on the haiku, Paz discusses some examples from Yamazaki Sokan (1465–1553) and compares the original haiku: "Summer moon / if you put a handle on it / a fan!" with Antonio Machado's paraphrase in *Nuevas canciones (New Songs)*: "A una japonesa / le dijo Sokan: / con la luna blanca / te abanicarás, / con la luna blanca / a orillas del mar" (To a Japanese woman / Sokan said: / with the white moon / you will fan yourself / with the white moon / at the seashore), and adds: "In spite of the fact that one of his virtues was innuendo, in this case Machado did not resist the very Hispanic and Hispanic American tendency for explication and reiteration. In his paraphrase the suggestion has disappeared, that part of the poem *not said* in which poetry truly lies." Perhaps this footnote, as a marginal commentary, is the most precise description of the meaning of poetry as a search in the meanders and spaces of silence. The first poems of *Libertad bajo palabra (Liberty on Parole)* exalt this silence, which is sometimes confused with a hermeticism through which modern poetry, and in particular French poetry, attempts to grasp the ungraspable, to express a signified which escapes the signifiers of language. In Paz, this search is a dialogue with silence from the very beginning of his poetic work, a path leading from "one silence to another": "desembocamos al silencio / en donde los silencios enmudecen" (we flow into silence / where silence says nothing) states the last line of "Silencio" in *Condición de nube (Cloud Condition*, 1944). At this stage of his poetry, the theme still appears as the first formulation of a true poetic of silence, as a program his later work will fully carry through:

¿Cómo decir los nombres, las estrellas,
los albos pájaros de los pianos nocturnos
y el obelisco del silencio?
. . .
¿Cómo decir, camelia,
la menos flor entre las flores,
Cómo decir tus blancas geometrías?
¿Cómo decir, oh Sueño, tu silencio en voces?

(How to speak of these names, these stars,
the white birds of evening pianos
and the obelisk of silence?
. . .
How to say camellia,
the least flower among flowers,
how to say your geometries of whiteness?
How to speak of, oh Dream, your silence in voices?)

Words are not an alternative to silence for Paz, but a transgression against words themselves. "It is not about the destruction of language, but an operation aimed at revealing the reverse of language, the other side of signs." This idea appears formulated with still greater clarity in his essay on Tantric art: "The sign, whatever it may be, has the property of taking us beyond, always beyond. A perpetual *toward* . . . that is never a here. What writing says is *beyond the written*, and what Tantric painting presents is not in it. Where the poem ends, poetry begins; the presence is not the painted signs we see, but that which the signs invoke." That *toward* . . . and that beyond the written is a space in whose boundaries the poem is resolved in the wake which words leave: a silence, yes, but different from that which precedes writing. The first is an empty space, amorphous, a void; the second is also a void, but full of suggestions: an empty space clipped by words which communicates from its invisible substance. The silence which precedes the poem is a sterile chaos; the silence which the poem depicts is a hole peopled by inaudible voices which, in the final analysis, are the true voices of poetry. "Piedra nativa" (Native Stone) traces this distance between the two silences:

Como las piedras del Principio
Como el principio de la Piedra
Como al Principio piedra contra piedra
Los fastos de la noche:
El poema todavía sin rostro

El bosque todavía sin árboles
Los cantos todavía sin nombre

Mas ya la luz irrumpe con pasos de leopardo
Y la palabra se levanta ondula cae
Y es una larga herida y un silencio sin mácula.

(Like stones from the Beginning
Like the beginning of Stone
Like stone against stone at the Beginning
The chronicles of the night:
Poem without a face yet
Forest without trees yet
Songs without names yet

But the light now bursts with leopard steps
And the word rises quivers falls
And is a long wound and a flawless silence).

Even more explicitly, the prose poem "Trabajos del poeta" (Works of the Poet) confronts these two silences and attempts to describe the "palctadas del silencio cayendo en el silencio" (the strokes of silence falling into silence). A good number of the poems which follow, in *Libertad bajo palabra*, are an effort to hear this silence which the poem inscribes on words. "El río" (The River), for example, opens long "galleries" of reasoning: "un río de tinta" (a river of ink), "un discurso incomprensible y jadeante, un tartamudeo de aguas y piedras batallando, su historia" (an incomprehensible and panting speech, a stuttering of waters and battling stones, its history). This history is a "larga palabra que no acaba nunca" (long word which never ends): "Es una explanada desierta el poema, lo dicho no está dicho, lo no dicho es indecible" (The poem is a deserted esplanade, what has been said no longer stands, what has not been said is unsayable). The poem celebrates its own failure: "que las palabras depongan armas y sea el poema una sola palabra entretejida, un resplandor implacable que avanza" (that words may lay down their arms and the poem be a single intertwining word, a relentless splendor advancing), but this failure is the poem's major triumph because this "long word which never ends" is like a watermark in the poem ("voices of water," one of the poems in Vuelta will say) which from silence names the unnameable:

> y sea todo como la llama que se esculpe y se hiela en la
>   roca de entrañas transparentes,

duro fulgor resuelto ya en cristal y claridad pacífica.

Y el río remonta su curso, repliega sus velas, recoge sus
    imágenes y se interna en sí mismo.

(and may everything be like a flame that sculpts itself
    and freezes into the rock of transparent bowels
harsh glow already firm in crystal and peaceful clarity

And the river goes back upstream, folds its sails, picks
    up its images and curls into itself).

In the final book of Libertad bajo palabra—*La estación violenta (The Violent Season)*—"Himno entre ruinas"—(Hymn Among the Ruins), the first poem, asks: "dónde desenterrar la palabra" (where are we to unearth the word?); the next to the last poem of this collection, "El cántaro roto" (The Broken Pitcher) tries to answer. It is an answer that goes back "hacia atrás, hacia la fuente, . . . siglos arriba / más allá de la infancia, más allá del comienzo, más allá de las aguas del bautismo" (backwards, toward the source, . . . centuries upstream / beyond childhood, beyond the beginning, beyond the baptismal waters), and toward the end urges: *hay que desenterrar la palabra perdida (we must unearth the lost word)*. But between this assertion and the question the poem runs like the imminence of an absent word, like a word incarnated in that silence which for Paz has more and more become the residence of poetry. This lost word does not appear in the poem as a physical presence because it is more than the sum of its words—it is what preceeded the words—but without naming it the poem names it, or at least it names one of its many faces.

In *Piedra de sol (Sun Stone)* this word is all words, "todos los nombres son un solo nombre" (all names are one name), a word which does not come to an end, like the poem itself which through the last six lines repeating the first six and together with the final colon suggest a circular reading of the poem. But in addition, this silence which leaves the poem unfinished is an invitation to the poetry inscribed in the poem. The poem continues in the reader. It is not a circle closing on itself, but a spiral which opens up. In "Fable" Paz intuits a "palabra inmensa / como un sol" (word as large / as a sin), a primeval word which contains all words. *Piedra de sol* is this word which speaks from the silence that confronts the reader. Word-silence which neither comments on nor summarizes itself. Not because of its extension (the poem) or the cosmic scope of its theme, but because the poetic experience lies in that encounter between the silence that comes after the reading of the poem and the silence of the reader. The one penetrates the other: one fertilizes the other, and from this fusion (a dialogue similar to lovemaking) emerges a meaning present neither in language nor even in the text of the poem. An experience which comes close to an illumination because the poem, when it hits its target, attains the impossible, blending language and silence, consciousness and innocence, reality and unreality: "Poetic illumination . . . consists of returning to the silence from which the poem began, only now weighed down with meaning." Paz alludes to this silence when he asks toward the end of *Piedra de sol*:

>   . . . y el silencio
> que se cubre de signos, el silencio
> que dice sin decir, ¿no dice nada?,
> ¿no son nada los gritos de los hombres?

>   (. . . and the silence
> which covers itself with signs, the silence
> which says without saying, does it say nothing?
> Are the cries of humanity nothing?)

Throughout the poem this silence curdles in images—words that are miniatures of the word, tiny mirrors where the poem folds over its own image—but the notion they convey escapes our cognition. If what "we really know is not reality, but that part of reality which can be reduced to language and concepts," poetic knowledge coins its own language by means of images and through them it can free itself from the tyranny of words and transcend them:

>   escritura del mar sobre el basalto,
> escritura del viento en el desierto
> testamento del sol, granada, espiga.

>   (writing of the sea on basalt,
> writing of the wind in the desert,
> testament of the sun, pomegranate, ear of corn.)

They are images of woman, indeed, but also images of the world, in the same way that the lines which follow—"todos los nombres son un solo nombre, / todos los rostros son un solo rostro, / todos los siglos son un solo instante" (all names are one name, / all faces a single face, / all centuries an instant)—are a cry for "our lost unity" and also images that offend scandalously the common sense of our consciousness, that disrupt the order and precisions set by logic to leave us facing a timeless time and an extraterritorial territory. What poetry proposes is no different than what Buddhism seeks: "The end of relations, the abolition of dialectics—a silence that is not the dissolution of language, but its *resolution.*" For Paz religion and poetry are separated by a thin wall. He has written extensively on this theme in *The Bow and the Lyre* and more recently in *Los hijos del limo (Children of the Mire)*: "Shelly's atheism is a religious passion. . . . In the Middle Ages poetry was the servant of religion; but in the Romantic Age, it is the true religion, the fountainhead of the Holy Scriptures. . . . And because poetry remains we can continue to read the Vedas and Bibles, not as religious but as poetic texts. . . . 'The Religions of all Nations are derived from each Nation's different reception of the Poetic Genius.'" Nevertheless, there is a difference between mysticism and poetry, though that difference may be the fulcrum common to both: at the end of the religious text God awaits as a revelation that the Psalm or the Veda brings forth; at the end of the poetic text a silence awaits like an "imminence of a revelation which does not occur." The religious text rests on the certainty of faith; the poetic text makes its faith out of uncertainty; religion is surrender, poetry, rapture; "Mysticism is an immersion in the absolute; poetry is an expression of the absolute or of the rupturing attempt to reach it".

After *Libertad bajo palabra*, a good part of Octavio Paz's poetry is an exploration through a timeless time and through a territory without space in which the geography of silence is found. In *Salamandra* that effort to define the indefinable and to touch silence continues through new stations of the same journey—stopovers that bring us nearer to the sought destination, ascents through "thought which becomes rusty / and gangrenous writing" toward "the silence of the sun" from which the Word glows:

> Los nombres no son nombres
> No dicen lo que dicen
> Yo he de decir lo que no dicen
> Yo he de decir lo que dicen.

> (Names are not names
> They do not say what they say
> I will say what they do not say
> I will say what they say).

In the poem dedicated to Cernuda, Paz returns to the notion that reading a poem is a creative (or re-creative) exercise in which the poem and

the reader exchange their silences in a symbiotic act from whose alchemy
true poetry is born:

> Con letra clara el poeta escribe
> Sus verdades oscuras
> > Sus palabras
> No son un monumento público
> Ni la Guía del camino recto
> Nacieron del silencio
> Se abren sobre tallos de silencio
> Las contemplamos en silencio
> Verdad y error
> > Una sola verdad
> Realidad y deseo
> > Una sola substancia
> Resuelta en manantial de transparencias

> (With clear handwriting the Poet writes
> His obscure truths
> > His words
> Are not a public monument
> Nor Guide to the true way
> Born out of silence
> They open up on stems of silence
> We contemplate them in silence
> Truth and error
> > A single truth
> Reality and desire
> > A single substance
> Resolved into a fountain of transparencies).

The next two poems—"La palabra escrita" (The word written) and
"La palabra dicha" (The word spoken)—are new meditations concerning the
problem of the word. The last two lines of "The word spoken" present a very
tight synthesis of two central notions of Paz's poetic thought: the vision of
poetry as a return from the language of science to the language of
innocence—"olvidar lo que sabemos" (to forget what we know)—and the
conception of silence as the firmest territory of the word ("thought of
smoke"):

Inocencia y no ciencia:
Para hablar aprende a callar.

(Innocence and not science
To speak learn to keep quiet).

One can understand that to Vasconcelos' warnings in "The Same Time" ("Dedicate yourself to philosophy") and to Ortega y Gasset's advice ("Learn German / And begin to think"), Paz would reply: "Un día sabré menos y abriré los ojos" (One day I will know less and open my eyes) and especially "Yo no escribo para matar al tiempo / Ni para revivirlo / Escribo para que me viva" (I do not write to kill time / Nor to relive it / I write so that it will live me).

In another poem, "Noche en claro" (Clear night), the poem is "gateway" and "bridge" and a river flowing by the other shore: "el río de los siglos, el río de los astros" (the river of centuries, the river of signs, the river of stars) and between this constellation of signs flows the "escritura silencio que canta" (writing—silence which sings). Woman is an image of the world, or rather, woman is the world which in turn is the song through which poetry resolves itself into silence:

. . .
Pero tu sexo es innombrable
La otra cara del ser
La otra cara del tiempo
El revés de la vida
Aquí cesa todo discurso
Aquí la belleza no es legible
Aquí la presencia se vuelve terrible
Replegada en sí misma la Presencia es vacío
Lo visible es invisible
Aquí se hace visible lo invisible
Aquí la estrella es negra
La luz es sombra luz la sombra
Aquí el tiempo se para
Los cuatro puntos cardinales se tocan
Es el lugar solitario el lugar de la cita

(. . .
But your sex is unnameable
The other face of being

The other face of time
The other side of life
All talk stops here
Beauty is no longer legible
Presence becomes terrifying
Fallen back on itself Presence is emptiness
The visible is invisible
Here the invisible is made visible
Here the star is black
Light is shadow light shadow
Time stops here
The four cardinal points touch
It is the secluded place the place of rendezvous).

The dominant theme of *Salamandra* is woman and the mystery of love. But woman is the natural world recovered, and love, the path of return to that world, buried by the mechanics of life and chattering: "We moderns, incapable of innocence, born in a society that makes us naturally artificial and that has stripped us of our human value in order to convert us into commodities, search vainly for lost humanity, for innocent humanity. All serious attempts of our culture, from the end of the eighteenth century, are directed toward recovering it, to dreaming it." Paz has said that in his adolescence the reading of Breton's *L'amour fou* and Blake's *The Marriage of Heaven and Hell* opened the doors of modern poetry for him like "an art of love" that later "life and the East have corroborated": the beloved woman as the way which leads to that time of innocence and human value; "the analogy, or rather, the identity between the loved one and nature." "The couple is time recaptured, time before time . . . Woman is a bridge, place of reconciliation between the natural and human worlds. She is language taking shape, revelation incarnate." Poetry emerges thus as a dialogue between the tangible language of the loved woman and the signs of the poem's language:

Te hablaré un lenguaje de piedra
(Respondes con un monosílabo verde)
Te hablaré un lenguaje de nieve
(Respondes con un abanico de abejas)
Te hablaré un lenguaje de agua
(Respondes con una canoa de relámpagos)
Te hablaré un lenguaje de sangre
(Respondes con una torre de pájaros)

(I will speak to you in a language of stone
[You reply with a green syllable]
I will speak to you in a language of snow
[You reply with a fan of bees]
I will speak to you in a language of water
[You reply with a canoe of lightning]
I will speak to you in a language of blood
[You reply with a tower of birds]).

The language of the poet—stone, snow, water, blood—stirs up a multitude of suggestions, but the attribute common to these four images is their condition of silence. There is a clear opposition between the sobriety of these substances (in their solid colors and in their restrained movement) and the exuberance of the images of the woman's language (intense and mottled colors, rapid and lively movements). In the poet's language there are elementary materials; in the language of woman there are creatures (birds, bees) and elementary phenomena (lightning, greenness). The first language lives in its silence; the second is inhabited by a song. The two, however, evoke and invoke a natural world in which human consciousness is absent except in the text itself that inscribes the poem. The poem, whose theme is an interwining of two languages in whose dialogue love speaks, is also "articulation of the duality consciousness/innocence" in whose synthesis Paz sees the final mission of poetry. The poem which began as a dialogue between man and woman reunited in love ends as a dialogue between that primordial world of nature (innocence) and that artificial world of consciousness (language) reunited in the poem. Words mute, silence speaks. Love whose nature is silence ascends to the text of the poem. The text crystalizes silence. This magic is called poetry.

But it is in *Ladera Este* where the perception of this theme reaches its fullest moment, and the questions set forth throughout his entire work are resolved in three of the most lucid and concentrated poems of the collection: "Letter to León Felipe," "Reading John Cage" and *Blanco*. "Letter to León Felipe," besides being a live díalogue with the Spanish Poet, is a reformulation of some of the concerns and quests of poetry. Paz opposes two green stains—"two parrots in full flight"—to language: a way of confronting metonymically the natural world with the artifices of culture, the innocence which the poet seeks and language as his only road of return to which he is forced by his condition as a creature of words. From this challenge, language inevitably ends in defeat because between words and things there is an abyss that has exiled humanity from the natural world. Language, incapable of communication with the world of things, creates a universe of signs and comments on itself never endingly:

> No nos queda dijo Bataille
> Sino escribir comentarios
> > Insensatos
> Sobre la ausencia de sentido del escribir
> Comentarios que se borran

> (Nothing remains for us said Bataille
> but to write foolish
> > Commentaries
> On the absence of meaning in writing
> Commentaries that erase themselves).

Things ("two parrots in full flight") defy movement, leap, fly; words, on the other hand, "dissipate themselves / their movement / is a return to immobility." Poetry is "a senseless undertaking" because it proposes to construct with language, which has created a breach between the natural world and humanity, a bridge of return to that world; it is madness because the poet asks immobility (language) to become movement. Modern poetry turns into a religion when it assumes the miracles denied to religion by the omnipotence (or rather arrogance) of the sciences. Its devotion to the word requires a faith in the (poetic) word greater perhaps than that which the pantheon of any religion required from its believers. If language represents the historic fall that separated humankind from its primordial world, it is understandable that the poetic endeavor should begin as a criticism of language and then proceed to rescue humankind from the traps of its own spell:

> > > La escritura poética
> Es borrar lo escrito
> > > Escribir
> Sobre lo escrito
> > Lo no escrito

> . . .
> La escritura poética es
> > > Aprender a leer
> El hueco de la escritura

En la escritura
No huellas de lo que fuimos
Caminos
Hacia lo que somos

(To write poetry
Is to erase the written
To write
On the written
The unwritten
. . .
To write poetry is
Learning to read
The empty space of writing
In the writing
Not the footprints of what we were
Paths
Toward what we are).

If writing poetry is "to write on the written the unwritten" and "learning to read the empty space of writing," the poem is inexorably "the unwritten," "the empty space," all that language is not and will never be, but which poetry compels it to be. Without mentioning the word silence, Paz names it in the most convincing way: keeping it quiet. But we already know that for Paz silence is not the absence of the word: "The West teaches us that Being dissolves itself in meaning and the East that meaning dissolves itself in something that is neither Being nor non-Being: it is a Same which no language except silence designates. So humankind is made up in such a way that silence becomes also language". How to say this silence? If the poem is, in the end, "the unwritten," "the empty space of writing," and language at the same time, then Paz is really saying the poem does not have to be either this or that, but "this and that," writing and silence, writing which says silence and silence which is manifested through writing. Not without reason did poets begin speaking of poetry as verbal alchemy.

Finally: what does this silence reveal? Before becoming a concern to modern poetry, the meaning of silence was a question placed at the heart of Buddhist thought; Paz sums it up in *Claude Lévi-Strauss* or the *New Feast of Aesop*:

The word of Buddha has meaning, though it asserts that nothing has, because it aims at silence: if we wish to know what he really said, we ought to question his silence. Now, the interpretation of what Buddha did not say is the crux of the great controversy which has divided schools of Buddhism from the beginning. Tradition tells us the Enlightened One did not answer ten questions . . .

For some those questions could not be answered; for others, Gautama did not know how to answer; and for still others, he preferred not to answer. K. N. Jayatilleke translates the interpretations of these schools into modern terms. If Buddha did not know the answers he was a skeptic or a native agnostic; if he preferred to remain quiet because to answer might have kept his listeners from the true way, he was a pragmatic reformer; if he kept quiet because there was no possible answer, he was an agnostic rationalist (the questions are beyond the limits of reason) or a logical positivist (the questions lack meaning and therefore, answers). The young Sinhalese professor favors this last solution . . . But this interpretation, not very far from Lévi-Strauss' position, forgets another possibility: silence itself is an answer.

What is not said is what is said: such is the answer that "Reading John Cage" suggests. Although the long reflection on silence in this poem alludes to music, the comments there are equally applicable to poetry. Silence which constitutes a response, silence which speaks, is not a wide barren plain of language; language invents silence in the same way "music / invents silence" and "architecture / invents space" and just as "music is not silence" but "silence is music," neither is language silence and, on the other hand, silence is the most powerful language our language is capable of eliciting. *Silence is an idea and is not an idea*: it is not an idea because in our logical thinking silence is a negation of ideas, but it is an idea because silence transmits *something*, though this *something* lacks a conceptual referent: idea that ideas cannot express, and which can only be conveyed through silence. *Silence is the space of music* and this space is the environment where music is made possible and where silence can generate its idea. The language of poetry also creates a space: residence and speech of silence. This space must not be confused with the new format of the poem which since *Un Coup de Dés* a good part of modern poetry has adopted, thought that new arrangement of space between lines far from being purely ornamental or visual, has a definite function as an expressive vehicle. More than the physical space of the poem, it deals with the mental space which the poem opens in the reader: empty space of writing which is perceived by the reader in the act of reading as a silence generating the only meanings denied to language:

                              No hay silencio
          Salvo en la mente

                              (There is no silence
          except in the mind).

Claude Lévi-Strauss and *Blanco* appeared in the same year; essay and poem
were written in 1966 in Delhi, India. The last pages of the essay can be read
as a brief meditation on silence; *Blanco*, or at least its central column, "is a
poem whose theme is the passage of the word, from one silence to the next,
passing through four stages: yellow, red, green, and blue." This poem
represents the culmination of that search. Culmination and conclusion, since
the next book, *Vuelta* (1976), hardly mentions it. It is present as context, but
with *Blanco*, this long reflection which began with Paz's first poems draws to
a close. What *Blanco* suggests is a meaning already anticipated partly in his
discussion on Lévi-Strauss and already found in a different form in *The Bow
and the Lyre*:

> Silence is in itself an answer. This was the interpretation of
> the Madhyamika School and of Nagarjuna and his disciples of
> what Buddha *did not say*. There are two silences: one, before
> speech, is an attempt at meaning; another, after speech, is the
> knowledge that the only thing worth saying cannot be said.
> Buddha said everything which it is possible to say with words: the
> errors and achievements of reason, the truth and lies of the
> senses, the illumination and the void of the instant, the freedom
> and slavery of nihilism. Words filled with reasons that cancel
> themselves and of sensations that consume each other. *But his
> silence says something different.*

Language is, as Wittgenstein said, "a picture of the world," but of
the world invented by human beings: an artificial world created by culture
that has its cornerstone in language. If "reason is language" as Johann Georg
Hamann said, it is through language that humankind knows the world, but
knowledge, as Ernst Cassirer has observed, "can never reproduce the true
nature of things as they are, but must frame their essence in 'concepts.' But
what are concepts except formulations and creations of thought, which,
instead of giving us the true forms of objects, show us rather the forms of
thought itself? Consequently, all schemata which science evolves in order to
classify, organize and summarize the phenomena of the real world turn out
to be nothing but arbitrary schemes—airy fabrics of the mind which express

not the nature of things, but the nature of mind. So knowledge has been reduced to a kind of fiction, to a fiction that recommends itself by its usefulness, but must not be measured by any strict standard of truth, if it is not to melt away into nothingness." More briefly, Jung has warned that "Western reality is in danger of losing its shadow altogether, of identifying itself with its fictive personality and of identifying the world with the abstract picture painted by scientific rationalism." But if, as Jung believes, we have become the slave of our own fiction and a purely conceptual world gradually replaces reality, how then can we return to reality if we are separated from it by a wall of symbols which represents the foundation of our culture? How can we relinquish this fiction which has made us into what we are, and with which we have constructed our world? Referring to contemporary science, a North American scientist said recently, perhaps with much reason: "We have created a kind of world from which we cannot return." Wittgenstein postulates in his *Philosophical Investigations* a thesis opposed to the one presented in his *Tractatus*: "Philosophy is a battle against the bewitchment of our intelligence by means of language," and adds: "The results of philosophy are the uncovering of one or another piece of plain nonsense and of bumps that the understanding has got by running its head up against the limits of language." Philosophy has always been a kind of X-ray of language, and consequently its limits and range are the limits and range of language; philosophical investigation moves on the tracks of language; if it abandoned those tracks, it would derail. It makes sense that Heidegger sought in Hölderlin, and poetry in general, the answers that his systems could not provide; his answer, one of his answers, is a line from Hölderlin: "Poetically man dwells." Where philosophy ends, poetry begins. If language has bewitched our intelligence, poetry will try to bewitch language. *Here to bewitch* means to force language to keep quiet so that from its silence—a momentary silence carved in the substance of language as its space—may rise its deepest voice: a bridge of return toward true reality. The East was in love with silence: "When the mind is silent," the *Maitri Upanishad* says, "beyond weakness or non-concentration, then it can enter into a world which is far beyond the mind: the highest End." In that silence, the chaos of the world becomes harmony. The god of Brahmanism is "eternal silence and cannot be seen by the eye nor can words reveal it," but Brahman reveals itself through silence: "It can be seen indivisibly in the silence of contemplation." To a certain extent, Paz's interest in Eastern thought lies in that cultivation of silence as the resolution of phenomenal reality and as the resolution of language itself. Toward the end of his essay on Lévi-Strauss, Paz says:

> Language is the kingdom of dialectics which ceaselessly destroys itself and is reborn only to die. Language is dialectics,

operation, communication. If Buddha's silence were the expression of this relativism, it would not be silence, but word. This isn't so: with his silence, movement, operation, dialectics, word, all cease. At the same time, it is neither the negation of dialectics nor of movement: Buddha's silence is the *resolution* of language. We come out of silence and return to it: to the word that has stopped being word.

Thus "Nirvana is Samsara" but "Samsara is not Nirvana" and "silence is music" but "music is not silence": "Silence is an idea / The fixed idea of music." There is silence before music—empty silence—but the true silence occurs after music, in music, or as a resolution of music. Such is the silence poetic language seeks: a silence that poetry achieves through the incantation of its word:

> el comienzo
>   el cimiento
> la simiente
>   latente
> la palabra en la punta de la lengua
> inaudita   inaudible
>   impar
> grávida   nula
>   sin edad
> la enterrada con los ojos abiertos
> inocente   promiscua
> la palabra
> sin nombre   sin habla

> (the beginning
>   the source
> the seed
>   latent
> word on the tip of the tongue
> unheard of   inaudible
>   odd
> gravid   void
>   ageless
> the woman buried with open eyes
> innocent   promiscuous
>   the word
> nameless   speechless).

The poetic word (silence) is "el lenguaje deshabitado," (uninhabited language), "sin nombre" (nameless) and "sin habla" (speechless). The poem is a ladder of words that, upon reaching silence, throws away the ladder and remains in that blank space which is not an absence of color, but the resolution of all colors. Like light, which integrates in its whiteness all colors, the second silence of poetry is not absence, but presence of words, though now integrated in the poem as the "resolution of language." The poem is an inverted prism which restores the myriad fragments in which language has been divided into that "one word, as large as a sun" which, like light, disappears into the transparency of its white silence.

Such an operation implies a sacrifice of language in whose ceremony—the poem—words atone until they are purified and melt away:

> El lenguaje
> Es una expiación,
>   Propiciación
> Al que no habla,
>   Emparedado
> Cada día
>   Asesinado,
> El muerto innumerable.
>   Hablar
> Mientras los otros trabajan
> Es pulir huesos,
>   Aguzar
> Silencios
>   Hasta la transparencia,
> Hasta la ondulación,
>   El cabrilleo,
> Hasta el agua.

>   (Language
> Is expiation,
>   Propitiation
> To whomever does not speak,
>   Imprisoned
> Each day
>   Assassinated,
> The innumerable dead one.
>   To speak
> While others work

Is to polish bones,
                    To sharpen
Silences
                    Into transparency,
Into undulation,
                    The rippling,
into water.)

The four states through which the central column of the poem travels, yellow, red, green and blue, point to a clarity—water—in which each singular color disappears in order to become transparent—"transparency is all that is left"—just as the "mujer tendida *hecha a la imagen del mundo*" (woman lying down *made in the image of the world*) is the world or rather, the world is the dispersion of woman, a bundle of over-flowing images which in woman cluster in one image, a primordial world: "tu cuerpo son los cuerpos del instante" (your body is the bodies of the instant), "presente que no acaba" (never-ending present). But woman is also part of this fragmented world, she is in it as silence is in words, as a "bridge," as a "place of reconciliation between the natural and human worlds;" she is language and silence, silence which becomes language: "tú te repartes come el lenguaje *espacio dios descuartizado*" (you divide yourself like language *space cut up god*). In his essay on Breton, Paz says: "Woman is concrete language, revelation incarnate: 'la femme n'est plus qu'un calice débordant de voyelles.' " Definition of woman which is at the same time a definition of poetry. Woman and poetry are for Paz different versions of the same silence full of meaning: poetry like woman "is a bridge, place of reconciliation between the natural and the human worlds."

Through the fiction of language, the poet seeks to recover the world's reality, and through love, reach his lost innocence: "entrar en mí / al entrar en tu cuerpo" (to enter myself / on entering your body). Is it by chance that the two great themes of Paz's poetry should be love and language? Yet his erotic stand is also a poetic stand. Woman is dispersed in her body and only through love does she disappear to become "time before time": her body, "lenguaje repartido" (dispersed language), dissolves into the fullness of silence, ceases to be dispersion and becomes harmony. Love, like the poetic act, begins in silence in order to reach another silence, begins on one shore to arrive at the other shore. Woman's body (and man's) is that language on which the poem rests to reach love (poetry). Love and poetry tear away the fiction of the world—human body dispersed in its functions, picture painted with words—in order to touch solid ground again. Departing from the unreality of language, poetry finds its way into reality: "La irrealidad de lo mirado / Da realidad a la mirada" (The unreality of the seen / Makes real the seeing). And what is the substance of that reality recovered by poetry? Isn't the poem but language, irrevocably language? The answer, from *Blanco*:

> El árbol de los nombres
> > Real irreal
> Son palabras
> > Aire son nada
> El habla
> > Irreal
> Da realidad al silencio
> > Callar
> Es un tejido de lenguaje
> > Silencio

> (The tree of names
> > Real unreal
> Are words
> > Air are nothing
> Speech
> > Unreal
> Gives reality to silence
> > Stillness
> Is a fabric of language
> > Silence).

What poetic language says is what it does not say: a silence that, like a love spasm, is nothing and everything, time in which the unreality of the world vanishes for an instant ("perpetual present") to leave us face to face with a primordial reality, a wholeness glimpsed like lightning, silence. Buddhism understood this silence with a lucidity rarely granted to the Western mind:

> What Buddha's silence says is neither negation nor affirmation. It says something else; it alludes to a beyond that is here. It says *Sunyata*: everything is empty because everything is full, the word is not a statement because the only statement is silence. Not nihilism but relativism which destroys itself and goes beyond itself. Movement is not resolved in immobility; it is immobility, and immobility is movement. The negation of the world implies a return to the world, asceticism is a return to the senses, Samsara

is Nirvana, reality is the loving and terrifying cipher of the
unreal, the instant is not a refutation, but the incarnation of
eternity, the body is not a window to infinity: it is infinity itself. . . .
To reduce the world to meaning is as absurd as reducing it to the
senses . . . Vibration, waves, signs and responses: silence. Not the
knowledge of emptiness: an *empty knowledge*. The Buddha's
silence is not knowledge but what comes after knowledge:
wisdom. An unknowing.

Paz's work rises toward that "coded silence": a road that travels
where "roads end." *Blanco* points toward that silence—where silence ends—
with sibylline rhythm, like a text that speaks from its blank space loaded with
meanings, from the reverse of the signs: not silence of language but language
of silence.

Paz's work, like the fig tree of his poem, has "countless arms." It
would be impossible (and preposterous) to attempt to trace one single line
that defines it, but I think that this counterpoint between language and
silence is the trunk from which his best poetry grows and branches out. We
must only reexamine the pages of *El mono gramático* to realize to what degree
Paz agonizes, like a seer, over that dialogue. The poet's plight is that of
Sisyphus'. "There is no end, everything has been a perpetual rebeginning.
What I say is a continuation of what I am going to say and which I never
finish saying. In writing, I walk toward meaning; on reading what I write, I
erase it, I dissolve the road. Each attempt ends in the same way: dissolution
of the text in reading, expulsion of meaning by the written. The search for
meaning culminates in the apparition of a reality that is beyond meaning and
which disintegrates it, destroys it." But the situation of the poet is also that
of a visionary. If the text is dissolved in its reading, and if writing expels the
meaning of the poem it is because poetry is a constant struggle between
language and a meaning beyond language. In that strange struggle, the poet
seeks to make language say what it cannot say. The poem is a testimony to
that struggle, and that testimony speaks not through language but through
space formed by the written text: "Poetic writing resolves itself in the
abolition of the written: finally it confronts us with an inexpressible reality.
The reality which poetry reveals and which appears behind language—that
reality visible only through the cancellation of language in which the poetic
operation consists—is literally unbearable and maddening. At the same time,
neither humankind nor language are what they are without the vision of this
reality. Poetry nourishes and destroys us, gives us speech and condemns us to
silence."

This silence *is* the most genuine voice of poetry because from it poetry communicates what language cannot say. Language is the "consequence (or the cause) of our exile from the universe, and it represents the gap between things and us. It is also our response to this gap. If that exile ceased, language would cease." As long as this exile exists, as long as humankind remains banished by the unreality of language, as long as the world remains an invention of the spirit, the silence which poetry invites will keep being a road of access to the transparency of the world. And that transparency "is all that remains."

MANUEL DURÁN

Irony and Sympathy in Blanco *and* Ladera este

> *To understand is to see patterns.*

Isaiah Berlin's statement in *Historical Inevitability* might well stand as a motto for my critical approach. Possibly the relative security with which literary criticism has tended to deal with poetry derives not only from long experience—we have been at it since Aristotle—but equally from the structural emphasis of Aristotle's work. In a more contemporary context, the impact of Paz's poetry derives in no small part from its perception of patterns (which Frye prefers to call schematic rather than systematic) relating the parts of a poem or a book to each other and to the larger literary contexts which subsume them. Dr. Johnson would have been pleased.

Blanco appears in 1966, *Ladera este* in 1968. The first is a long, tight poem about a seemingly abstract subject, language. A philologist would turn to yards of gray prose. Paz explodes technicolor fireworks. *Ladera este* is a longer book, not more complex than *Blanco*, but rather less tightly composed, more varied. In both cases a yes and a no, enthusiasm and irony, provide a framework of polarities, and beat like the expansion and contraction of a heart. One does not pretend here, to make criticism (in this case criticism of Paz's poetry) what Harry Levin rightly observes it cannot be, an "exact science." What I rather propose to do is to explore structural units more systematically and fully than criticism has so far done. Insofar as literature is

From *The Perpetual Present: The Poetry and Prose of Octavio Paz*, edited by Ivar Ivask, © 1973 by University of Oklahoma Press.

idea-form, a grasp of recurrent form is as essential and integral to a total literary comprehension as is a grasp of recurrent ideas or archetypes. My students have long since decided that to find patterns in a work is to please Professor Durán. I would make bold to suggest that in the intersecting of those patterns lies a unity: they are not a scaffolding but an inner frame holding the building erect.

To state that Paz is a living poet implies that he is subject to all the pressures, both positive and negative, that our time generates in abundance. Among them is an increase in the tempo, the rhythm, of change. The period of Paz's production that concerns us now is the decade of the sixties. During this time Paz discovers two facts that are bound to affect his writings. On the one hand, a fact which has its roots in a personal experience: his residence in India. He gains a direct access to the reality of the orient in a most specific form. On the other hand, another fact influences his conscious life, his life as an intellectual: this is the impact of a theory, the nucleus of ideas that we can describe under the general label of "structuralism." Without ceasing for a moment to be a surrealist and moreover without dismantling the superimposed existentialist canopy that had been placed upon the surrealist background, Paz becomes a structuralist.

We are therefore dealing with a complex multilayered reality. It is perhaps impossible to sort out the strands; the labyrinth of influences challenges our ingenuity when faced with any poem written by Paz in the decade of the sixties. Yet there are certain basic facts that will help us. Change is always superimposed upon an enduring continuity. If we compare the latest poem by Paz with one, with any one of his early poems, we shall immediately see the difference between the two poems, but we should also be capable of seeing the line that unites them, the stylistic and ideological factors that allow us to recognize both poems as being the result of the same personal vision, of the same poetic mind. Therefore I think it prudent not to overemphasize the originality of Paz's latest poetry: it is, of course, a new departure, a fresh look at the world, a new definition of reality, which is what we can and should expect from a new book from a great poet, and yet the man who has written this poetry is the same man, the same writer, who gave us *Libertad bajo palabra* and the early Paz essays. "Plus ça change, plus c'est la même chose."

On the other hand, there are periods where evolution steps up its pace, where *ça change* at a new rhythm. This is what happens for Paz, I think, during the decade of the sixties. We still do not have a biography, official or otherwise, of Paz as a man and as a writer. Usually one has to wait until the death of a man in order to have a complete image of his life. (Isn't this observation the same one made by a character created by Cervantes in *Don*

Quixote, where Ginés de Pasamonte explains that he could not possibly write the story of his life, since he had not stopped being alive?) Some day, however, some day which I hope is still very far in the future, we shall have a biography of Octavio Paz. If it is a good one, it shall underline the importance of the decade of the sixties in his life. If I may be allowed for a brief moment to place my explanation within a Jungian framework, I shall remind my readers that according to Jung's interpretation of the evolution and maturing of the human psyche, a man cannot be considered as having successfully become an adult until he has killed a dragon and married a princess. These terms are of course symbolic and have to be translated into the language and the circumstances of the twentieth century. Yet it is clear to me, in my interpretation of what we know of Paz's activity during this period, of his long and courageous battle with what we can define as the ugly dragon of Mexican official institutions, and his having found in India a woman he loved and made his wife, that Paz has finally fulfilled the Jungian requisites: he has done victorious battle with a dragon and married a princess. No wonder his poetry has gained in depth: it is now the fully mature poetry of an adult poet.

The decade of the sixties is crucial for Paz in another field, the one that should concern his readers most. During these years he discovers simultaneously the vast reality of India—and the intellectual tool of structuralism, specifically in its French version as represented by Lévi-Strauss. Of his discovery of India we find abundant traces in Paz's poetry, and also in his prose essays on Hindu art. His structuralist avocation has found a lucid outlet in essays such as *El nuevo festín de Esopo* and *Conjunciones y disyunciones*. I think it is significant, and helpful to us as readers of Paz, that these two discoveries took place at the same time. They seem to balance each other, to "need" each other. India is the place—the culture—in which borderlines are erased, identities blend, sharp lines become as blurred as colors in a bleeding Madras cloth. A gigantic cauldron, the original melting pot, much more efficient and hotter than its American equivalent. Any Westerner who lives in India not as a tourist or as a mere diplomat, but rather as a man sensitive to his environment, is bound to have his sense of identity, himself, his ego, both expanded and eroded. Paz was fully prepared for such a change. I do not know whether Paz has read Martin Buber or not. What matters is that Paz was always interested in the "I—Thou" relationship, and therefore was already prepared to surrender some sharp edges of the self, to make his self more available to dialogue and projection toward others, toward the world in general.

"Everything the artist invents is true," Flaubert said—a more profound remark than it might appear. Yet the emphasis in Flaubert's sentence is placed upon man, as an artist, as a cultural hero. From Descartes on, it is man's rational self which occupies the center of the stage—at least in the Western tradition. This view is reflected in the early Paz as a critic: in the first edition of *El arco y la lira*, published in 1956, the emphasis is upon the self, the poet as a cultural hero: "There is no poem," Paz writes, "without a creating mind." "Poetry is an act of free creation." "Poetic creation is merely the exercise of human freedom. What we call inspiration is only the manifestation or unfolding of such a freedom." Emir Rodríguez Monegal has carried out a careful confrontation of this first edition of *El arco y la lira* and the second edition of 1967. The changes are numerous and important. Under the twofold impact of structuralism and the oriental experience, Paz reaches conclusions which in many respects differ from his previous statements. As Monegal states, "now the orient is for him something more that a dazzling vision or an intuition captured reading between the lines of texts by Western specialists. This does not mean that Paz has ever ceased being a Western man. On the contrary, he is more Western than ever. But the East has now become part of his vision as a Western man. . . . Through the mask, or disguise, of Oriental culture, Octavio Paz can now reach the true face of his Western world." Summing up: as a critic of literature, Paz has recently de-emphasized the magic or heroic role of the poet, underlining instead a new role of language which has been suggested by structuralism—and probably also by the emotional impact of his oriental experience. He writes in *Corriente alterna*: "The problem of meaning in poetry becomes clear as soon as we notice that the meaning is not to be found outside, but rather inside the poem; it is not to be found in what the words have to say, but rather in what the words *have to say to each other*." (". . . en aquello que *se dicen entre ellas*"). In his essay on André Breton, published in *Mundo Nuevo* (December 1966), Paz states: "A man inspired, a man who really expresses himself, does not say anything that belongs only to him: through his mouth it is language that speaks to us." And in *Festín de Esopo* he states that for Lévi-Strauss "it is nature that speaks to herself through man, without man being aware of it." Flaubert's sentence should now become: "Everything language invents is true," and man would be a mere vehicle, a bystander. We are now in a properly humble frame of mind. Paz is ready to show us, in *Blanco*, a poem which seems to be self-creating, self-sustaining, a slow and painful—but also graceful—dialogue in which one word seems to give birth to another, until a whole army of words marches on. His approach is subtle, modern, humble: the act of creation is displaced from poet to the language itself. Mallarmé, Valéry, and structuralism, are an obvious background. I can think of another image that comes to my mind: a boastful young boy riding a bicycle: "Look, Ma, no hands!"

And yet a break with the past has not taken place, at least if by the past we understand the role of the poet as *vate*, as the one who expresses the yearnings and the visions of the tribe, the anonymous sayer of lines and creator of myths. For this vision, which the German romantic poets were to resuscitate, puts its emphasis not upon the self, the individual man, but upon the obscure forces of collective inspiration. By his retreat from the center of the stage, by his giving the dominant role to the forces of language, Paz in *Blanco* has succeeded in modernizing and updating one of the oldest and most basic interpretations of poetry. When the composition of *Blanco* begins we are surrounded by silence. When it ends we go back to silence. What happens between these two moments is not clearly willed and controlled by a conscious mind, at least not one that is visible to the reader. (We are reminded of a Japanese Noh play, in which the prop men, all dressed in black, may move furniture around without the public becoming aware of it.)

Blanco is possibly the most difficult poem written until now by Paz. The author himself seems to challenge us, to taunt, to tantalize us, by offering a series of elusive clues. The poet, the true poet, he says elsewhere (in his book on *Lévi-Strauss*) is a man in love with silence—but one who cannot keep himself from talking. He partakes of silence and language, is suspended half-way between an acute feeling of loneliness and the need to share his vision with others. While describing the world around him and inside himself he not only recreates this world but gives us the clues so that we can do the same thing while reading his poem. These clues are necessary if we want to approach a poem such as *Blanco* through analysis—and let us add here, through an analysis that has gained some insights from the structuralist approach. As Roland Barthes himself has stated,

> the goal of every structuralist activity, whether reflective or poetic, is to reconstitute an 'object,' in a manner that will make clear, through this reconstruction, the rules of functioning (the 'functions') of this object. The structure is, therefore, in fact, a *construct [simulacre]* of the object, and yet a construct which has a goal, a purpose, since the imitated object makes evident for us something that seemed . . . natural object [which is being translated by art]. Structuralist activity takes what is real, analyzes it and then synthesizes it. This seems to amount to very little—which suggests to some that structuralist activity is 'insignificant, uninteresting, useless.' Yet from a different viewpoint this little effort is decisive, for between the two objects, or the two 'strokes' of structuralist activity, something new is brought to light . . . the representation is the object plus

the human intelligence added to it, and this addition has an anthropological value, inasmuch as it is man himself, his history, his situation, his freedom, and the very resistance which Nature opposes to his spirit, which is being defined. (*Essais critiques*)

After this "structuralist cameo," let us return to *Blanco*. The poem carries an epigraph of Hindu origin: "By passion the world is bound, by passion too it is released," and one from the West, "Avec ce seul objet dont le Néant s'honore." They give us two clues. First, that Paz's mind is now operating as a meeting ground of East and West. Second, that the poem is about a meeting between passion and silence. Since we soon discover that the poem deals with language, with the birth of words, this point is not without significance. The poem unfolds in several ways: we can read it as a whole, from beginning to end; we can choose the central column, which deals with the birth of language; we can find to its left another column, an erotic poem divided into four sections standing for the four elements in nature; to the right, another column also divided into four parts deals with sensation, perception, imagination and understanding. Briefly, this is a poem in which space, the interaction of these segments within the framework of the blank space of a book, is as important as time. Language cannot be born, Paz seems to tell us, if space, time, passion, and silence are not combined into one single unit. The Hindu *Mandala*, the squaring of the circle, the labyrinth which points toward infinity but also toward the here and now, is its emblem.

As Paz himself has written in *Corriente alterna*, "modern poetry is an attempt to abolish all meanings because poetry itself appears to be the ultimate meaning of life and of man himself." If the German philosopher Ernst Cassirer defined man as the animal who could create language and myths, we can also state that it is language, myths, poetry, that have created man, that have made modern man into a poetic, myth-making, speaking animal.

Blanco begins with an untranslatable pun:

> el comienzo
> > el cimiento
> la simiente

(Beginning, foundation, seed: all are the same thing, all are contained in words.) In the beginning was the Word, according to St. John. Not action, the will, the deed, as Goethe claimed, but the Word. The people who usually discuss words and language are philologists and linguists, and although language in itself is fascinating, language as analyzed and classified by linguists and philologists (without mentioning psycholinguists) becomes sometimes extremely boring. But Paz is a poet, and we sense the newness of his approach right away: where the philologists use black-and-white, mostly gray, Paz plunges into technicolor and images. This is how he recreates for us the birth of the word "sunflower," and with it the birth of the flower that the word allows us to see:

> Superviviente
> Entre las confusiones taciturnas,
> > Asciende
> En un tallo de cobre
> > Resuelto
> En un follaje de claridad:
> > Amparo
> De caídas realidades.
> > O dormido
> O extinto,
> > Alto en su vara
> (Cabeza en una pica);
> > Un girasol
> Ya luz carbonizada
> > Sobre un vaso
> De sombra.
> > En la palma de una mano
> Ficticia,
> > Flor
> Ni vista ni pensada:
> > Oída,
> Aparece
> > Amarillo
> Cáliz de consonantesy vocales
> Incendiadas.

The word "sunflower" appears after a long preparation, after we have images, sounds, light and darkness. It is a painful birth, yet it creates in turn other images, sounds, in a loud explosion which we could compare to the second stage of a rocket: the poem unfolds into two columns, eroticism and sensations of sound and light open up right and left: Paz has organized a *son et lumière* spectacle around the magic blessed event, the birth of a word which is a symbol for the birth of language.

The yellow of a sunflower is replaced by the blue of a river. Once more we realize that color, movement, the anguished presence of a man surrounded by "something"—something we may have to name, we may call it "river"—are not merely steps that unfold slowly and logically but rather simultaneous, interacting realities. By translating so closely human experience, sounds, colors, images, into a frenzied sensual embrace, Paz seems to abolish time and history, or at least to tell us that the interaction of these spatial and temporal elements is so fast and furious that the neat Western projections of historicism, rationalism, positivism, are to the real world what gray ashes are to a living body. New visions, red deserts, frenzied screams of *yes* and *no*, seem to shake the entrails of this poem like a vast earthquake. More than once we feel we are drowning in a sea of intoxicating sensations. Yet Paz is too great a poet not to know that every work of art needs a center. He has provided one, and of course this center is in tune with the rest of the poem: it is an explosion of paradoxes out of which, if we look closely, if we are not blinded by the light of the explosion, a crown—or is it a halo, or a mushroom-shaped cloud—of meaning will momentarily appear:

> El espíritu
> Es una invención del cuerpo
> El cuerpo
> Es una invención del mundo
> El mundo
> Es una invención del espíritu

A blind alley? A vicious circle? Rather, a self-sustaining irony. It is not always easy to tell apart irony and enthusiasm in *Blanco*. When we come to *Ladera este* the operation is much simpler. The whole book is organized around two poles, the ironic look and the enthusiastic, ecstatic vision. The world around the poet contracts, then expands, pulsating evenly from beginning to end of the book. Most of the short poems, at least a good many of them, are wrapped around a core of irony. The long ones offer us a look into vast spaces, timeless vistas. Perhaps the basic irony, the original joke (the joke is on the reader) is that a book which deals with essential being and transcendental beauty reads also most often as a travelogue, as a tourist's notebook. Paz has also taken care to provide bridges in order to make his contrasts less painful. Thus for instance in "Madurai," a short ironic poem:

> En el bar del British Club
> —Sin ingleses, *soft drinks*—
> *Nuestra ciudad es santa y cuenta*

> Me decía, apurando su naranjada,
> *Con el templo más grande de la India*
> (Mainakshi, diosa canela)
> *Y el garaje* T.S.V. (tus ojos son dos peces)
> Sri K.J. Chidambaram,
> *Yo soy familiar de ambas instituciones.*
> Director de The Great Lingam Inc.,
> Compañía de Autobuses de Turismo.

An inane monologue around soft drinks—and the reader knows that "lingam" means "phallic symbol of Shiva" or simply "male organ." Yet behind the tawdry boasting of a Hindu Babbitt there lurk the eyes of a beautiful goddess.

And yet the contrast between some of the short ironic poems and a long poem such as *Viento entero* is still powerful. Paz knows the world is made up of pettiness and infinity, of saints, madmen, clowns, mediocre people. His goal is not only to see infinity in a grain of sand, as William Blake proposed, but at the same time not to forget the size, texture and color of the grain of sand. *Viento entero* is a love poem and a metaphysical poem *and* a description of a journey through the Hindu subcontinent:

> El presente es perpetuo
> Los montes son de hueso y son de nieve
> Están aquí desde el principio
> El viento acaba de nacer
>   Sin edad

And yet we have concrete glimpses, snapshots of everyday reality, "los gritos de los niños / Príncipes en harapos / A la orilla del río atormentado / Rezan orinan meditan." Fragments of history, legend, literature, merge with the eternal present. Opposites become fused: "Eres la llama de agua / La gota diáfana de fuego." Images and sacred presences lift up the present to a higher level: "En el pico del mundo se acarician / Shiva y Parvati / Cada caricia dura un siglo." Enthusiasm has won the day, irony recedes. Ambiguity becomes a shifting, shimmering change of focus in the human eye, as when the poet describes the subtle trembling of a poplar: "Entre el cielo y la tierra suspendidos / Unos cuantos álamos / Vibrar de luz más que vaivén de hojas / ¿Suben o bajan?" A chord is struck, the world vibrates, enthusiasm wins over the ironic eye. As in *Blanco*, so in *Ladera este*: words, mere words, tightly organized in endless dialogue, can create a world—which in turn will give birth to new languages: the present never ends.

RICARDO GULLÓN

Reverberation of the Stone

In an anthology of modern poetry limited to the ten best poems of the twentieth century, two written in Spanish would rightfully take a place. Next to Rilke and Pessoa, not far from Eliot and Ungaretti, near Yeats and Pasternak, close to Seferis and Valéry, I (anthologizing is always a personal matter) would include works of Juan Ramón Jiménez and Octavio Paz. (If it were a matter of books rather than poems, neither Jorge Guillén's *Cántico* nor César Vallejo's *Trilce* could be kept from this list). And the poems which in my judgment would best represent Jiménez and Paz (though I believe he would not agree) are "Espacio" (Space) and *Piedra de sol (Sun Stone)*. In the first instance the selection seems indisputable; in the second, perhaps there is room to show *Blanco* can vie with *Piedra de sol* in its modernity. Yet it is precisely the assimilation and interpretation of the modern in the eternal which makes me prefer the latter.

   Piedra de sol has been widely discussed and commented on; but occasionally someone like José Emilio Pacheco, who like Paz, being both a poet and a Mexican, gives an account of things most other critics have neglected. Pacheco, in his essay, "Description of *Piedra de sol*," begins by noting the noble quality of the poem—which is no exaggeration since it is a masterpiece. I've used the adjective "eternal"; this is a word not to be used carelessly. Open poetry and closed poetry; line and circle; limpid and

From *Octavio Paz: Homage to the Poet*, edited by Kosrof Chantikian, © 1980 by Kosrof Chantikian and KOSMOS.

hermetic. A space as immense as Blake's "grain of sand," with horizon and time before and after the word. Having placed *Piedra de sol* under the invocation of Artemis and, more precisely, under the enigma created by Gérard de Nerval in his sonnet "Artémis" (his four lines serve as an epigraph to Paz's verses), the poem shows clearly it is intentionally and necessarily mysterious. Mysterious, but as I said, also limpid. Images that suggest the one and its contrary, verticality and horizontality; for example; "sauce de cristal" (willow of crystal), "chopo de agua" (poplar of water), "surtidor que el viento arquea" (gushing fountain curved by the wind), "árbol . . . danzante" (tree . . . dancing), opening up to a poetic space in which all evocations and transformations will be possible.

They will be possible thanks to the poetic activity of an imagination whose shape expresses symbolically that which, by taking root so deeply, cannot be verbalized in any other way. Symbolization: reversion toward the outside of interiorized intuititions, certainly, but actually caused by exterior impulses. Paz writes with a passion scarcely masked by the beauty of the writing which proves that intuition, although it comes from shadow, is genuinely illuminating, and conversely obscures and clouds the translucent: "voy por las transparencias como un ciego" (I go through transparencies like a blindman). It could not be any other way since the universe through which the Poet passes is a body: "piernas de luz, vientre de luz" (legs of light, belly of light); woman is his city: his womb, "plaza soleada" (sunny plaza); her breasts, "iglesias donde oficia la sangre" (churches where blood is celebrated). The inversion of the images serves an identifying function: the world is an organism and the female body a world: "ciudad" (city), "muralla" (wall), "paraje de sal, rocas y pájaros" (place of salt, rocks and birds). World and woman are labyrinths as well as inventions of the voice which speaks them, of the vision that courses through them and dreams them. Thus the expression has cosmic force and desire, and the innocence and ferocity of an animal: "los tigres beben sueño en esos ojos" (tigers drink sleep in those eyes), a desire made gentle as it touches this body in thoughts. Rarely has love been expressed with such total consciousness. And even if there were no other evidence, these six or seven verses which I am reading would be enough to place Octavio Paz among the finest erotic poets of our time— where sadly, the female body has been degraded into a thing.

Woman in this beautiful constellation is energetic and energizer. If by desiring woman men fertilize and transform her, they are at the same time fertilized by her "boca de agua" (mouth of water), by contact with the nature and spirit which she embodies. Expanding these quotations would simply show the extent to which Paz's verses are impregnated and determined by a metaphorical chain in which image on image illuminates a conception of woman as universe.

The poem revolves while the poet roams through the galleries that Antonio Machado scoured in dreams. Paz's are "corredores sin fin de la memoria" (corridors of endless memory), memories that are forgotten and arrive from very far to install themselves in the image of the poem, in the images which are the poem. To search for the form of these forgotten memories intending to recover them without their being altered seems a desperate attempt; but it is not since the text summons a continuity of evocations that creates and re-creates them. We read: "busco sin encontrar" (I search without finding). Such a declaration is inexact; through writing Paz has discovered the space and time through which the poem flows and in it his own image and likeness: weighed down by mystery, feeling his way, falling, accidentally slipping—all truly marvelous since to stumble is to hit against something—the revealing word, the flash of vision, symbol that defines exactly the imprecise, which gives shape to the ineffable.

Characters added to the text first as images, now appear with a face and name: Melusina, Laura, Isabel, Persephone, Mary, . . . allusions within the text that expand prodigiously the space within the poem; prodigious because how otherwise explain legend, myth, history, suddenly turning up to add complexity to the cipher of the text. We now are made to recall the potentiality of woman as magic: Melusina as fairy and serpent; Persephone as clear youthfulness and springtime (Kora) and queen of Hades; Mary—carpenter's wife and queen of the heavens. Myths, legends—and poetry; poetry of love incarnated in Laura de Noves (who loved Petrarch) and Isabel Freyre (who loved Garcilaso). Archetypes of absolute authenticity, characters of a metamorphosis provoked by the variation of myth. For Paz, this woman has "todos los rostros y ninguno" (all faces and none). It is Woman, Eternal Female, and immortalized in this way it is not strange that the Poet should turn to forms of expression tinged with religiosity. Pacheco has pointed out that the invocations found in this passage form a litany like Catholics appealing to the Virgin to intercede for us before God. "In *Piedra de sol*," he observes, "the *I* addresses a remark to the beloved one, mediator between humanity and nature in the language of divine affection just as mystics have elevated their prayers to God in the language of concerned humans." This attitude and method of composition are suggestive of San Juan de la Cruz, Fray Luis de León and even of that passionate and wise king who wrote the "Song of Songs." And here one gives up a temptation much explored by criticism: that of singing the human to the divine, exalting passion to the dignity of God's love. It is clear, as well, that the litany of the lyrical voice does not reverberate in one direction alone: "reina de serpientes" (serpent queen), "fuente en la peña" (fountain in the rock), "pastora de los valles submarinos" (shepherd of underwater valleys), "guardiana del valle de los muertos" (guardian of the valley of the dead), correspond to mythical figures mystics never thought of.

The Poet conceives the poem as a struggle against time, a structure built with the most elusive material, the word, resistant to a vision, which acquires consistency and reality only through that word. Inventive word, instrument and substance from which verbal space is born, from which vision finds its privileged zone. The function of verse, Paz has said, "consists in reinventing time" and in reinventing it in order to transform the instant into the eternal. Poetry, Antonio Machado had warned, is "word in time." Never more so than in *Piedra de sol*, but with this addition: in the time and space of transfiguration. Slowly experience emerges in form; that is, form is the form of experience which goes on inventing itself in the poem. At this stage the poem "gives of itself," grows from itself and is as much energy as movement. Each line responds to the preceding one and postulates the next. A system in which the metonymical chain strengthens its links in unusual ways: name requires face, instant seeks centuries, dream asks for image, and from these requests correspondences emerge that emphasize reiteration in the variation:

> todos los nombres son un solo nombre,
> todos los rostros son un solo rostro,
> todos los siglos son un solo instante

> (all names are one name
> all faces a single face
> all centuries an instant)

The repetition in the first two lines suggest, even demand, an equivalence in the third. Perfection of the verse in which neither rhythm nor tone nor intuition vary. The connection is perfect as it was before in the presentation of the litany. Behind the reduction of diversity into harmony, the word we have waited for enters the poem: "death," antithesis and complement of love. Time resolves itself in death, destroys itself by the only act of being (". . . madura hacia dentro de si mismo / y a si mismo se bebe y se derrama") (. . . ripening inward / drinking and scattering itself) and in its mortality humankind recognizes and identifies itself with it. The most dramatic exclamation emerges now: "oh vida por vivir y ya vivida" (oh life to live and already have lived).

The voice that is saying and making the poem returns from present to future, burns the stages of time and feels itself already outside the abode of the instant, in a duration that is a pure going beyond, dust and smoke. Who guides the poet in this descent to the depths of time? Woman from the beginning is not yet light but faithfully shadow, instrument of destruction. The lover has seen in Melusina the serpent which she reverts to periodically (tu atroz escama . . . brillar verdosa al alba") (your cruel scale . . . shining greenish at dawn) and has recognized in this fairy-tale monster the emblem of the human condition. Change of tone and vocabulary—in order to record the drama of the situation, the ambiguity of the times: the mother sees the father in the son; life is death and death "vida verdadera" (authentic life).

Can the voice which invents the poem identify itself? Is it one voice only? It knows neither its name nor who it is nor who that woman is nor the other who may walk at its side. But history saves it and gives it a past, a past of tangible reality touched by the fingers of memory. The name of this past is Carmen; it happened in Oaxaca or in Paris or more tense and unequivocal, in Madrid in 1937, amidst a war and on a square where there was then and is still a hotel for the Poet. All of this—facts, figures—is like the artist's signature in the corner of a painting, authenticating and identifying it.

Five lines are enough to introduce a situation, summarize a drame: the Spanish Civil war, the irruption of violence in calmness, the death of innocent ones. Death and love are joined; an exercise in continuity that brings together contraries and complements: bombs fall and bodies bind themselves together in copulation that will engender new life. And to whom does this spirit of passion speak? To woman, to its shadow, to itself? Mainly to itself, to its "others," emerging specters in the writing and at times determinants of its direction. What it says of love, of transfiguration in and through love, does not extend to reconstitute a personal experience but to discover in the potentiality of the word the greatness of this transformation of love. What a shock that this emotion is invented and made sacred this way ("todo se transfigura y es sagrado") (everything is transfigured and sacred) in this center of the world which is the bedroom!

I am opening myself up to a level of meaning that does not present major difficulties of interpretation, but it is advisable to warn the complexity of *Piedra de sol* is greater than has up to now been noted. Perhaps the visionary temptation should be emphasized and the peculiar texture of this vision, as in Lorca's *Poet in New York*, made up of threads of visible and invisible reality. Octavio Paz puts his hand into this clarity and contagion of his ardor, almost driven by its fever, raising it to the enigmatic to which I referred in the beginning.

Finally, Héloïse arrives. Paz was, I believe, waiting for her. (As he waited for her in Jiménez's "Espacio" where she appears and later Abélard, whose castrated condition is recalled by both Poets). Héloïse—absolute love and sex—sacrificed by an imbecile. This is the point where Paz, in speaking of love, oscillates between gentleness and burning passion and raises Abélard's curse to eloquence.

>   mejor ser lapidado
>   en las plazas que dar vuelta a la noria
>
>   (better to be stoned to death
>   in the town square than tread the mill).

Again and again myths. History makes and unmakes them; analogous in its expressiveness (in its meaning); different in its literalness. Assassins, victims, heros . . . , the text incorporates and makes them equal in value: Cain-Abel, Agamemnon, Cassandra, Socrates, Brutus, Moctezuma, Robespierre, Churruca, Lincoln, Trotsky, Madero, . . . Closely woven allusions in which each of the characters contributes their visible touch, constituting a dramatic, bloody altarpiece. Voices and shouts are heard including the one on "Friday afternoon"—possibly God complaining of being forsaken.

The meditation on time, based on historical incident and myth, is like a deep structure under whose fluid framework it reveals itself. That the meditation is selective and crystallizes in an anthology of images as well as anecdotes is something good for poetry: Robespierre with his jaw broken carried to the guillotine: Churruca dying in Trafalgar with his smashed leg in a barrel of flour; Lincoln's, Trotsky's, Madero's, assassins synthesized in an instant, in one gesture. Thus the Poet declares his belligerency, his assumption of a moral attitude, very precise and convincing of course, safe for those who put truth ahead of dogma. The past is part of the present: yesterday's crimes are happening now and will happen tomorrow; that's why the lyrical voice asks: "doesn't anything happen as time passes?" and it (or the other) responds:

>   —no pasa nada, sólo un parpadeo
>   del sol, un movimiento apenas, nada,
>   . . .
>   los muertos están fijos en su muerte
>   y no pueden morirse de otra muerte,
>   . . .
>   su muerte ya es la estatua de su vida
>   un siempre estar ya nada para siempre,
>   cada minuto es nada para siempre
>   . . .
>
>   (—nothing happens, just a blinding
>   of the sun, hardly a movement, nothing
>   . . .

the dead are fixed in their death,
and cannot die any other death,

. . .

their death is already the statue of their life,
endless being and nothingness forever
each minute is nothingness forever).

Nothing, death, forever, the irreversible declared insistently. The form of speech responds to the aesthetic necessity of preserving the moment in all the intensity of experience and at the same time sharing the moment with a continuity that fulfills the difficult paradox of absorbing and enhancing it. If memory is capricious, its whims were not arbitrary here but answers to the call of a consciousness which, as in "Espacio," is simultaneously the setting and agent of representation. Images, figures, forms of oblivion, all evoked by the poetic consciousness, which receives and plunges these images into currents, guiding them in such a way that yesterday's occurrences will continue flowing in the word which draws them up in a superior sphere of the same consciousness.

The poem nears its end as the ontological question is answered: I am who I am when I recognize myself in others, from them I receive the fullness of existence and to them I return it. Héloïse, Persephone, Mary—three women, three figures, who are one: astonishing and immortal woman, lover, mother, of a thousand faces, who takes us by her hand to the most secret of kingdoms. And the song of a never ending beginning: the last six lines of *Piedra de sol* are the same as the first six. This end is a beginning: the circle closes and the poem again unfolds the chain of propositions as if neither author nor reader are able to escape its fascination. Under the skin of the poem is heard the furious beat of Octavio Paz's heart.

MANUEL DURÁN

Towards the Other Shore: The Latest Stage in the Poetry of Octavio Paz

In the final pages of Carlos Fuentes' novel *Terra Nostra*, several mysterious events occur which leave most readers baffled. A hermaphroditic character appears. It is twelve noon in Paris, but clocks everywhere remain silent, refusing to give the time. Everything is shrouded in a pale solar light, in a white, supernatural light. I would like to suggest that here, as in other earlier instances in Fuentes' work, the poetry and *oeuvre* of Octavio Paz are able to make clear to us the meaning of these strange presences in Fuentes' novel. And conversely, these final pages of *Terra Nostra* help us in defining the meaning of Paz's poetry.

In an esoteric and at times grotesque form, Fuentes' novel in the end, offers us a series of symbols of transformation and transcendence. We approach the other side of reality, of history, of everyday life. Behind innumerable pages dedicated to history, philosophy, theology and magic, we are ready for the mortal leap, the definitive transformation: the contraries make a pact—the two sexes fuse into a single hermaphroditic being, a complete and visible symbol of androgynous life, and we prepare to abandon historical time, the time of chaos and mortality. And here Fuentes does nothing but follow in the footsteps that have left in our literary history some of Paz's greatest poems. The overcoming and abolition of time for example, is a theme that appears several times in Paz, especially in *Viento entero* whose

From *Octavio Paz: Homage to the Poet*, edited by Kosrof Chantikian, © 1980 by Kosrof Chantikian and KOSMOS.

191

recurring theme is "the present is perpectual" where temporality is transcended through the merging of male and female gods:

> El presente es perpetuo
> En el pico del mundo se acarician
> Shiva y Parvati
>> Cada caricia dura un siglo
> Para el dios y para el hombre
>>> Un mismo tiempo
> . . .

> (The present is perpetual
> At the top of the world
> Shiva and Parvati caress
>> Each caress lasts a century
> For god and for humanity
>>> The same time)
> . . .

The pale sun of Fuentes also finds its source in the fusion of colors, whose union—light, is one of the facets of Paz's complex poem, *Blanco*. Fuentes' novel and Paz's poems (which are prior to it and the probable source of its inspiration) start from disintegration and advance toward a unity. As Juan Garcia Ponce has written:

> It is not difficult to see that two principal parallel lines run through the poetry of Octavio Paz within which the poet carries out and at the same time constructs his creative work, making as firm as destiny, the word's ultimate meaning. One of these lines is knowledge of the Fall, caused by an absence of natural Grace in the life of humankind, resulting in a feeling of uprootedness and a separation from a world before which humanity feels strange as a consequence of having lost original innocence. The other, partly a result of the attitude with which Paz confronts that consciousness of the Fall, is a faith in the power of artistic creation, in the power of poetry—to reconcile us with a world fundamentally outside us—by its ability to restructure and reorder the world through the power of the world.

Already in 1948, in "Himno entre ruinas" ("Hymn Among the Ruins"), we catch a glimpse of a solution in which words play a primordial role:

. . .
La inteligencia al fin encarna
se reconcilian las dos mitades enemigas
y la conciencia-espejo se licúa,
vuelve a ser fuente, manantial de fábulas:
Hombre, árbol de imágenes,
palabras que son flores que son frutos que son actos.

(. . .
Intelligence becomes incarnate at last,
the two enemy halves are reconciled
and the miror of consciousness is liquified,
to become a fountain again, source of fables:
Humankind, tree of images
words which are flowers which are fruits which are deeds.)

We begin with a paradox expressed again and again by Octavio Paz himself—the tradition of contemporary poetry is a tradition of rupture. Style and vision of the world change with the rapidity of growing, negating the earlier styles, the previous visions, not allowing them to continue in any way. The poet, just like the chimera the ancients spoke of, on changing, remains the same; and it is in this changing that the poet's fidelity lies, the poet's being is to become. In this way we can refer to a second period in the poetry of Juan Ramón Jiménez, to various stages in Neruda's poetry, to a "latest" style in the poetry of Antonio Machado,

Paz's poetic work is so rich and varied that in order for us to go deeply into it, it is essential to mark the boundaries of certain zones on this vast map. I propose a rather simple division in three parts. "Himno entre ruinas" will form the first period of the poetry collected in *Libertad bajo palabra*. This will be followed by a transitional period composed again of "Himno entre ruinas," and by *Salamandra* and *Piedra de sol*. Finally, the second period will include everything from 1962 on, especially *Viento entero* (1965), *Blanco, Ladera este* (1969), *El mono gramático* (1974) and *Vuelta* (1976).

Paz himself seems to have foreseen the direction his poetic evolution was going to take in a youthful phrase he wrote: "The poet driven by desire abandons solitude for communion." Communion through comprehension, reconciliation, love—is to see our existence revealed in another being and partly merged with it. The other reveals and defines us. A solitary heart, Machado said, is no heart.

The path traveled by Paz in these last years is so considerable that we might speak of a complete transformation. I see rather a process of intensification and above all, the fulfillment of a poetic program already latent and sometimes explicit, in his earlier work. The Poet, in abandoning solitude, arrives at communion with beings, things and the world. If the earlier themes of freedom, destiny, death and eroticism do not entirely disappear, they are nevertheless transformed, surrounded by a new attitude, a new sensibility.

The typography also becomes modified, spread out as in the experiment in *Blanco*, which might be the first adaptation of Chinese scrolls in modern western poetry and even approaches at times, concrete poetry whose typography sketches an image. For Paz, as for Mallarmé, the silences and empty spaces also speak, are also meanings. The use of alternating and complementary fragments in the same poem, already present in *Salamandra*, is systematically amplified in *Ladera este*, in which Oriental influences remain purged, transformed and synthesized through a contrasting opposition between short poems with frequent irony, mysterious at times, bringing to mind Japanese poetry and the long poems, sensual and pantheistic, inspired by Hindu culture. Pantheism and irony then are the two principal ingredients of this latter book, the two voices with which the Poet directs at his situation, the ebb and flow of the present.

This evolution and dialogue are carried out without Paz losing touch with his Western, Hispanic and Mexican roots. The memory and presence of the West intervene in a receptive form and integrate the Oriental experience. Paz's poetry stretches out to the universal in this second period because of it, not as an abstraction, but as a creative synthesis. Finally, we find in *Blanco* the most advanced, most ambitious example, may be even the most successful, of this poetry of communion and synthesis. It is not necessary to point out that the more ambitious Paz's poetic program becomes, the more difficult it is to read his poems. I believe *Blanco* is his most difficult book so far.

A good example of a short poem is "Aparición" in *Ladera este*:

> Si el hombre es polvo
> Esos que andan por el llano
> Son hombres

> (If humankind is dust
> Those who walk through the plains
> Are human)

It would be difficult to say more with fewer words. This brief, concentrated form reminds us, on the one hand, of Japanese haiku and of a syllogism, on the other. The beginning words "humankind is dust" are reminiscent of a

Western Christian, medieval, ascetic tradition lasting until the Golden Age. But this abstract definition is modified immediately by the double impact of the title "Apparition" and the two final lines. We are suddenly reminded that the Poet writes from India, perhaps opposite a burning, dusty plain and those apparitions, those tiny, remote shapes covered by dust are our counterparts. Dust as a symbol of death remains transformed—until what point depends on the reader, and in it resides in part, the riches of the poem; not in vain has Paz written that there exist as many poets as readers—in real dust, of a desolate plain. (We avoid, let it be said in passing, exaggerating the Oriental traces in this latest period of Octavio Paz. Already in his first period he was writing excellent "lapidary" or "Japanese inspired" poems such as are found in *Libertad bajo palabra*:

> Roe el reloj
> mi corazón
> buitre no, sino ratón.

> [The clock gnaws at
> my heart
> not a vulture, but a rat.]

The evolution is then rupture but also continuation.)

The contrast between the short poems with their load of mystery or irony, and the long ones, with their vision of a cosmos in a rough swirling of activities that influence and interpenetrate, is probably what constitutes the internal organization of Paz's latest books, especially *Ladera este*. If we may compare a short poem to a photograph of the outer world, a photograph deformed and transmuted by the mind, experience, irony or the philosophical spirit of the Poet, then a large poem would have to be like the projection of a color film onto a screen of vast dimensions, in the course of which the mind and sensibility of the Poet speak with things and each time expand in order to embrace more aspects of an external world which is at the same time shaped and modified by the Poet's ego, until the bounds between inside and outside, you and I, above and below, begin to fade.

In these poems of Octavio Paz, the three roads to revelation, according to Ramón Xirau, are image, love and a sense of the sacred. Very close to Machado and Heidegger, Octavio Paz sees the poem as a being shaped by pharases whose intimate makeup is time. But if the poem is temporal, how does one specify its significance clearly?

Like Heidegger, for whom the essence of poetry may be given from a few of Hölderlin's verses, Paz chooses a particular image formed by two phrases: "heavy as a stone," "light as a feather." What is the poetic image? Undoubtedly, the union of contraries. "The poet," Paz has said, "names things: these are feathers, those are stones. And suddenly affirms—the stones are feathers, this is that. The elements of the image do not lose their concrete and singular character. The stones continue being stones, rough, hard, impenetrable, sunny yellow or mossy green—heavy stones. And the feathers, feathers: light. The image turns out to be shocking because it defies the law of non-contradiction. To declare the contrary entity assaults the foundation of our thinking. And Ramón Xirau observes:

> In other words, the image for Paz is essentially paradoxical and reveals stimultaneously the unity and the vexing paradox which we are. The image discloses the contrary of logical thought that has dominated the West since Parmenides. It reveals our sameness and our otherness. It ends up by demonstrating that we are at the same time, ourselves and another. For Paz, the poetic experience resembles the experiences of the Orient—for which the horror of the "other" doesn't exist—and the expression of a few mystics of the West.

Paz himself, in his "Carta a León Felipe" (Letter to León Felipe), points out some characteristics of his poetics:

> . . .
> Como los saltimbanquis
>   Andan por el aire
> Dos loros en pleno vuelo
>   Desafian al movimiento
> Y al lenguaje
>   !Miralos
>   Ya se fueron!
> Irradiación de unas cuantas palabras
> Es un aleteo
>   El mundo se aclara
> Sólo para volverse invisible
> Aprender a ver oír decir
>   Lo instantáneo
> Es nuestro oficio
>   ¿Fijar vértigos?
> Las palabras
>   Como los pericos en celo

Se volatilizan
        Su movimiento
Es un regreso a la inmovilidad
. . .
La poesía
        Es la ruptura insantánea
Instantáneamente cicatrizada
                Abierta de nuevo
Por la mirada de los otros
            La ruptura
Es la continuidad
. . .

             (Ladera este)

(. . .
Like acrobats
        Flying through air
Two parrots in full flight
           Defy motion
And language
        Look at them
                Already gone!
Irradiation of a few words
Is a flapping of wings
           The world making itself clear
Only to becoming invisible again
To learn to see to hear to say
           The instantaneous
Is our trade
        To get hold of vertigos?
Words
      Like these parakeets in heat
Dissipate themselves
        Their movement
Is a return to immobility
. . .
Poetry
      is instantaneous rupture
Instantly healed
        Cut open again

Through the meeting of another's eyes
                                                    Rupture

Is continuity
. . .)

Poetry is then, a form of approaching close to "the other shore" "there where contraries make a pact," a way of transcending solitude and the poverty of the ego locked up in itself. Which leads us to observe that the Orient for Paz, expressed as a lived and cultural experience in which his poetry has reached its prime, has a tendency radically opposed and contrary to the Oriental experience of Pablo Neruda. The Orient absorbed Neruda, locking him up in the treasures of his subconscious. Paz is opened up by the Orient, fusing his experience and personality with a vaster and vaster present and horizon. At the end of "Vrindaban," Paz writes:

. . .
Tengo hambre de vida y también de morir
Sé lo que creo y lo escribo
Advenimiento del instance
                                        El acto
El movimiento en que se esculpe
Y se deshace el ser entero
Conciencia y manos para asir el tiempo
Soy una historia
                                Una memoria que se inventa
Nunca estoy solo
Hablo siempre contigo Hablas siempre conmigo
A oscuras voy y planto signos
                            (*Ladera este*)

(. . .
I am hungry for life and for death too
I know what I believe and I write it
Coming of the instant
                                    The act
The movement in which whole being
Is sculpted and destroyed
Consciousness and hands to seize time
I am a history
                        A memory that invents itself

I am never alone
I always talk with you
You always with me
In the dark I go and plant signs)

Contrast Paz's "I am never alone" with Neruda's phrase in *Residencia en la tierra*, a book directly influenced by his Eastern experience: "Estoy solo entre materias desvencijadas" (I am alone among broken down substances).

    Viento entero, one of Paz's longest, most important and characteristic poems of this "Eastern period," is a good example of the technique with which the Poet articulates and by saying it in this way "ennobles" a series of experiences appearing at first sight, disordered and chaotic. The link in the end concludes by means of a repetition of a central theme—"El presente es pertetuo" (The present is perpetual). Each incident is like a brief notation in a travel diary:

. . .
En los claros de silencio
                  Estallan
Los gritos de los niños
                    Príncipes en harapos
A la orilla del río atormentado
Rezan orinan meditan
                  El presente es perpetuo
Se abren las computers del año
                    El día salta
    Agata
. . .

(. . .
In the clear silences
                  Explode
The children's cries
                  Princes in rags
On the shore of the tormented river
They pray they piss they plan
                  The present is perpetual
The floodgates of the year are opened
                  The day bursts
    Agate
. . .)

The dignification of the material is carried out through images and mythology (I believe this is one of the modern poems Góngora would have understood immediately). The beloved woman is described briefly: ". . . Si el fuego es agua / Eres una gota diáfana . . ." (. . . If fire is water / You are a limpid drop . . .). The mountains are: ". . . Soles destazados / Petrificada tempestad ocre . . ." (. . . Carved out suns / Petrified ochre storms . . .).

> El puño de la sangre golpea
> > Puertas de piedra
>
> . . .
> (The fists of blood pounded
> > Doors of rock
>
> . . .)

> La noche entra con todos sus árboles
> Noche de insectos eléctricosy fieras de seda
> . . .
> (The night comes in with all its trees
> Night of electric insects and beasts of silk
> . . .)

And we enter in this way into a zone of vertigos and mystery in which everything is possible beneath the remote gaze of the gods:

> . . .
> > Los universos se desgranan
> Un mundo cae
> > Se enciende una semilla
> Cada palabra palpita
> > Oigo tu latir en la sombra
> Enigma en forma de reloj de arena
> > Mujer dormida
> . . .
> Emigran los espacios
> > El presente es perpetuo
> En el pico del mundo se acarician
> Shivay Parvati
> > Cada caricia dura un siglo
> Para el dios y para el hombre
> > Un mismo tiempo
> Un mismo despeñarse

. . .
Yo veo a través de mis actos irreales
El mismo día que comienza
                              Gira el espacio
Arranca sus raíces el mundo
No pesan más que el alba nuestros cuerpos
                                        Tendidos

(. . .
        The universes separate
A world crashes down
                          A seed is ignited
Each word throbs
                      I hear your pulse in the shade
Riddle shaped hourglass
                          Sleeping woman
. . .
Spaces migrate
                  The present is perpetual
At the top of the world
Shiva and Parvati caress
                          Each caress lasts a century
For god and for humanity
                              The same time
To hurl yourself down
. . .
I see through my unreal acts
The same day that begins
                          Goes around spaces
The world tears up its roots
Our stretched out bodies weigh no more
                                  Than the dawn)

Flow and return of consciousness and the external world, point and counterpoint and the eternal, the latter reinforced by the words "always" and "perpetual" that appear repeatedly, Paz's poem is made up of contrary elements coordinated in a unity, a synthesis that leaves undestroyed each concrete experience except order and meaning. The eternal and fleeting come to an agreement and coexist. The erotic and sacred experiences strike us very closely, since, as Paz has written:

. . . These are acts that spring forth from the same fountain. At different levels of existence we leap wanting to reach the other shore. Communion, to mention a familiar example, brings about a change in the nature of the believer. The sacred food transmutes us. And that being "others" is nothing but a recapturing of our original nature or condition. "Woman," Novalis said, "is the highest bodily food." . . . The idea of the return—present in every religious act, in every myth and even in utopias—is the force of the gravity of love. Woman exalts us, makes us get out of ourselves and simultaneously makes us return. To fall: to be again.

And finally we reach *Blanco*, perhaps Paz's most difficult poem. If *Viento entero* expressed a precarious yet sparkling plenitude, a cosmic confidence, *Blanco* might seem to us at the beginning a cautious and solipsistic poem, a poem of words and about the word, the word that looks at itself in the mirror, the word that bites its tail and withdraws into itself. On this poem are cast the shadows of Mallarmé, Georges Bataille, and maybe even Zen Buddhism with its instinctive mistrust before intellectual constructions of language.

If we could see the world through words, if only with words we could get hold of and seize the chaos that surrounds us, what then would the very foundation of the word be? Let us reread another fragment from "Carta a León Felipe" that might well serve as prologue for *Blanco*:

> . . .
> Las palabras
>   Como los pericos en celo
> Se volatilizan
>   Su movimiento
> Es un regreso a la inmovilidad
> No nos queda dijo Bataille
> Sino escribir comentarios
>   Insensatos
> Sobre la ausencia de sentido del escribir
> Comentarios que se borran
>   La escritura poética
> Es borrar lo escrito
>   Escribir
> Sobre lo escrito
>   Lo no escrito

Representar la *comedia* sin desenlace
Je ne puis parler d'une absence de sens
Sinon lui donnant un sens qu'elle n'a pas
La escritura poética es
                        Aprender a leer
El hueco de la escritura
                        En la escritura
. . .
(Ladera este)

(. . .
Words
        Like these parakeets in heat
Dissipate themselves
                    Their movement
Is a return to immobility
Nothing remains for us said Bataille
But to write foolish
                    Commentaries
On the absence of meaning in writing
Commentaries that erase themselves
                            To write poetry
Is to erase the written
                    To write
On the written
                The unwritten
To perform the *comedy* without an ending
Je ne puis parler d'une absence de sens
Sinon lui donnant un sens qu'elle n'a pas
To write poetry is
                Learning to read
The empty space of writing
                        In the writing
. . .)

Blanco is a poem that, like the novel *Rayuela* by Julio Cortázar, can be read in many ways. The large central poem (about 80% of the text) is a long discourse on the word and silence, on the foundation of the word. To the right and left rise, like short walls, like flanked towers, two other poems—a love poem and a poem dedicated to the sensations. As if with the presence of love and the sensations Paz should want to give life and sensualize what in some other way would result in an exceedingly intellectual and dry exercise. The word leans on itself, it questions itself about its own being. We see born, slowly, with effort, the words "sunflower," "river." But Paz's flower is much more concrete than Mallarmé's *l'absente de tout bouquet*:

> . . .
>   Alto en su vera
> (Cabeza es una pica),
>   Un girasol
>
> . . .
>   Flor
> Ni vista ni pensada:
>   Oída,
> Aparece
>   Amarillo
> Cáliz de consonantes vocales
> Incendiadas.
> . . .
> (. . .
>   High on its shaft
> |Head on a pike|
>   A sunflower
>
> . . .
> Neither seen nor thought:
>   Heard
> Appears
>   Yellow
> Chalice of consonants and vowels
> Burning.)

The Poet advances by means of paradox:

> . . .
> La irrealidad de lo mirado
> Da realidad a la mirada
> . . .
> (. . .
> The unreality of the seen
> Makes real the seeing
> . . .)

One must know how to say No and Yes at the same time. We got out of trouble not by using the traditional linear logic, but thanks to an ambiguous, circular one:

> . . .
> El espíritu
> Es una invención del cuerpo
> El cuerpo
> Es una invención del mundo
> El mundo
> Es una invención del espíritu
> . . .
>
> (. . .
> The spirit
> Is an invention of the body
> The body
> An invention of the world
> The world
> An invention of the spirit
> . . .)

And the philosophical poem is contaminated at last by eroticism before a young woman ". . . desnuda / Como una silaba . . ." (. . . naked / As a syllable . . .) whose body ". . . Visto / Desvanacido / Da realidad a la mirada" (. . . Seen / Vanished / Makes real the seeing). And the mirror breaks: the image lives. Through the presence of another human being, a presence seized and aroused by the word and its meanings, language remains well-founded, established, in this poem. And in it, as in all Paz's poetry, contraries make a pact and are reconciled and in so doing reach the plenitude of their own being.

ALLEN W. PHILLIPS

Octavio Paz: Critic of Modern Mexican Poetry

In view of the proverbially comprehensive nature of Octavio Paz's literary criticism, it is perhaps amazing to recall that he has devoted so much time to his own literature. It is equally true that for this very reason he is genuinely universal in his outlook, at the same time rejecting forcefully any spurious nationalism. Paz clearly does not believe in Mexican literature in the abstract, but rather in certain Mexican authors and in certain poems written by Mexicans who are progressively taking a major role in the literary dialogue of our times. However, from the decade of the thirties when he began to practice what he modestly called literary and artistic journalism, up to the panoramic prologue to "Poetry in Movement" (1966), he has not failed to be deeply concerned with Mexican literature, its past and its present.

To begin with, let us venture a rapid description of Octavio Paz's literary criticism in its general lines, taking as a special base his works on Mexican literature, but without at the same time excluding others on different themes. As an essential note I should like to emphasize that his is a creative criticism, inseparable from poetic activity, always highly personal and the product of wide and careful reading. It is an *open* criticism, made in lively response to the works studied, which establishes the multiple resonances they wake in his spirit. To read his pages is to embark on a voyage through all cultures and all literatures, although it is not difficult to perceive

From *The Perpetual Present: The Poetry and Prose of Octavio Paz*, edited by Ivar Ivask, © 1973 by University of Oklahoma Press.

certain preferences or families of writers that especially attract him. Without speaking of oriental sources, there are among the French: Baudelaire, Mallarmé, Lautréamont, Rimbaud, Apollinaire and the surrealists; Novalis and the German romantics; Blake Donne, Whitman, Eliot and other figures in poetry of the English language; the Spanish baroque writers (reading Góngora and Quevedo was decisive for him) and certain contemporary writing in Spanish from Darío and Lugones to Cernuda and Guillén. Among the Mexicans to whom he is devoted alongside Pellicer, Villaurrutia and Cuesta, three national authors seem to be particularly distinguished by his preference: Alfonso Reyes, José Juan Tablada and Ramón López Velarde.

Paz's criticism is also in a certain sense fragmentary, which is not to say that he has not written organic books like *El arco y la lira*, revised in later edition, or *El laberinto de la soledad*, with its *Posdata* of 1970. Usually he chooses the form of brief notes and approaches authors who awaken his enthusiasm or admiration: fluctuation between direct commentary on some specific poem, the concentrated essay embracing the work of a single author; or more general topics like surrealism or pointed definitions of the modern literary adventure. Such, for example, are the pages collected in *Las peras del olmo* (1957), a selection of early works that have lost none of their freshness and mastery of direction in spite of having been written, for the most part, some twenty or twenty-five years ago. The book is composed of essays of various kinds, in which certain clichés of criticism undergo fresh examination, their partial truth failing to correspond with reality; ("Emula de la llama . . ."); studies in revaluation; ("La estela de josé Juan Tablada"); or texts which perfect and complete earlier studies of other critics ("El lenguaje de Ramón López Velarde"). And it is appropriate to recall Octavio Paz's interest, still persistent, in the plastic arts, evident on many pages of this same book.

These brief essays were followed by a companion volume *Puertas al campo* (1966) intimately related to the earlier title and then at a later date by *Corriente alterna* (1967). In my judgment the prologues to the last two books are particularly significant. In the one to *Puertas al campo*, Paz explains that the volume is an extension of the earlier essay except that time separates them. He further states that this volume of 1966 coincides with a moment of great richness in Mexican letters, as opposed to one of indecision in the preceding volume of 1957, and in this flowering he takes great faith and joy.

In the brief introduction to *Corriente alterna* he defends the fragmentary nature of his criticism, only superficially disperse, and in the same pages he insists on two key ideas: the moving reality of which we are part and books as a system of relations and interrelations. The critical fragments of Octavio

Paz have an internal unity and a consistent train of thought holds them together. It is important to note how certain critical themes and concerns appearing in early pages are later more fully developed, a question of a clear process of growth and maturing; a constant return and an enrichment; a prolongation and refining of what was in him already from the first stage of his literary criticism.

Paz has never proposed arranging Mexican poetry in a systematic or systemized history. In this connection I am not forgetting his introduction to the *Anthology of Mexican Poetry* (Indiana University Press, 1958) which covers the Colonial Period up to and including Ramón López Velarde. Here he reveals his enthusiasm for some Mexican baroque poets as well as his lack of sympathy for the very limited success of Mexican romantics. With a few exception, (among them the fascinating personality of Sor Juana), it is only natural that he is more interested in the poetry after modernism and especially contemporary expression. If he frequently condemns the novel of the *Revolución*, he is attracted to its more modern counterpart (Yàñez, Rulfo, Fuentes and some of the younger novelists). Paz also gives importance to the essays of certain Mexicans, above all to those of Reyes and Cuesta. Nonetheless, the critical texts of Paz, indeed partial, tend to form a rather complete panorama of modern Mexican literature, above all from modernism to today.

Another element inseparable from his literary criticism and in effect of all his prose work, is the synthesis, sure and brilliant, often expressed in a terse phrase, almost aphoristic, which sums up or lights up clearly the meaning of his critical thought. I believe, in fact, that to characterize this criticism, based on a precise play of queries and answers (he questions himself and the works) there are two words of equal significance: illumination and revelation. I dare even propose two others: self-examination and self-portrait. Paz's literary criticism is the recreation of the poem by a poet-critic exceptionally gifted and committed to the practice of literature, who knows how to identify himself in feeling (which does not at all exclude lucidity) with the experience of another, make it his own and communicate to the reader a personal response to it.

The foregoing description of Octavio Paz's criticism corresponds to my personal way of reading it and being enlightened by it. Now, more objectively, I find myself forced to refer to a few texts in which the writer himself speaks of the function of that criticism. It is not surprising that a spirit so clear and passionate at the same time should have always had full consciousness of its mission and should now and again have complained of a certain poverty of good critical writing in Spanish. He rejects, naturally and immediately, the journalistic criticism full of facile enthusiasms and useless conformism, and sees great danger lest criticism be prostituted by commercialism and politics (*Puertas*, 1966). Nor is he a defender of a traditional science of literature and classifications imposed by traditional rhetoric ("to classify is not to understand"), although he may write: ". . . rhetoric, stylistics, sociology, psychology and all the other literary disciplines are indispensible if we wish to study a work, but they can tell us nothing about its intimate nature". There are, however, texts to which one must refer here: in one Paz explains the inner process of his criticism; in the other he defines the role of criticism, offering at the same time recommendations for Spanish language critics.

In his pages written in 1960 about the painter Rufino Tamayo, Octavio Paz reflects on the esthetic experience which is essentially pleasure, and since in the critical act of judging (and he judges, he confesses, to add pleasure to pleasure, which is or should be the starting point of all criticism) there enter reflections and the senses, thought and feeling, activities of diverse origins, but complementary in the adjustment of a truly critical vision. The senses cannot be eliminated; they must be guided and made more lucid. And then, as Paz says, judgment, sometimes an ally, at others an adversary, but always an incorruptible witness, "teaches how to distinguish living works from the mechanical. It reveals to me the secrets of clever fabrications and traces the frontier between art and artistic industry. In short, in enjoying works, I judge them; in judging, I enjoy. I live through a total experience, in which my whole being participates". Lastly in the same essay Paz speaks of how he takes possession of the work with careful scrutiny and how he conceives criticism again, always as an active and creative experience. In the critical act, he says, the work of art becomes a part of him. In judging it he also judges himself. No longer passive, he tries to go back to the origin of the artistic expression and rebuild the road which the creator has traced. Criticism, then, for Paz is always creative in nature and in the ultimate analysis is the description of a personal esthetic experience.

A second fragment, highly significant and collected in *Corriente alterna*, is entitled "About Criticism." His point of departure is partly negative: he laments that there is not in Spanish what he calls "intellectual space," which would permit a meeting of works, one with another, in true dialogue involving its extension or negation: ". . . Criticism is that which constitutes what we call a literature and is not so much the sum of the works as the system of their relationships: a field of affinities and contrasts." Once again Paz insists on the close relation between criticism and creation, criticism as nourishment for modern artists and as literary invention.

The mission of the literary critic, then, is to relate works of art and discover their place in the totality of literary expression. The function of criticism is to invent a perspective and an order. This points precisely to the failure of criticism in Spanish America; Spanish American critics must describe the frontiers, the forms, the structure, the dynamic movement of their literature and place its work in communication with one another, reading them in a universal context. Although Latin America still lacks a literary center ("Argentinian Europeanism and Mexican nationalism are distinct forms with a common infirmity: deafness"), Paz seems to glimpse the possibility of establishing authentic communication at some future time. Inasmuch as good literary criticism, operating by negation and associations, affinities and oppositions, brings order and stresses relationships, he even goes so far as to say that in our epoch criticism is the foundation of literature.

In an article about Paz as a critic of modern Mexican literature one cannot evade another idea conceived as fundamental and reiterated with marked frequency in his criticism of recent years. It is possible that Paz believed vaguely at an initial stage in the possibility of defining and differentiating the specifically Mexican in its literature. It seems to me now that he has doubts about the conception of what is truly Mexican. At one moment he asks himself: what is it that unites poets so different as López Velarde, Lugones and Laforgue? It is not, it cannot be, the so-called national genius but the *spirit of the time* and he goes on to say:

> The existence of a French, a German or an English poetry is debatable; the reality of baroque, romantic or symbolist poetry is not. I do not deny national traditions nor the temperament of peoples; I affirm that style is universal, or better, international. What we call national traditions are almost always versions and adaptions of styles that were universal. In the last analysis a work is something more than a tradition and a style: a unique creation, an individual vision. To the extent to which the work is most perfect, tradition and style are less visible. Art aspires to transparence. (*Poesía*)

Literary styles are not national but international, and the individual accent of each artist is more significant than elusive national character.

Paz does not tire of repeating that styles travel; they are temporal in nature and "do not belong to the land but to the centuries"; they are, in a word, more ample than any geographical frontiers. And even more: in his opinion, modern literature is a single literature, and, now that time and space have become intermingled "a synchronic vision of art is superimposed over the diachronic."

There definitely exists a Spanish American literature, different from the Spanish above all because of its destructive and polemic attitude with reference to language and tradition, but the plurality of nations, each with their own peculiarities, does not destroy a unified culture and language. But this unity does not imply uniformity. Literary tendencies do not correspond to geographical labels, to political or ethnic entities. If an artistic movement is important, it does not take long to go beyond national boundaries. And Mexican literature is, after all, a portion of that literary dialogue, and the Mexican writer of today feels himself to be not only a part of Spanish American literature but also immersed in the universal artistic expression of our modern world.

In *Cuadrivio* (1965) are collected four long essays on Rubén Darío, Ramón López, Velarde, Pessoa and Cernuda, dissident poets whose "creation was also critical, breaking with the language, the esthetics or the morality of their time" and their work, according to Paz, establishes a tradition of scission, the characteristic note of modern poetry. In the essay on Darío, "El caracol y la sirena," definitive pages and in my opinion among the best written by Paz as critic, modernism is correctly presented as what it really was: the great beginning, the end of which is not yet, the importance of which is double: ". . . on the one hand it produced four or five poets who renewed the great hispanic tradition, broken and detained at the end of the 17th century; on the other hand, having opened all doors and windows, revived the language." It is enough to say that Paz emphasizes the most lasting and vital of that splendid movement, seeing it as a linguistic renewal without neglecting its profound ideological content. In summary, then, with modernism is created a new poetic language and in Hispanic America a dialogue with other literatures is really begun.

In modernism Paz usually and with good reason isolates the importance of Lugones and above all of his great *Lunario sentimental*, a book of open revolt already in a position outside of modernism. I believe, however, that Paz would be little interested in Lugones's final poetry, more narrative and traditional, but one cannot insist too much on the significance of the *Lunario*, in which a new poetic vision and extraordinary language have held so transcendant a place in the evolution of Hispanic-American poetry, from López Velarde to the *ultraístas* of Argentina and beyond. It surprises me a little that Paz has not given more attention to Herrera y Reissig, who is mentioned occasionally in lists, for this is another unconventional poet, moving surely toward the vanguard by way of metaphor and a language that mingles with lyricism certain prose elements that give new tension to his poetic expression. Naturally, Octavio Paz has at various times concerned himself with Mexican modernism, and he does not consider its poets to be of the same stature as the great figures of the movement. He believes that the Mexicans were not aware of the profound meaning of modernism and that their work was usually limited to the exoticism and purely external aspects of this tendency. An example, not mentioned by Paz, could be Efrén Rebolledo, perhaps the most faithful of all Mexican poets to the modernist esthetic, with all the defects and virtues implied in such a statement. The verdicts of Paz on Gutiérrez Nájera as a poet (he does not refer to his prose) and Amado Nervo are not on the whole favorable (at one point he even calls them "authors of some of the clumsiest and most prosaic of our poetry") his reticences are equally eloquent. Personally, I believe that his opinions are correct and will stand the test of time. More kindly are his brief words about Othón and Salvador Díaz Mirón, and we can see how he relates them to each other in the following admirable summary: "If Othón is an academic who discovers romanticism and thus escapes from the Parnassianism of his school, Salvador Díaz Mirón undertakes a voyage in an opposite direction: he is a romantic aspiring to classicism . . .". Paz all the same notes how Icaza and Urbina, less applauded in their time ". . . approach more nearly the electric zone of poetry." There is, naturally, one modernist Mexican poet saved from this almost total condemnation: Enrique González Martínez who closes the period before the break that comes with the work of Tablada, López Velarde and Pellicer. Paz's opinions about the serious and austere González Martínez are definitive: he does not break with modernism, he strips it bare; he veils its light; makes from it a consciousness; and with the work of this writer from Jalisco "poetry ceases to be description and plaint to become again spiritual adventure." His strength and example is to have returned to poetry what Paz calls the gravity of the word. This is the positive side of González Martínez, but the critic is not slow in referring to his moralistic symbolism and notes how his verse sometimes lapses into sermonizing. Furthermore: his poetic work lacks the unexpected and lacks movement, being essentially hostile to innovations. The treatment given González Martínez is courteous but distant and hardly enthusiastic.

Among the special predilections of Octavio Paz are three Mexican writers, very different one from the other, but each in the best of his work existing outside the modernist stream: Alfonso Reyes, José Juan Tablada and Ramón López Velarde.

In many pages, from some of the earliest to others of more recent date, Paz never stints his praise of Reyes as a writer and an example. "It is enough to say," he once wrote, "that without him our literature would be half a literature." In his vast and varied writing, Paz praises the humanist and the universal writer, the erudite scholar refined by humor and the poet in love with words. In his literary output he fuses criticism and creation (another devotee of Mallarmé); prose and poetry mingle (for example, Vision de Anáhuac); and even in a few poems the direct language is infused with a secret poetic tension. The key and summit of Reyes, *Ifigenia cruel*, a dramatic poem commented on extensively in the beautiful essay "El jinete del aire" was written directly after Reyes's death.

And in summation of these statements about Alfonso Reyes, which sometimes take the form of enthusiastic portraits, it is important to remember what Paz says about his books dealing with poetic theory. In the final section of the introduction to the first edition of *El arco y la lira* Paz writes this great tribute:

> Stimulus from him has been double: on the one hand his friendship and his example gave me courage; on the other, the books dedicated to subjects closely related to these pages . . . and so many unforgettable essays, scattered in other works–made clear to me what had seemed obscure, the opaque transparent, the wild and tangled easy and orderly. In a word: they enlightened me (*Arco*).

In another way Tablada awakened in Octavio Paz enthusiasm and fascination, an attitude not shared by many commentators on modern Mexican poetry. And more: certain poems of Tablada have been, without doubt, on more than one occasion a model for Paz's own poetry. It is not hard to explain what he found in a part of Tablada's work: movement and severance, surprise and humor, adventure and travel, cosmopolitanism and curiosity. It is important to add to these substantives, already become commonplaces with reference to Tablada that he is always in the vanguard, friend of painters and devoted to prehistoric culture. With the exception of El Abate de Mendoza and, to a lesser degree, Villaurrutia, no Mexican or foreign critic has done more than Paz to revaluate the almost forgotten work of Tablada so that it can be said that he has created a poet whose work, nonetheless, is still awaiting complete evaluation. Octavio Paz has not only done this but has also separated the worthiest part of his poetry from the more lifeless part, in accord with what Villaurrutia asked for in an earlier time. Dissenting with González Martínez, unmoved in his classicism. Tablada and at his side his young friend López Velarde, who was one of the very few who understood Tablada's attempts in spite of his grave doubts about certain poetical experiments of the older poet, broke with the language of modernism and initiated a new lyric adventure. And it is not irrelevant to recall that in 1914 Tablada was one of the first to recognize the originality and worth of López Velarde. Nor is Paz unaware that between these two poets and the next generation of *Contemporáneos* there exists an obvious continuity. Paz's most complete essay on Tablada dates from 1945, but it is enough to mention here what Paz wrote about possibly "our youngest poet" in 1966 and his opinion has not changed:

> In Mexico the tradition of the open work, not in the strict sense but in the broadest and most general, begins with Tablada. One part of his work fascinates me: that written at the end of his poetic life. There are not many poems but nearly all are amazing. Haiku and ideographic poetry, humor and lyricism, the natural world and the city, women and travel, animals and plants, Buddha and insects. His poetry has lost none of its freshness, none of its novelty . . . (*Poesia*).

The longest essay that Paz devotes to a Mexican poet is "El camino de la pasión" (1963) on Ramón López Velarde. It is difficult for me to summarize my judgments on this brilliant work. They shift from frank and unqualified enthusiasm to certain minor disagreements (perhaps the most pertinent is in reference to the slight value Paz seems to give the poems collected posthumously in *El son del corazón*, excepting "La suave patria"). What I have already said in print, is that after this memorable study by Paz there is practically nothing new to say of the Zacatecan poet, even in this year 1971, the fiftieth anniversary of his death, which has produced critical writing to the saturation point. Yet in my own inescapable share in the homages presented in the month of June, I had the uncomfortble feeling that I was repeating in another form many things said already, and better, by Paz.

His was an early interest in López Velarde. Exemplary is his note about this writer's innovations in language, and this work of 1950 completes and continues an earlier essay of Villaurrutia. Here for the first time something fundamental is studied: Lugones and Laforgue as fruitful stimuli to López Velarde's own original instrument of expression. I believe that Paz's statements made twenty years ago have not lost their freshness and they have passed, with hardly a correction, into his more extensive work of 1963. In parenthesis, if Paz has not changed his word on Laforgue, the pages on Baudelaire and López Velarde have undergone some fundamental modifications.

"El camino de la pasión," always precise and illuminating, places López Velarde on the threshold of worldwide modern poetry (and in the Spanish language, according to Paz, this saw the light in Hispanic America earlier than in the peninsula). The essay is important also for what it tells us of the modern poem, its form and structure; of the esthetic of López Velarde and the metaphor which reveals and strips bare; of his eroticism and his love; of his beliefs and his literary tradition. Especially meaningful also are the textural commentaries on one of López Velarde's most intense poems, "El sueño de los guantes negros," where the central verse is a question ("is not your flesh preserved in each bone?") and one with no answer.

This essay seems to be the happy climax of long years spent with the brief and concentrated work of López Velarde; it succeeds in illuminating many obscure corners that characterize the poet's mature work in prose and verse. Having commented thus upon some of the friendly judgments Paz gives on Reyes, Tablada and López Velarde, three writers related, though differently, to later poetry, we are in a position to move on to two ultimate nuclei in our long voyage through Paz's criticism of modern Mexican poetry: the generation of the *Contemporáneos* and that of the young who follow them.

In this final part of our subject it would be little short of impossible to make a complete collection of the critical judgments given by Paz on the poetry of the twenties to the present. They are, with a few notable exceptions, more fragmentary, but not for this reason less authentic or penetrating. This is the literary period that critic and poet lived through intimately. Above all I should like to avoid a sort of catalogue, and therefore will be content with pointing out certain enthusiasms and reservations that influence his personal way of evaluating or placing in focus the evolution of the national lyric in some fifty years of intensified production.

To the decade of the twenties belong the beginnings of the generation of *Los contemporáneos*, a group of distinguished writers, accused of being neglectful of Mexico but united by their absorption with universal questions and their high esthetic ideals, by their critical position and their tireless activities in behalf of culture (reviews, experimental theater, love for the plastic arts). Among these writers Paz seems to be enthusiastic about four in particular: the three great poets (Pellicer, Villaurrutia, Gorostiza) and the essayist Jorge Cuesta. He is less interested in two figures slightly more to the right: Torres Bodet and Ortiz de Montellano, although as regards the latter he does mention his sympathy for the prehispanic. All the same he points out the importance of Gilberto Owen, because his work is a milestone in the development of the prose poem in Mexico. As for Salvador Novo, only his first stage seemingly merits Paz's praise.

In *Las peras del olmo* two critical essays are collected, from 1951 and 1955, devoted respectively to Gorostiza and Pellicer. There is no specific article on Villaurrutia, whom he greatly admired, none that we know of, except that he excuses himself for not having written one. Certainly he comments warmly on his poetry on many occasions, and I believe, besides, that Villaurrutia's literary criticism on Mexican and foreign authors was always stimulating to Paz. He perfects and prolongs in more than one sense Villaurrutia's critical appraisals. And in 1966 Paz offers a splendid summary of his poetry.

In the case of Cuesta, who claimed Paz's intellectual sympathy because of the originality of his thought and his capacity for analysis, he valued him above all as an essayist preoccupied with research in the meaning of the Mexican tradition. Paz writes of him in a page of *El laberinto de la soledad*, alongside other thinkers (Vasconcelos, Ramos, Reyes and others), and besides a few other brief phrases alluding personally to Cuesta, Paz explains his exclusion from *Poesía en movimiento* as follows: ". . . The influence of his thinking upon the poets of his generation was very deep, and on my own also, but his poetry was not in his poems but in the work of those lucky enough to have heard him."

In an early note (1942) entitled "Emula de la llama . . ." that received a prize in the Editorial Seneca contest, the earlier title being "Pura, encendida rosa," Octavio Paz undertakes a critical examination of Pedro Henríquez Ureña's often abused statement about Mexican sensibility and its twilight tones. Here are delineated the hour of Pellicer (the brilliant light of morning), of Gorostiza (early morning) and of Villaurrutia (night). In a later essay on Pellicer he goes deeply into the work of this poet of sun and sea; sees in him the first really modern poet of Mexico, already far from the manner of González Martínez; and completes his judgment by stating: ". . . he is the richest and most vast of the poets of his generation. There are more perfect poets; or more dense and dramatic; keener or deeper; but none has his deep breadth, his dazzled and dazzling sensuality. . . ." I cannot resist the temptation to copy an opinion of 1966 about Pellicer in which Paz reiterates with increased certainty some earlier points of view:

> We also grow enthusiastic about this poetry which puts the world in flight and turns rocks to cloud, the woods to rain, a puddle to a constellation. Word-kite, word-helix, word-stone to fling at the sky. We shall never tire of this winged reality. Each time I read Pellicer, I truly *see*. To read him clears the eyes, sharpens the senses, gives body to reality. Speed of a glance into diaphanous air; to arrest that moment in which energy flows invisibly, matures and bursts into tree, house, dog, machine, person. Like the rivers of his land, Pellicer's work is broad and, like them, true to itself: his latest book could be the first. In another poet this might be a defect. In him it is a virtue, the greatest of his gifts. He preserves intact the original force: enthusiasm and creative imagination. (*Poesía*)

The reflectiveness of Villaurrutia is contrasted with the magic of Pellicer, but in a revealing earlier page, Paz believes that there are wings in the poet of Tabasco ". . . but not a 'somersault,' nor change from one state to another." And on various occasions he repeats that those three poets, the best of their generation and each with his own remarkable, distinguished personality, were condemned to staying within the frontiers of their poetic universe. Gorostiza, sparing and complex, is according to Paz, the author of "one of the most important works of modern poetry in the Spanish language," a poem ". . . summoned to last as long as the loftiest creations of the language." In his introduction to *Poesía en movimiento*, he gives us, as in the case of Pellicer and Villaurrutia, another admirable measure for establishing what "Muerte sin fin" represents in the modern tradition.

After the generation of the *Contemporáneos* comes that of Octavio Paz himself, which in its time, the thirties, was grouped around various ephemeral reviews before the founding of *Taller* in 1938, its principal and most permanent organ. In 1954 Paz wrote his polemical reply to *La poesía mexicana moderna*, the anthology published by Castro Leal. He did it because it seemed clear to him that in the second part the compiler failed to understand and therefore did not represent the latest generation of Mexican poets very well. In this text, as opposed to the desires and predilections of the earlier group—many of them certainly admired and sympathized with by Paz—he defines clearly the ideals of his own generation of *Taller*. I confine myself to a short summary at best risky: poetry as an action and experience lived through, in which the writer realizes and transcends himself; repudiation of the earlier intellectualism; new influences (the young Spanish poets, the surrealists, Neruda, et cetera); and, as Paz says, "love, poetry and revolution were three burning synonyms." A new conscience vis-à-vis the world, society and the word.

In two brief essays written in 1959 and later collected in *Puertas al campo*, Paz first hails the "verbal explosion" of the first book of Marco Antonio Montes de Oca and next the appearance of *La paloma azul* of Manuel Durán. This is a cordial and sympathetic critique, enthusiastic but demanding, implying certain slight disagreements with the authors. In the same volume there appears a long essay "El precio y la significación" (1963) which includes in its last part an extensive list of young writers (Rulfo, Arreola, Sabines, Xirau, Segovia, García Terrés, García Ponce, Fuentes and others) who contributed toward 1950 to the birth of a new epoch in Mexican literature, after the relative pause in the decade before. From the fifties must be mentioned also the experimental group of *Poesía en voz alta* and the publication of the *Revista mexicana de literatura*, both undertakings animated by the presence of Octavio Paz in Mexico.

There was a delay of a few years, indeed until 1966, when Paz wrote his most organic pages about Mexican poetry of the last fifty years. This constitutes the introduction, already quoted, to *Poesía en movimiento*, an experimental anthology compiled in collaboration with Alí Chumacero, Pacheco and Aridjis. The anthology incorporates a total of forty-two poets, among whom about thirty belong to recent generations.

Certain basic ideas govern the selection of poets and poems. The aim is to show poetry in all its mobility and mutation; indicate the spirit of adventure and search which characterizes it from the point of view of the break initiated years before by Darío and Huidobro, the break which for Paz is the mark of modern poetry. Their criterion then, is change, not the stalemate implied by the collecting of the best poems of an author and not necessarily those showing an intention to do something distinctive. The method used to reflect this dynamic quality is not completely exclusive, and therefore, to the benefit of the whole panorama, some poets are included who have sought novelty in only a few instances (I am thinking at the moment of Torres Bodet, Rosario Castellanos). Besides in constructing this book, there is a departure from traditional order, since the authors do not regard the past as a beginning, but the reverse: "to see in the present a beginning, in the past an end." Hence the order of the poets. The work begins with Homero Aridjis and Pacheco (the youngest), and ends with López Velarde and Tablada (the oldest). Lastly it seems to me highly proper to include poems in prose of Julio Torri, Owen, Paz, Aridjis and Pacheco, and I wonder, in parenthesis, why not some of López Velarde?

In his introduction, solid and complete, Paz moves freely, treating historical or chronological schemes and general historical groups (*Los contemporáncos*, *Taller*, *La espiga amotinada*), but, as he himself confesses, he lets himself be guided not by an objective criterion but by his own preferences and even his caprice. His judgments are always personal and imaginative and in them can often be seen the play of oppositions and affinities helping to determine the exact position of the authors. While individualizing them, he establishes contradictory and complementary relationships among them. Remember, for instance, the stratagem of using for the younger poets the system of coordinates derived from the *I Ching*. Paz insists that his opinions do not belong to literary criticism; clearly I do not agree; but let me repeat the closing words of the introduction:

> . . . the significance of poetry, if it has any, is not in the judgments of the critic or the opinions of the poet. The significance is changing and momentary: it flowers from the encounter between poet and reader. (*Poesía*)

One final word: Octavio Paz believes fervently in youthful Mexican poetry (he would probably say in some poets and their work); youthful Mexican poetry believes in him. He has oriented many of them, from Montes de Oca on; he is an inciting presence among them; they read and study him. It would be tiresome to recount here what during different periods of his wandering life Paz's sojourns in Mexico have meant to literary youth. They have acted as a catalytic agent. Even more: they are become a fundamental presence.

Chronology

1914   Octavio Paz born on March, 31, in Mexico City. Brought up in Mixcoac where he attends primary school.

1927   Attends secondary school in Mexico City.

1929   Completes secondary education.

1931   Publishes first poem. Founds *Barandal*, first literary review.

1933   Publishes *Luna silvestre*, first book of poems.

1936   Visits and works in Yucatan.

1937   Marries Elena Garro.

1937   Attends Writer's Congress in Republican Spain. Meets Neruda, Vallejo, Bunuel, and Miguel Hernandez. Publishes *Raiz del hombre*.

1938   Meets Robert Desnos in Paris. In Mexico he founds *Taller* (1938-41), a literary review.

1942   Publishes *A la orilla del mundo*.

1943   Helps found and edit *El hijo prodigo* (1943-45), a literary review.

1943   Comes to the United States on a Guggenheim fellowship, where he stays until 1945.

1945   Moves to Paris.

1946   Becomes Mexican cultural attache. Befriends Andre Breton and
           his surrealist group.

1949   Publishes *Libertad bajo palabra*.

1950   Publishes *El labertinto de la soledad* (second revised edition in
           1959).

1951   Publishes *¿Aguila o sol?*.

1952   Visits India and Japan.

1954   Publishes *Semillas para un himno*.

1956   Publishes *El arco y la lira. La hija de Rappaccini* (play) is performed.

1957   Publishes *Piedra de sol*.

1959   Takes residence in Paris where he lives until 1962.

1960   Publishes *Libertad bajo palabra* (revised edition in 1968).

1962   Publishes *Salamandra*.

1962   Becomes Mexican ambassador in India until 1968.

1963   Receives International Poetry Prize, Brussels.

1964   Marries Marie-Jose Tramini.

1967   Publishes *Blanco*. Enters Colegio National, Mexico.

1968   Resigns his post in protest at the massacre of students just before
           Mexico hosted the Olympic Games.

1969   Publishes *Ladera este; Conjunciones y disyunciones*.

1970   Publishes *Posdata*. Becomes Simon Bolivar chair at Cambridge
           University.

1971   Founds *Plural*, literary review.

1971   Charles Eliot Norton Professor at Harvard University.

1972   Publishes *Renga*.

1974   Publishes *Los hijos del limo*, his Harvard lectures.

1975   Publishes *Pasado en claro*.

1976   Founds *Vuelta*, literary review.

1977   Receives the Jerusalem Prize.

1979   Publishes *Poemas* (1935-1975). Receives Golden Eagle Prize,
           Nice.

1980   Receives Olin Yoliztli Prize, Mexico. Receives an Honorary degree, Harvard.

1981   Receives Cervantes Prize, Madrid.

1982   Publishes *Sor Juana Ines de la Cruz o las trampas de la fe*. Receives Neustadt Prize, University of Oklahoma.

1984   Receives Peace Prize, Frankfurt.

1990   Receives the Nobel Prize in Literature

1998   Dies, April 20, in Mexico City

Contributors

HAROLD BLOOM is Sterling Professor of the Humanities at Yale University and Henry W. and Albert A. Berg Professor of English at the New York University Graduate School. He is the author of over 20 books, including *Shelly's Mythmaking* (1959), *The Visionary Company* (1961), *Blake's Apocalypse* (1963), *Yeats* (1970), *A Map of Misreading* (1975), *Kabbalah and Criticism* (1975), *Agon: Toward a Theory of Revisionism* (1982), *The American Religion* (1992), *The Western Canon* (1994), and *Omens of Millennium: The Gnosis of Angels, Dreams, and Resurrection* (1996). *The Anxiety of Influence* (1973) sets forth Professor Bloom's provocative theory of the literary relationships between the great writers and their predecessors. His most recent books include *Shakespeare: The Invention of the Human*, a 1998 National Book Award finalist, and *How to Read and Why*, which was published in 2000. In 1999, Professor Bloom received the prestigious American Academy of Arts and Letters Gold Medal for Criticism.

KOSROF CHANTIKIAN lives and works as an editor and writer in San Francisco, California. He edited and wrote an introduction for the literary volume *Octavio Paz: Homage to the Poet*.

RACHEL PHILLIPS did her scholarly work at the University of Kentucky. Her publications include the highly regarded study of Octavio Paz's work *The Poetic Modes of Octavio Paz*.

JASON WILSON has been a Professor of Latin American Literature at Kings College, University of London. He has published several articles and

225

reviews on Latin American writers such as Julio Cortazar and Felisberto Hernandez, and the critical volume *Octavio Paz, A Study of his Poetics*.

JULIA A. KUSHIGIAN was the recipient of a grant from the Tinker Foundation and a fellowship from the Yale/Mellon Foundation. She is a scholar of Latin American Literature whose works include *Orientalism in the Hispanic Literary Tradition: In Dialogue with Borges, Paz, and Sarduy*.

DJELAL KADIR is a scholar of Latin American Literature. Kadir has written articles on such authors as Gabriel Garcia Marquez, Vargas Llosa and Octavio Paz, as well as the collection of essays *The Other Writing: Postcolonial Essays in Latin America's Writing Culture*.

FRANCES CHILES holds degrees in Latin American Studies and Hispanic Literature from the University of Colorado and Stanford University. She has taught at the University of of Idaho and Pomona College. Her articles and essays have appeared in such journals as *Latin American Literary Review and World Literature Today*.

JAIME ALAZRAKI lives in Cambridge, Massachusetts and teaches at Harvard University. Alazraki's work has appeared in several scholarly collections and journals, including KOSMOS.

MANUEL DURÁN has been the chairman of Yale University's Spanish Department. He has published several essays and collections of poetry, some of which have been translated by Willis Barnstone for the journal KOSMOS.

RICARDO GULLÓN lives in Chicago, Illinois where he teaches at the University of Chicago. His work has appeared in several literary journals and scholarly anthologies, including a volume devoted to the work of Octavio Paz.

ALLEN W. PHILLIPS has spent much of his life living and teaching in Santa Barbara, California. He is a literary scholar whose work has been anthologized in various collections, including *The Perpetual Present: The Poetry and Prose of Octavio Paz*.

Bibliography

Abrams, M.H. *Natural Supernaturalism: Tradition and Revolution in Romantic Literature*. New York, 1973.

Alquie, Ferdinand. *The Philosophy of Surrealism*. Ann Arbor: University of Michigan Press, 1965.

Bernard, Judith A. "Mexico as Theme, Image, and Contribution to Myth in the Poetry of Octavio Paz." Doctoral Dissertation, University of Wisconsin, 1964.

_____. "Myth and Structure in Octavio Paz's Piedra de sol." *Symposium*, 21, (1967): 5-13.

Bly, Robert. "At best new anguish, at worst old mush." *The New York Times Book Review* (April 18, 1971).

Brooks, Cleanth. *Modern Poetry and the Tradition*. Chapel Hill: University of North Carolina Press, 1965.

Brotherston, Gordon. *Latin American Poetry: Origins and Presence*. Cambridge: Cambridge University Press, 1975.

Caso, Alfonso. *The Aztec People of the Sun*. Trans. Lowell Dunham. Norman: University of Oklahoma Press, 1958.

Cassirer, Ernst. *An Essay on Man*. New Haven: Yale University Press, 1962.

Cea, Claire. *Octavio Paz*. Paris: Editions Pierre Seghers, 1965.

Chantikian, Kosrof, ed. *Octavio Paz: Homage to the Poet*. San Francisco: KOSMOS, 1980.

Chiles, Frances. Octavio Paz: *The Mythic Dimension*. New York: Peter Lang Publishing House, 1987.

_____ . "'Vuelta': The Circuitous Journey Motif in the Poetry of Octavio Paz." *Latin American Literary Review*, Vol. VI, No. 12 (Spring-Summer 1978): 57-67.

_____. "The *Bildungsreise* of Octavio Paz." World Literature Today, Vol. 56, No. 4 (Autumn 1982), 626-631.

Fein, John. "The Mirror as Image and Theme in the Poetry of Octavio Paz." *Symposium* 10, no. 2 (Fall 1956): 251-70.

Flores, Angel. ed. *Aproximaciones a Octavio Paz*. Mexico City: Joaquin Mortiz, 1974.

Fowlie, Wallace. *Age of Surrealism*. Bloomington: University of Indiana Press, 1966.

_____. *Love in Literature*. Bloomington: University of Indiana Press, 1965.

Gallagher, D.P. *Modern Latin American Literature*. Oxford: Oxford University Press, 1973.

Gimferrer, Pere, ed. *Octavio Paz*. Madrid: Taurus, 1982.

Ivask, Ivar, ed. *The Perpetual Present: The Poetry and Prose of Octavio Paz*. Norman: University of Oklahoma Press, 1973.

Kadir, Djelal. *The Other Writing: Postcolonial Essays in Latin America's Writing Culture*. West Lafayette: Purdue University Press, 1993.

King, Lloyd. "Surrealism and the Sacred in the Aesthetic Credo of Octavio Paz." *Hispanic Review* 37 (July 1969): 382-93.

Kushigian, Julia A. *Orientalism in the Hispanic Literary Tradition: In Dialogue with Borges, Paz, and Sarduy*. Albuquerque: University of New Mexico Press, 1991.

Leal, Luis. "Octavio Paz: El laberinto de la soledad." *Revista Imberoamericana*, 49 (January-July 1960): 154-186.

Nugent, Robert. "Structure and Meaning in Octavio Paz's *Piedra de sol*." Kentucky Foreign *Language Quarterly* 13, no. 3 (1966): 138-46.

Phillips, Rachel. *The Poetic Modes of Octavio Paz*. Oxford: Oxford University Press, 1972.

Prescott, F.C. *Poetry and Myth*. New York, 1927.

Remley Rambo, Ann Marie. "The Presence of Woman in the Poetry of Octavio Paz." *Hispania*, Vol. LI, No. 2 (May 1968): 259-264.

Rodriguez Padron, Jorge. *Octavio Paz*. Madrid: Jucar, 1975.

Roggiano, Alfredo, ed. *Octavio Paz*. Madrid: Editorial Fundamentos, 1979.

Rukeyser, Muriel. *Selected Poems: A Bilingual Edition*. Bloomington: University of Indiana Press, 1963.

Souza, Raymond D. "The World: symbol and synthesis in Octavio Paz." *Hispania*, XLVII, no. 1 (March 1964): 60-65.

Tomlinson, Charles. "Translations from Octavio Paz." *Hudson Review*, Vol. XXI, No. 2 (Summer 1968): 457-462.

Vickery, John B. ed., *Myth and Literature: Contemporary Theory and Practice*. Lincoln: University of Nebraska Press, 1966.

Wheelwright, Philip. *The Burning Fountain*. Bloomington: University of Indiana Press, 1968.

Williams, Thomas A. *Mallarme and the Language of Mysticism*. Athens: University of Georgia Press, 1970.

Wilson, Jason. *Octavio Paz: A Study of his Poetics*. Cambridge: Cambridge University Press, 1979.

_____. "Abrir/cerrar los ojos: A Recurrent Theme in the Poetry of Octavio Paz." *BHS*, XLVIII (1971): 44-56.

_____ . *Octavio Paz*. Boston: Twayne Publishers, 1986.

Acknowledgments

"The Poetry and Thought of Octavio Paz: An Introduction" by Kosrof Chantikian from *Octavio Paz: Homage to the Poet*, edited by Kosrof Chantikian, © 1980 by Kosrof Chantikian and *KOSMOS*. Reprinted with permission.

"The Surrealist Mode" by Rachel Phillips from *The Poetic Modes of Octavio Paz* by Rachel Phillips, © 1972 by Oxford University Press. Reprinted with permission.

"Mentalist poetics, the quest, 'fiesta' and other motifs" by Jason Wilson from *Octavio Paz: A study of his poetics* by Jason Wilson, © 1979 by Cambridge University Press. Reprinted with permission.

"Flowing Rivers and Contiguous Shores: The Poetics of Paz" by Julia A. Kushigian from *Orientalism in the Hispanic Literary Tradition: In Dialogue with Borges, Paz, and Sarduy* by Julia A. Kushigian, © 1991 by University of New Mexico Press. Reprinted with permission.

"Arborescent Paz, Interlineal Poetry" by Djelal Kadir from *The Other Writing:Postcolonial Essays in Latin America's Writing Culture* by Djelal Kadir, © 1993 by Purdue Research Foundation. Reprinted with permission.

"The Poetic Revelation" by Frances Chiles from *Octavio Paz: The Mythidc Dimension* by Frances Chiles, © 1987 by Peter Lang Publishing, Inc. Reprinted with permission.

"Octavio Paz—Poetry as Coded Silence" by Jaime Alazraki from *Octavio Paz: Homage to the Poet*, edited by Kosrof Chantikian, © 1980 by Kosrof Chantikian and KOSMOS. Reprinted with permission.

"Irony and Sympathy in *Blanco* and *Ladera este*" by Manuel Durán from *The Perpetual Present: The Poetry and Prose of Octavio Paz*, edited by Ivar Ivask, © 1973 by University of Oklahoma Press. Reprinted with permission.

"Reverberation of the Stone" by Ricardo Gullón from *Octavio Paz: Homage to the Poet*, edited by Kosrof Chantikian, © 1980 by Kosrof Chantikian and KOSMOS. Reprinted with permission.

"Towards the Other Shore: The Latest Stage in the Poetry of Octavio Paz" by Manuel Durán from *Octavio Paz: Homage to the Poet*, edited by Kosrof Chantikian, © 1980 by Kosrof Chantikian and KOSMOS. Reprinted with permission.

"Octavio Paz: Critic of Modern Mexican Poetry" by Allen W. Phillips from *The Perpetual Present: The Poetry and Prose of Octavio Paz*, edited by Ivar Ivask, © 1973 by University of Oklahoma Press. Reprinted with permission.

Index